The Way it Was

GRAMPIAN - the little TV station with the BIG reputation

Compiled by
Jimmy Spankie
Graham Mcleish
Edited by
Ted Brocklebank

First published in Great Britain in September 2021
by SNB Publishing Ltd
57, Orrell Lane,
Liverpool L9 8BX

Copyright 2021 Contributors

First edition published September 2021
Second edition published November 2021

Photographic credits

Our thanks to all the copyright holders of the photographs used in this book, especially to DC Thomson and STV. Also Pete Moran, Mike Kinnersly-Taylor, William Brown, ConocoPhillips, Scotavia Images and Interactive Media Services Bulgaria.
Every reasonable effort has been made to fulfil requirements with regard to reproducing copyright material: the publisher will be happy to rectify any omissions at the earliest opportunity.

Cover design by Stuart Cameron design100
Cover photo : Jimmy Spankie, Selina Scott, Calum Kennedy, Isla St Clair

Contents

Contents (cont'd)

Acknowledgements

This book was the brainchild of Jimmy Spankie. Without his inspiration and perseverance it would not have happened. Jimmy and Graham Mcleish collated and commissioned the 50-plus contributions which were then edited by Ted Brocklebank. We would like to thank all contributors without whose enthusiasm and anecdotal skills 'The Way It Was' would have remained a pipe dream. Also thanks to those whose names have been omitted or changed to protect the innocent!

Thanks also go to Nick Broadhead, our publisher, to Stuart Cameron who designed the cover and to Murray Thomson for his sage advice on publishing and distribution matters.

Special thanks to Alex Mair, George Mitchell, Colin Lawson and Cilla and John McKenzie for generous financial support.

Many of the photographs used in the book were taken by crew members, but others were the work of Grampian's staff photographer, the late Johnny Thomson. STV now own the copyright to these and we are extremely grateful that they have given us permission for their use here.

Many thanks too, to our wives, who have been a constant source of support - Frances Brocklebank, Allain Mcleish and Jay Spankie.

We apologise for any omissions or mistakes which, of course, are entirely the fault of the aforementioned commissioners and editor. This is a charitable venture. Please don't sue!

Editor

Foreword
Jimmy Spankie

WELCOME! Thank you for your interest in Grampian Television. I'm delighted to pen this introduction and to act as your guide through a host of memories by those who helped make Grampian the little TV station with the big reputation. The following chapters tell a story of drama, excitement, humour, inspiration and dedication.

Born in 1961, Grampian Television as such actually existed for only 36 years - from 1961-97. After its 'merger' with the Scottish Media Group in 1997 it later became the Northern TV news service for the Glasgow-based STV. But as the original ITV regional provider for North and North East Scotland it built up a remarkable reputation for quality broadcasting among its fiercely loyal viewers.

Producing programmes for an area as big as Holland and one including the remote Highlands and Islands of Scotland was no easy task. To a remarkable extent, with a programme budget initially dependent entirely on advertising revenue (later supplemented by programme sales), and constantly adopting the latest broadcasting technology, Grampian kept its viewers and shareholders happy.

What Grampian also produced were some of the nation's finest broadcasters, many of whom went on to become network household names. Older viewers and readers will remember the brilliantly articulate Donny B. Macleod, Renton Laidlaw, who found fame as an international TV golf pundit and Donald MacCormick, the 'Andrew Marr' of his day. More recently the list includes TV's golden-girl Selina Scott, broadcaster and MP Anna Soubry, as well as the BBC's Swiss correspondent, Imogen Foulkes and the award-winning BBC politics presenter, Anne Mackenzie. Along with Isabel Fraser, Martin Geissler, Isla Traquair (all BBC) Al Jazeera's Alan Fisher and Sky's Mark White, and not forgetting top Tory politician, Michael Gove, all cut their broadcasting teeth with Grampian.

However, for Grampian to succeed YOUR loyalty was key. I

can still recall that only a year after it was launched, Grampian faced bankruptcy. When the station opened in September 1961 it served a potential audience of 332,000 across 98,000 homes. In its first year it presented viewers with seven regular regional programmes – *News and Views* (a thrice weekly magazine), *Country Focus*, *Women's World, Serenade, Scotland For Me, Points North* (local politics), *Grampian Golf*, local news programmes and monthly church services. At the time viewers in Dundee and Tayside tuned into Scottish Television thanks to the strong signal from the Blackhill transmitter.

However, this led to furrowed brows in the Grampian boardroom when, after the first three months on air, the station was attracting only 13% of the available viewers in Tayside while audiences across the whole viewing area turned out to be less than hoped for. But came the hour came the man. James Buchan had been a senior producer with BBC when he was appointed Grampian's first Controller of Programmes. Jim it was who decided that the way to build a local audience lay in light entertainment with a distinctive Scottish flavour. This strategy, along with a strong news presence, guided by the redoubtable Charles Smith, including a Tayside-based reporter and news film crew, proved a winning formula.

These early programmes and the loyalty of you the viewers saved us from going to the wall. As audiences grew advertisers flocked to our rescue. I recall that in one six-month period in 1963 Grampian had no fewer than fifty shows in the most popular local Top Ten programmes. By the end of the 60s, boosted by a new Angus transmitter situated immediately north of Dundee, the station's potential audience reached a million viewers and Grampian was employing more than 200 staff at studios in Aberdeen, Dundee and Edinburgh. Later the company's reach extended all across Northern Scotland and out to the Hebrides with staffed studios and crews in Inverness and Stornoway. THANK YOU for making that possible.

I spent twenty of the happiest years of my working life with Grampian. Here, some of my former colleagues and close friends join me in recalling our stories about the little station with the big, big heart. In its previous and present guise 'Grampian' has been around for sixty years. I'm proud to have been a part of that history.

The way Grampian was
Ted Brocklebank

In terms of a human lifespan four decades isn't long. Yet much can be achieved within 40 years as Jesus of Nazareth, Robert Burns and Martin Luther King might have testified had any reached the age of 40. Grampian Television existed in its original form for only 36 years - the publication date of this book celebrates 60 years since the original GTV was founded. Yet in the view of many in its 36 years of existence Grampian reflected the character and lifestyle of Northern Scotland more faithfully than far larger media organisations with far greater resources.

During the 60s the mainstays of the North-East economy, farming and fishing – or 'tatties and herrin' in the local vernacular – were not in the best of health. By the mid-sixties Tom Johnson's North of Scotland Hydro-Electric Board had built no fewer than 54 main power stations and 78 dams, meaning that 90% of the population of the north was connected to the national grid. Yet it wasn't until the Highlands and Islands Development Board was set up in 1965 that the economy of the North and West began to stir from what seemed like terminal slumbers.

Things were looking a bit better on Tayside where by the late 60s the Timex Corporation employed about 5,000 people in Dundee making watches, more than the traditional industries of jute, jam and journalism combined. The Ohio-based National Cash Register Company also set up a plant in Dundee. And indeed had the Independent Television Authority not allocated the new Angus transmitter to Grampian, with a corresponding surge in advertising revenue from Tayside, the fortunes of Aberdeen-based Grampian TV would have been even bleaker. However, by the end of the decade branch factory economics saw the start of a downturn in watch and office equipment production on Tayside that would eventually see the collapse of Timex and NCR and years of economic stagnation for Dundee in particular.

But, as I relate elsewhere, everything was to change on an October night in 1970 when BP announced that oil in commercial quantities had been discovered under the North Sea. Within a matter of months the economy of Grampian's transmission area was transformed, with hundreds of oil-related companies setting up throughout the North. The new industry needed office space but it also needed engineering and service facilities. It needed pipe storage and handling for the undersea pipelines that would transport the oil and gas from more than a hundred miles offshore to terminals along the Aberdeenshire coast. It needed deep water inlets like Nigg in Easter Ross and Kishorn on the west coast to build the steel and concrete platforms from which the oil wells would be drilled. It also needed lots of new houses for the workers attracted north by the big wage packets paid by the oil companies. These new houses would be built not only around Aberdeen, but in Peterhead and Banchory and Montrose, in Alness and Invergordon in Easter Ross, and in Orkney and Shetland, as thousands moved up from the central belt.

Totally unexpected a multi-billion pound industry had landed literally on Grampian TV's doorstep. By some divine intervention the oil strikes were all geographically situated within Grampian's transmission area – from offshore Montrose in the south to offshore Peterhead in the North-East, then round to the Moray Firth, and north again to Orkney and both East and West of the Shetland isles. Clearly, God had decided that STV, Scotland's other commercial television company, wasn't to share in this great gift of nature. Otherwise, surely He'd have allocated a couple of strikes somewhere in the Clyde estuary. Or maybe He felt they had enough strikes down there!

Anyway, I remember chairing a TV debate in the early 70s between a rookie industrial journalist called Andrew Neil and the Upper-Clyde veteran trade unionist, Jimmy Reid. Neil had written an explosive piece in The Economist entitled 'Eastward Ho, Westward Woe' which predicted that the industrial heart of Scotland was moving East and North-East away from strike-riven Clydeside. As I recall this was probably young Mr. Neil's TV debut. And perhaps his prediction wasn't to come true in its entirety. But oil and gas would certainly transform the economy of the North – and indeed the UK – for the next three decades. It would also transform the political landscape.

'It's Scotland's Oil' was a persuasive slogan, and the Scottish National Party which for years had been a fringe political force now began to be taken seriously. The economic situation wasn't helped by the fact that the staple industry of the North-East, fishing, was going through its own turbulent times. Forced to accept the restrictions of the Common Fisheries Policy, as part of the Conservative government's joining of the EEC, fishermen felt betrayed when they were forced to share 'Scottish' waters with foreign vessels. Over-fishing led to a ban on catching herring in the 70s. Demersal stocks like cod and haddock, were also in short supply, and once-prosperous ports like Arbroath, Peterhead and Fraserburgh went into recession. It was the perfect scenario for the emergence of a new political force. In due course Nationalist MPs would replace Conservatives in virtually every Scottish coastal constituency.

These were dynamic times for the North and for Grampian news teams. Offshore disasters like Piper Alpha were on a far larger scale than the fishing and lifeboat tragedies Grampian had grown sadly accustomed to covering. Yet time and again Grampian reporters and producers rose to the challenge, vigorously competing with the BBC, servicing ITN, producing network documentaries from the region and regularly winning awards for the local *North Tonight* news magazine.

While the first Scottish Parliamentary Elections were not held until 1999, two years after the takeover by SMG, the wind of political change was blowing throughout the 90s. The pivotal role of the North of Scotland in the ongoing independence debate is a story Grampian was uniquely qualified to tell. It's a story, regrettably from the viewpoint of this veteran, that is now being told by others. But while Grampian Television may be no more, sixty years on the Grampian spirit still endures. Readers can judge for themselves as they share the memories of some of those who helped create the wee TV station with the big reputation.

Fond memories

Selina Scott
Reporter and Presenter, 1977-1980

It was half a lifetime ago. I can still hear the voice of an anxious helicopter pilot, rising and crashing with the waves as I leapt on to the gale-lashed oil platform north of Shetland, "You have one minute max. We have to be out of here. It is too dangerous."

Cameraman Alistair Watt steadied himself on the swaying deck, as I delivered one of the most bizarre, one-take, pieces to camera in my entire broadcasting career. Whose idea it was to send us to the most northerly outpost of the British Isles in a raging storm, to show off a revolutionary newsgathering tool, ENG, I never discovered. But this was typical of Grampian in those days.

ENG, Electronic News Gathering, as it was known, soon made film and the laborious process of cutting and splicing stories for broadcast, redundant. It changed the entire TV news industry in the blink of an eye. Little Grampian was the first in the UK to use it and had the chutzpah to make a song and dance about it.

Forty years ago, with the coming of Oil, the North of Scotland and the Highlands and Islands regularly found national exposure on ITN, in those days run by David Nicholas, a Welshman and Alastair Burnet, a Scot. It was Burnet who turned up in the middle of a snow storm (booking incognito into an out-of-the-way Aberdeenshire hotel) to offer me the coveted role of news anchor on *News at Ten* after seeing me on one of Grampian's news stories broadcast nationally.

I had arrived at Grampian from The Sunday Post, lured by memories of my grandparents who were both born in Aberdeenshire. I was the first signing by the new Head of News and Current Affairs, Ted Brocklebank, who would later make household names of Anna Soubry, Alistair Yates, the gentle John Duncanson, Anne MacKenzie and Angus Peter Campbell, of the quixotic Gaelic charm.

I was, as usual, the only woman on the news team which comprised reporters Alan Cowie and Bill Mackenzie, producer Bill Mackie and news editor Alistair Gracie. They did a nice line in dead-pan humour. Bill Mackenzie was stick-thin, had thick curly hair and high-waisted, grey trousers which he was forever hoisting up, fearful, I suppose, that they might fall down at any minute.

Alan Cowie would saunter off on news stories, his gait a bit like Charlie Chaplin's, head down, muttering mischievously.

Selina Scott and Ron Thompson

Alistair Gracie was Mystic Meg. He could read minds, especially that of Alex Ferguson, then working his magic at Aberdeen Football Club. He was a weekly fixture on Grampian's news agenda. It usually fell to me, who didn't know the first thing about football, to interview him. To help, Alistair would give me the questions and even wrote down what Alex would say in response. To my astonishment, Alistair was able to predict Alex's reply, word for word.

Grampian taught me life lessons which have carried me through my career. Like switching to red alert whenever I hear politicians say they are doing something "in the national interest". *In the National Interest* was the title of a documentary Bill Mackie and I made about Dounreay. Bill had secured unprecedented access to the secretive goings-on within the fast breeder reactor. In the cavernous, space-age interior, clad in a white hazmat suit, Dounreay's boss assured us on camera that the reactor was safe and totally impregnable. Even while we were filming and although we obviously didn't know it, the reactor was spewing out radioactivity on to the Caithness coast, contaminating its sea bed possibly for all eternity – 'in the national interest'.

My primary role at Grampian was to present the nightly news bulletin *North Tonight* with Ron Thompson, the first of what would be many pairings with older men in my TV career. But I had to cover news stories too. And that meant heading out into Aberdeenshire each day, with an ENG crew. Ian Murray was normally the electrician, lighting me when I did pieces to camera. But Ian wasn't content with just lighting me. He also directed me. The moment I began, Ian would either shake his head dismissively if he didn't think I'd got the tone right or nodding vigorously with a toothy grin if he thought I had. In this way, by pleasing 'director' Ian, I got the hang of talking directly to viewers on camera.

Another person to whom I owe a debt of gratitude, although she infuriated me at the time, was Ellie, our autocue operator who hailed from Tayside. Ellie said the funniest things in her broad Dundonian accent, and was a powerful presence because she was in total control of the autocue in the studio. Autocue is supposed to be a hidden tool for the presenter, an aid to help him or her appear fluent. At Grampian, in Ellie's hands, it became a rod to beat you with. Sometimes it would be there. Often not. Ellie regularly got words and sentences the wrong way round, Tippexing madly to make last minute editorial changes to the script. Instead of taking the blame when I ended up on live TV with egg on my face, having tripped up over her missing words, Ellie would brazenly blame me for the pressure SHE was under. I could never hold it against her for long, but I developed a deep mistrust of all autocues no matter how slick or automatic they were supposed to be.

On the fortieth anniversary of the D Day landings in Normandy when *BBC Breakfast* went live from Juno Beach, for example, and also at the Royal Albert Hall, in front of the Royal Family, I was asked by the producers of both events, to rely totally on autocue. I was so struck with a kind of Ellie terror that I risked their ire and walked on with my notes. When the opening words on the autocue failed to appear, the screen went blank, but I was able to seamlessly skip along and save what could have been a TV disaster thanks to Ellie's misfiring autocue tutelage all those years before. To the everlasting gratitude of the producers, I might add, on both shows!

Selina walks with Prince Charles on Berneray's famous west beach

Before Grampian disappeared into TV oblivion I returned to Aberdeen to make an interview series on global newsmakers for ITV. It meant I was happily reunited with cameraman Alistair Watt, capturing a pivotal moment in the Prince of Wales' life before his divorce from Diana. His feelings very much on display, the Prince agreed that Alistair could film him as he set up his painting easel on the tiny Hebridean island of Berneray. Through his lens, in close-up, Alistair told me he had never witnessed a sadder-looking man. The Charles movie attracted twelve million viewers. It was swiftly followed in 1992 by *A Year in Spain*, with a young King Juan Carlos and his family, during Spain's Barcelona Olympics year. Shot by Grampian's Steve Horrocks, it too got record viewing figures.

But my final network documentary, with Donald Trump didn't go quite so swimmingly. Donald, battling bankruptcy, had whisked us across America in his private plane, bragging about his real estate acquisitions. We ended up in Mar a Lago in Florida for the final set piece interview. Steve Horrocks was again the cameraman. The interview went well and I returned to my hotel room to pack and fly back to the UK. And then Steve arrived. He had discovered that Grampian's camera had inexplicably switched half way through the interview, from colour to black and white. It meant the footage was apparently unusable.

We had to ask Trump to do it again. If he refused the entire documentary would have to be scrapped. Donald's lawyer advised him not to do it, but Trump thought he could improve on the first interview and agreed. Unfortunately for the tycoon, when we got back to Grampian, not only did the company's brilliant in-house engineers manage to restore colour, but the second interview completely contradicted the first. We had captured Donald telling two totally different tales. Which meant we had a dilemma. Which one to use? We decided to juxtapose one against the other, leaving it to the viewers to judge which version, if any, was the truth. And we, naughtily, underscored it with the sound track to the *Porgy & Bess* hit 'It ain't necessarily so'.

Selina Scott, Donald Trump and his then wife, Marla Maples

When the documentary aired Trump went ballistic and blamed me. ITV and Grampian bosses ducked for cover as 'the Donald' threatened them with legal action, even demanding a right of reply, which ITV granted. Trump made a special air trip to Britain to denounce me live on ITV's morning show, and demanded that the documentary was never aired Stateside. The US networks were clamouring for it, but sadly Grampian and ITV bent the knee and lost themselves valuable programme sales as a result.

Looking back, and in spite of the debacle over Trump, it is with much affection that I remember Grampian and the many talented people I worked with. Many, sadly, no longer with us. The experiences I was gifted, the joy of working in one of the most beautiful landscapes in the world was, and remains, one of the great privileges of my life.

How do you get into TV?

Anne Mackenzie
Reporter and Presenter, 1981-1994

People have asked me lots of times how to get into TV, and the truth is I have absolutely no idea. I got into Grampian, and that was not the same thing at all. Grampian, I now realise, having experienced 'TV' on another channel was something altogether healthier and more rooted in humility and reality and people. Grampian was something from another age, and in my view those of us who worked there were lucky to have had the chance to experience it.

My accidental route in came via one of the best news presenters Grampian ever had - John Duncanson - whom I met at my granny's dining table. I was home on the Isle of Lewis on holiday before my final exams at Glasgow University; John was there in his capacity as the husband of a fairly distant cousin. It was a nice lunch and that was that.

But a few weeks later, John contacted my father to ask if I'd consider auditioning for a vacancy that had come up after one of the current presenters of *North Tonight*, Selina Scott, had been head-hunted by ITN. I was totally amazed. I wasn't confident or used to public speaking, I didn't like being the focus of attention, I took no part in student politics or student journalism. I was as unlikely a candidate for TV as they came. But not, John thought, unlikely for Grampian.

John worked on wearing me down, mainly through my dad, until I finally agreed to try an audition after my exams. And by some insane happenstance, and although I still wasn't at all sure I wanted it, or what he saw in me, the then Head of News & Current Affairs, Ted Brocklebank, gave me a job as Grampian's first news trainee with a knowledge of Gaelic, even though I didn't really speak the language. I soon discovered that little problems like that were just hurdles to be overcome at Grampian. We made do with what we had.

I think, before I worked at GTV, like everyone else, I'd had preconceptions of what a job in TV would be like. This was not it. There was a surreal feeling, almost of DIY, of putting it all together in the shed, because resources were so tight and the company was so small you were party to just about everything that happened. In reality, looking back, it was entirely professional, and very soon after arrival I was putting together news bulletins, having never done any journalism before. I was also witnessing the endless things that could go wrong in a time before technology became close to failsafe.

John Duncanson

When I first started, onscreen people on *North Tonight* needed nerves of titanium and no embarrassment gene. Things dropped off the studio set behind the presenters. Guests didn't turn up. Edits were so cumbersome - old-fashioned film that had to be physically cut and spliced - that reports sometimes barely made it on air. Regularly they were shuffled down the running order, with much padding by the presenters, until they arrived or time finally ran out. And in the worst scenario, telecine machines malfunctioned, losing all the filmed stories. This left John and his co-presenters, Alistair Yates and another new girl Anna Soubry (yes, that one) filling airtime with nowhere else to go.

Soon after I arrived, our urbane, unruffled political correspondent Bill Mackenzie was waiting in reception to get a lift home, watching that night's carnage unfolding in the studio on the house TV, when a floor manager burst out of the bowels of the building, dragging Bill bodily back down the corridor to the studio. Bill, still in his coat, paused only to grab whatever bit of script was in his typewriter. From that scrap of paper Bill somehow filled 5-10 minutes of dead air with something close to coherence. I think that ruffled even Bill's urbanity. It terrified me.

But madness like this became part of the seduction. In the way of these things, Grampian's small size and relative poverty spurred innovation and inventiveness. We had fewer resources, so we took more risks, and that could go horribly wrong or brilliantly right, but it was always exhilarating. The people I worked with at GTV, from the journalists to the engineers, the directors to the producers, to the camera and tech crews and the editors, were probably the best and most talented and resourceful I've ever worked with. I didn't understand that at the time, but after working with the licence-funded lot I came to realise it with a certain sense of shame.

As for the newsroom, the journalists running it were 'old school': men and women who'd come up through newspapers, not straight out of universities like me, and as a result they had an instinctive understanding of the area and of how people thought and felt. There was also a genuine political neutrality and lack of intellectual arrogance. Much of that seems to have been lost now that journalism has become a graduate profession. The Grampian newsroom drummed into me that it was my responsibility to the audience to keep my own opinions and feelings out of reporting and interviewing - to give everyone the same chance and the same grief - and that's something that I still believe should be the gold standard. I was incredibly lucky that these were the journalists I learned from - Bill Mackie, Alan Cowie, Bob Kenyon, Bill Mackenzie, Alistair Gracie, Jennifer Malcolm, Alan Saunders, Ron Thompson and Frank Gilfeather.

Management had their moments of brilliance too - tiny, relatively cash-strapped GTV was the first news operation in the UK to pioneer videotape - ENG. And it was one of the first newsrooms in the UK to become fully computerised. But none of that changed the basic aura of the place - a sense almost that we were making programmes for our own sake and for those few who could be bothered to peer through the glass at our antics. Did the audience even notice our disasters or our triumphs? In the days before Twitter, we didn't really know, because so few people bothered to phone or write to tell us. Dour Northerners indeed. True, we got little praise, but this also cushioned us from hair-trigger criticism or malice.

Rehearsal

The apparent lack of interest in Grampian from the press, the view of us as 'couthie' and not really a 'proper' TV or news operation, plus the relative absence of feedback from the audience, all allowed us to maintain that conceit of isolation. I was always startled and a bit unnerved if anyone recognised me in real life. Fan mail was a rare and often peculiar thing for all of us on screen, all too often, cliched as it may seem, written in green ink. It was vanishingly rare to be asked for an autograph to a signed pic - the selfies of the day. Celebrity was never part of the GTV deal. Well... apart from Jimmy Spankie!

That sense of doing it all in a vacuum was such, that when the live interactive current affairs show *We The Jury* launched its first show, courtesy of our mad and brilliant new Director of Programmes, George Mitchell - 'Should Smoking be Banned?' - we were so used to absence of feedback and so sure that no one would bother to phone in, that all of us on the production team primed our families to call in, pretending to be unaffiliated members of the public. As it turned out, they couldn't get through. We received something like 13,000 calls that night which was just the beginning of several highly-successful series of *We the Jury*. George hadn't been unhinged after all. And that was the moment I think I began to get some vague notion of how many people really were silently but loyally devoted to GTV.

And, probably because of GTVs almost pathologically down-to-earth atmosphere, it was next to impossible for anyone, no matter how famous, to maintain any aura of special apartness for long. A trip to the canteen was always a great leveller. Grampian was where I learned that celebrities and the powerful really are just ordinary people underneath the veneer.

Anne MacKenzie interviews Prime Minister Margaret Thatcher

Some random moments out of hundreds that stand out: interviewing Margaret Thatcher at the height of her power as the Berlin Wall was coming down, and watching the Iron Lady's delight when our makeup artist Jane Jones described her daughter's reaction on being told that Jane was going on a hush-hush assignment to make-up the most famous and important woman in Britain. Who was she? "Is it Kylie Minogue?"

Then there was the time the Bishop of St Andrews happily departed in a shared taxi with Britain's most famous dominatrix, Miss Whiplash, clad in a very brief metal-spiked leather bustier. They hit it off debating 'Should Prostitution be banned?' on *We the Jury*. She'd already offered myself and my husband a job.

Then the night that Marian Hepworth, the inspired producer of *We The Jury* organised a debate and viewer-vote on whether there is life after death (we're alright — Grampian viewers decided there is). One of the guests was a prominent past-life regressionist, who informed DJ Ally Bally (manning the studio phones) that he used to be a Chinese peasant and I used to read out the scrolls in Atlantis. Marion, Carrie Watt our researcher, Graham Mcleish our director, and Babs Dickie our PA apparently all drowned with me when Atlantis was destroyed. That was why none of us liked to feel water on our faces. Who knew?

I well remember the night of the first-ever *National TV Awards*, which George Mitchell had cooked up at GTV, waiting at Wembley with George and his team to see if any of the famous folk they'd invited would actually turn up. And wondering what to do with one and a half hours of live national airtime if they didn't. Thankfully, they did. Everyone likes an award!

Then there was the time I was ordered by the splendidly-bonkers Alan Cowie to interview a quadriplegic American evangelist for six minutes, but not, under any circumstances, to let her talk about God. Michael Gove (yes, that one) who was observing and assisting in the newsroom, timed it at 38 seconds before she quoted Jeremiah, which even Alan had to admit wasn't bad going.

But most hilarious of all was a live OB interview conducted by Isabel Fraser, our Inverness reporter, with the renowned ornithologist, Roy Dennis. It was in the aftermath of the Braer oil tanker grounding off Shetland. Isabel asked him what he thought of the government's new grant package to help clean up the oil spillage and its effect on wildlife.

"Well" said Roy, "I welcome it of course. It's very necessary. But in the end money can't compensate for all we've lost. I mean… what price a gannet? What price a cormorant? What price a shag?"

Back in the Aberdeen studio I looked at John Duncanson and he looked at me. For a moment no one could believe what we'd heard. Always the consummate professional Isabel turned back to the camera, totally deadpan, "Roy Dennis, thank you. Back to Anne in the studio."

Out of the corner of my eye I could see John covering his face with his hands, trying not to put me off. The floor manager cued me with his back turned. In a split second I had to decide whether to reference the faux-pas or pretend it hadn't happened. Remembering the demographic of our audience I decided on the latter and went straight into the introduction to the next item which was meant to be long and involved. I cut it to two strangled sentences. When we went into the next report the whole studio finally erupted. When I see an older Roy on TV these days discussing his latest

Anne and John

project – something like the reintroduction of Sea Eagles – I often wonder if it occurred to him what he'd said. If he ever reads this perhaps he'll let me know!

But what of John, who got me into it all? Well, I ended up presenting alongside him for quite a few years and I've never felt safer on air. John could deal with anything that happened, smoothly and gracefully. He was the ultimate presenter and a hugely generous and genuinely kind man.

One of the many occasions he saved me on live TV was the night I got so caught up taking instructions from the gallery for dealing with an upcoming outside broadcast, that I didn't register the *North Tonight* opening credits or the usual introduction over the chatter in my ear. John said, "Good evening and welcome to *North Tonight*. I'm John Duncanson..." The only reason I realised something might be wrong was the sudden silence in the gallery and in the studio. I stared into the camera trying to work out what I should be saying. "And she's Anne Mackenzie," John said smoothly before going into the opening headlines, as if I hadn't just forgotten my own name!

Then again, he regularly wound me up too, telling stories with punchlines timed for the exact moment we went on air. The one I remember with particular horror was his tale of his time as an assistant stage manager in the theatre, fighting off a pass from an amorous elderly actor. John protested that he was unfortunately straight. "Dear boy," the actor returned with full theatrical grandeur and perfect enunciation. "Man, woman or rough-haired terrier. It's all. The same. To me." Tiny beat. "Good evening and welcome to *North Tonight*. I'm John Duncanson..."

Reader, I corpsed. And John had to rescue me again. On reflection, it's probably surprising I didn't forget my name more often. I still miss John. And I still miss Grampian Television.

When Grampian was champion!
George Mitchell
Director of Programmes, 1988-1997

I was both angry and sad. I had led a team of talented programme-makers and technicians for nearly a decade during which time Grampian had been consistently voted the most popular TV station in Britain, attracting huge audiences for programming but also managing to turn in increased profits every year.

Now here I was one October morning in 1997 clearing out my desk and leaving the company along with other directors after a 'merger' with Scottish Media Group which was in reality a takeover. As I wrote a long 'handover' document of my forthcoming programme plans to my successor, Alistair Gracie, I couldn't help thinking of the opportunities that lay ahead but might now be lost. Our consultants and advisors had counselled us that we had a fiduciary duty to act in the interest of all shareholders. Nobody mentioned the interest of the viewers!

I always knew money could talk. But now I found it could also insist. Andrew Flanagan, then managing director of SMG, was not keen when I asked to bid farewell to my staff. He said it might upset them. But I could insist too, and was touched by how sad many of them seemed to see me go. And I knew just how much I was going to miss Grampian TV. But the game moves on. So, tomorrow to fresh woods and pastures new. But in the meantime, and nearly a quarter of a century later, a moment to pause and reflect on my days at Queen's Cross when Grampian really was Champion.

Over the last six decades Grampian Television has taken the credit for many things, but starting broken clocks wasn't one of them! Time had stood still until the controversial mind-reader and illusionist Uri Geller worked his magic in a Hallowe'en special *All Fright on the Night* in the autumn of 1994. After Uri's performance 36 alarmed and astonished viewers phoned the studios, then in

Aberdeen's Fountainhall Road, to report that their watches or clocks had mysteriously started to work again after Uri's performance.

But it seemed time was already running out for Grampian TV. Joining Britain's most northerly TV company and covering the largest geographical area from Fife to Shetland and Aberdeen to the Outer Hebrides, it was threatened with extinction within weeks of my arrival. The Conservative Government's Broadcasting Bill of 1989 was the cause of our distress. I well remember as one of the executive team going off for an intensive two-day strategy conference at Maryculter House to plan our fight for survival. Chief Executive Donald Waters, Bob Christie, Graham Good, Alec Ramsay, Alistair Gracie, Ted Brocklebank, Mike McLintock, Eric Johnstone and myself planned our strategy to win renewal of the TV franchise for the North of Scotland due for renewal in 1991 and coming into effect at the beginning of 1993.

Roy Thomson, the buccaneering Canadian tycoon who owned The Scotsman newspaper and had set up Scottish Television in the mid 50s, told potential investors in the new station that owning a TV franchise was like having a licence to print money! It was a statement that was to come back and haunt him.

Certainly TV companies in the early 1980's knew how to spend the cash. With strong trade unions, film crews for feature programmes consisted of seven or eight members and included a 'location assistant' whose job was solely to move props around on an interviewee's desk. I always thought it would have been more polite to invite the desk's owner to do it himself. So overmanning was rife. And it was always 'manning' back in the early 80s. Thankfully times have changed!

Many years ago as a new TV producer working at Central TV in the Midlands the first piece of advice I was given by one of the older hands was "always spend every penny of your programme budget. If you don't, it will be chopped for the next series." So this encouraged a culture of waste, totally out of step with Mrs Thatcher's economic mantra of living within your means. Conspicuous consumption was certainly out of fashion for the daughter of a careful Grantham grocer.

I was one of the very few at Grampian, or indeed throughout the whole ITV network, who believed in the blind auction of the TV franchises to the highest bidder. It seemed to me entirely fair that the TV companies who ran their businesses most efficiently would be the most profitable and therefore be able to bid the highest. But at the last moment the Arts minister, David Mellor, inserted a clause in the Broadcasting Bill that there was to be a 'quality threshold' which applicants would have to pass first. This was in effect a Becher's Brook which would sort out the thoroughbreds from the tired old nags who should be sent off to the knacker's yard or retired to give rides at the seaside. It was this clause that, later on, was to come to Grampian TV's rescue. We were seriously outbid by both our rivals for the new franchise. But thankfully were judged by the TV regulator to be the only one to pass the quality threshold.

Every TV company in the world keeps a keen eye on its audience ratings performance. But this is particularly crucial for broadcasters funded by TV ads rather than TV licences or subscription. No viewers, no dinner! But another key question is, left to themselves, what would viewers actually CHOOSE to watch? That's where attitude surveys come in. One held not long after I joined Grampian revealed families in our transmission area would like to see more programmes on natural history and social history of the region. I responded immediately coming up with *Country Matters*, giving the inside stories on outdoor pursuits and exploring the issues 'that make the greens see red' and produced by Grampian's fishing, shooting and hunting enthusiast, Paul Adderton. I got veteran local broadcaster Gerry Davis to don the mantle of 'raider of the lost archive' for *The Way it Was*, combining grainy black and white film with fascinating personal memories of those who'd lived through the good old days - but for some maybe not so good!

Gerry Davis

One of my biggest scheduling headaches was when a local football team like Aberdeen or Dundee had an important replay arranged at short notice. Do I abandon the advertised schedule of drama and entertainment or stick to that and risk the ire of mainly male soccer-loving viewers who tended to be harder to reach? (Those in the advertising department were always quick to remind me that so called ABC-1 men were the perfect target audience for drink and car advertising, but tended to be light ITV viewers and therefore more elusive).

As a child my family took regular summer holidays in the Hebrides, particularly Tiree where it was windy but also nearly always sunny! In addition while at Edinburgh University I had chosen to do my dissertation for my MA economic history degree on 'The Rise and Fall of the Scottish Kelp Industry'. So when the Thatcher government approved an £8m per year fund for Gaelic programming you'd expect me to be all in favour. But I wasn't!

Being in the business of broadcasting - not narrowcasting - it seemed crazy to me to be compelled to transmit 'a due proportion' of Gaelic programmes in peak time when statistics showed there were only around 40,000 Gaelic speakers. A bespoke studio was built in Stornoway to house a new Gaelic soap opera *Machair*. Repeats are still running on the Gaelic TV channel, BBC Alba!

Growing up in the 60s we had only two TV channels, BBC1 and ITV. Now my digital set brings me more than 500 channels. But I still have only two eyes and 24 hours in my day! But having abundant choice has empowered the viewer. They are our masters now. Because they control the zapper! But the downside of more channels meant TV advertising was in short supply and it was clear advertising couldn't sustain fifteen individual regional companies in ITV.

Mergers and takeovers were the order of the day. Grampian had been one of two distinct franchise areas in Scotland for more than 30 years. But times change. ITV companies in England were merging or being taken over and Scottish broadcasters could not maintain the way it was.

So discussions started about combining with SMG. Consultants were brought in to advise on the new structure. The beloved Grampian name and logo disappeared and not surprisingly there were severe job losses, including that of my own and fellow board member, finance director Graham Good. SMG honoured our contracts and we left with two years salary. It was not the finish I had wanted but to the victors belong the spoils, as they say.

But there was a happier postscript. Back in 1994 a friend and former colleague of mine at Central TV had come up with an idea for a TV awards show she had seen in Australia. Called *The Logies* after the Scottish inventor of television John Logie Baird, its distinctive feature was that all the winners were chosen by viewers in a huge nationwide poll. This was a dramatic departure from the norm where juries comprised of TV professionals sat in smoke-filled rooms to decide who won what.

Over the years I had been critical of ITV for lack of access to programme ideas from the smaller TV companies. In one angry article in Broadcast magazine I wrote that ITV regarded itself as a centre of excellence when in truth it was a cartel of arrogance. Looking back this seems a bit cheeky!

So to shut me up they jointly commissioned Grampian and London independent producer Indigo Television to make *The National Television Awards*.

Twenty five years later it is still running, and has consistently held its position as Britain's number one awards show. Hollywood royalty like Julie Andrews and Dustin Hoffman have graced the NTA stage. And real royalty like Prince Philip and the Prince of Wales have made appearances in the ceremony, as well as three Prime Ministers - Blair, Brown and Cameron.

I still have a loose connection with the show but, going on 72, I am content to be a viewer these days. But as I look back on all my years in broadcasting I can say with absolute certainty that my time at Grampian was champion. I loved it there.

How did a piper frae Dundee get on the telly?

Jimmy Spankie
Presenter and Newscaster, 1961-1980

Here's the question I am most often asked. "How did you get into television?" If asked aggressively my answer invariably is 'sheer talent'. If asked in a normal friendly manner the answer is longer – and more truthful. Looking back I find it interesting to discover odd signposts of what lay ahead.

I start with National Service. In the 50s most young men had to spend normally two years in the Armed Forces. I spent my time with The Black Watch. Having learned to play the bagpipes at school, joining my local regiment turned out to be a smart move. Well, a lucky move. Following basic training I joined the Pipes and Drums of the 1st Battalion Black Watch in Berlin. The summer months were spent preparing to embark in September on a three month tour of the USA and Canada.

While in Berlin I started to consider the possibility of a broadcasting career. Why? Well, come with me to the place where we all relaxed on a Saturday night. On second thoughts perhaps better NOT to come. Just take my word for it. Our relaxation was in the NAAFI where, allegedly, beer was taken. Sometimes not a pretty sight, I have to confess. My 'party piece' was to find an empty beer glass and pretend it was a microphone.

Jimmy fourth right

I would then commentate on an imaginary soccer match. Invariably it was a Scottish Cup Final - Rangers v Celtic at Hampden Park. Was that empty beer glass a sign of things to come? Using it as a mike, I mean!

The tour of the USA and Canada was an amazing experience and, apparently, a huge success. In twelve weeks we played sixty three cities and towns with five performances in Madison Square

Gardens. With our Military Band, Pipes and Drums plus Highland Dancers we were ninety eight in total, beating out a message of goodwill and no doubt bringing tears to many ex-pat eyes. These early dreams of making a career out of entertaining and informing the public suddenly seemed tantalisingly closer. That US tour also introduced me to lifelong friends, Whitney and Marshall Hardy and Jo Lynn. At the concert in Louisville, Kentucky I bumped (literally) into the Hardys, and our families have been friends ever since, with holidays and vacations on both sides of the Atlantic.

Our friendship led to some work for me in Atlanta GA, then in 1976 I was honoured at being made a Kentucky Colonel. P.S.There are only 113 Kentucky Colonels in the United Kingdom!

On the flight home from America I plucked up courage to write a note to one of the stewardesses, inviting her to dinner in London. She agreed. Jo Lynn, from Waco Texas, and I have been friends for over 50 years. But I digress.

My second year was at Redford Barracks, Edinburgh. Once again the band was busy with public performances in many parts of Britain. News programmes apart *Sunday Night at the London Palladium* was just about the only live programme on ITV. The Pipes and Drums were invited to perform. It was to be my first live television appearance! I couldn't wait to repeat the experience.

A final anecdote from my days as an army piper. We were practising for the Tattoo in the barrack room, and the Pipe Major (boss piper) made me stand opposite him - less than a couple of yards away. Normally the P/M didn't see me play because he marched in the front row and my normal position was in the back row. When on parade we had seven rows of four pipers. Being opposite the PM didn't exactly make me nervous - more like petrified!

Of course, the inevitable happened. All pipers changed from tune 'one' to tune 'two'. That's to say all pipers bar one. Spankie changed to tune 'four' all on his own. Pipie (as the P/M was called) stepped forward and held up his hand. Instead of all pipers finishing together we had just about 28 individual halts. The Drum Corps came to an untidy finish. There was a deathly hush. Pipie took a pace towards me, waxed moustache bristling with emotion. "Spankie" he cried, "You again. The Tattoo Producer asked me only last week how many pipers I had for this year's Tattoo. I told him I had 27 pipers and a fellow called Spankie." The barrack room erupted! In the Army discipline is key. Not a bad example for the broadcasting world either.

After Army life I returned to my native Dundee. Following my 'Beer Glass in Berlin' episodes my thoughts about a broadcasting career were strengthened by my interest in sport.

In those Dundee days one of my sporting weekly highlights was football commentating. There was a hospital broadcasting service in the city with part of its schedule involving live football commentary from either Dens Park (Dundee F.C.) or Tannadice (Dundee United). My usual involvement was as a half time and full time summariser.

On one occasion, however, the match commentator was called away. I had to perform my 'Beer Glass in Berlin' act but this time for real. Celtic were the visitors at Dens Park. Play was held up by an injury to a Celtic player. A stretcher was summoned. My voice became almost conspiratorial as I described the drama surrounding the exit of Bobby Collins. I even ventured to suggest Mr Collins had not been at his best that day. Imagine my embarrassment the following day to read The Sunday Post claiming that Bobby Collins had played a pivotal role in Celtic's win and what a shame about the leg gash that had forced Willie Fernie to leave the pitch. Okay, Celtic's players did not wear any identification on their shorts or shirts in these days. Not even numbers. But I'd got it horribly wrong. Commentating, I decided, was not as easy as shouting into a beer glass! It was a lesson for my later career: two lessons actually - 'do homework' and 'if in doubt say nowt'.

Hospital radio sport apart, the career vacuum created post-National Service needed filling. I borrowed a tape recorder and began interviewing people in pubs about local issues. Two evenings a week I worked (unpaid) in Dundee's Palace Theatre doing all the jobs no one else wanted, occasionally having to operate a spotlight. Terrifying. I joined a club which necessitated speaking in public. I became a member of the Repertory Theatre's Playgoers Club. That meant slightly cheaper seats every second Monday (first nights) and meeting the cast.

But what became my biggest commitment? Am/Dram! Ah Yes.

Amateur Dramatics – a pastime designed to bring out the best in human beings! A near neighbour ran a School of Drama for children of all ages (including me!). Ella Rutherford, a character indeed. In her sixties she sat and passed her driving test. Weeks later she achieved local fame by driving onto the Tay bridge between Dundee and Fife - on the wrong carriageway! In the dark!

Ella's three sons Harvey, David and Howie, myself and a school chum called Michael Duncan were often called upon to play adult roles. We had enormous fun. Hairy Moments - but fun.

We did have some success. The Scottish Community Drama Association organised a national One Act Festival and on two successive years we reached the Divisional Final. The first took place in Stonehaven Town Hall. The adjudicator was BBC Scotland's Howard M. Lockhart. He did not like us. A public adjudication was followed by a private one. At the private one he tore us into little strips and threw them into the local harbour.. The second was held in the Carnegie Hall, Dunfermline. This time Raymond Westwell was judging. Raymond happened to be the principal producer at Dundee Repertory Theatre. Out of three finalists we were the only ones from Dundee. How on earth could he nominate us as winners without showing bias? He couldn't - and didn't. Where Mr Lockhart had been negative and nasty, Mr Westwell was positive and helpful. But we still didn't win!

To be able to learn lines and move on stage when asked while delivering these lines isn't a bad introduction for a career in front of a camera. One day I saw an article in the newspaper about the arrival of a new television station in Aberdeen. It was called Grampian and it was looking for on-screen talent. No mention of piping skills being required. But still.

Another story - another day!

The launch of the good ship Grampian

Douglas Kynoch
Announcer/Newsreader/Presenter, 1961-1967

The announcement that an Independent Television station was to open in Aberdeen in 1961 was exciting enough to bring me scurrying back from Germany where I was teaching English. My audition was straightforward. Applicants interviewed one another on topics of their own choosing, read old news scripts and addressed the camera off-the-cuff for one minute. Production Controller, James Buchan conducted the audition and, before long, I was appointed as one of the new station's three announcer/news-readers. I was to remain with Grampian for the next six years.

Appointed at the same time were my university friend, June Imray (who, like me, had a background in drama). June was later to find fame as 'The Torry Quine', and later still as a BBC network news presenter. Three months after we opened we were joined by an affable Dundonian, Jimmy Spankie, whose many talents included playing the bagpipes! Other announcers I recall from the beginning were former Aberdeen actress, Daphne Penny, and, in due course, Graham Roberts, an actor from Cheshire, later to become nationally known playing the gamekeeper in *The Archers*.

Recruited in August, I was unexpectedly sent off to Border Television, just opened at Carlisle, where a newly-appointed male announcer had had a nervous collapse. This was not exactly encouraging; but I deputised until they could find a replacement. I returned to Grampian's Queen's Cross studios in time for the launch on September 30th. The foyer, I recall, was seething with humanity. A freelance cameraman said to me somewhat melodramatically, "Today is a day that will either make you or break you!" Thankfully it did neither. They tell me mine was the first voice heard on Grampian. For the life of me I can't remember what I said.

The programme schedule was then revealed for all. As well as network material, there were locally produced programmes such as

News and Views. This was a nightly magazine of news and sport edited by Charles Smith and presented first by the actor Jimmy Copeland and later by the polished June Shields from BBC radio. For the farming community, there was *Country Focus*, presented by a local farmer, Michael Joughin. For the young there was *Romper Room* with Lesley Blair and later with Daphne Penny.

James Buchan presenting the Bothy Nichts Brose Caup

There were programmes in the local vernacular, such as *Bothy Nichts*, in which teams such as the Kennethmont Loons and Quines and the Kingseat Bothy Billies competed for the Grampian Brose Caup. *Ingle Neuk* was another couthie entertainment set round the rural hearth, with the popular entertainer, John Mearns, regularly assuring us, "Fit a graan nicht we're haein!"

The announcers' lot in these days was not an easy one. Programme promotions today are short and to the point; and the announcer is never in vision. In those days, when local businesses had still to be persuaded of the value of television advertising, any shortfall in sales meant that commercial breaks had to be filled in some other way. Sometimes that meant a short film from the Central Office of Information like *Don't Be a Boot-Bumper* or *Drive As If You Had a Glass of Water on Your Bonnet*; but more generally, it meant that the continuity announcer had to fill the gap with programme information. When a programme under-ran (and, unlike today, many of the programmes were live), the hapless announcer had to fill in as required. It still sends a chill up my spine to recall the not-infrequent instruction at the end of *Sunday Night at the London Palladium:* 'Programme under-running. Prepare to fill for 2 minutes. No more cues!' With one eye on the clock and the other on your script, you then had to fill in for as long as necessary without looking as if a mouse had run up your leg.

This was actually good training as the newsreader-announcers were also encouraged to present programmes. It wasn't long before Jimmy Spankie was fronting the sports programme every week, aided by such local sporting heroes as Archie Glen and Freddy . June Imray and I jointly presented *Aye Yours*, a music programme featuring Jack Sinclair and his Band and the singer Dave McIntosh. For this, viewers were invited to submit dedications. The programme was certainly popular; and after June left for London, I continued to present it with Fiona Cumming from Border TV and a former Miss Scotland, Elizabeth Burns, from St Andrews.

Another of the programmes James Buchan devised was the Scottish quiz series, *A' the Airts*. The ubiquitous Mr Spankie presented it for several years. But one year (perhaps it was his turn for a breakdown), I was asked to deputise. Asking the questions was easy enough (the answers were on a card); but what with bells and buzzers going off at unexpected moments, I found it all a bit baffling. When a gong sounded during my first programme, I was completely flummoxed. What's that?" I exclaimed in alarm. A long-standing contestant, Mr Munro, came to my rescue "That's the end of the programme, Mr Kynoch." Nearly the end of the presenter, I thought!

Unlike the on-screen staff, the programme directors I remember were all imported: the exuberant Eddie Joffe from South Africa; the intellectual Adrian Malone and a light entertainment specialist, Mike Bevan, both from London. Only later were Scottish directors appointed: Hector Stewart from Aberdeen, a former cameraman, and Alan Franchi from Dundee, who was recruited initially as a sound technician. Both brought local credibility as well as technical skills to the production department.

Eddie Joffe vision mixing and directing with Alan Franchi (background right)

An important part of the work of the on-screen staff at Grampian was the public engagement, which, in the early days, was really an unofficial part of the company's PR. We all undertook these engagements, which made a pleasant change from being shut up in a continuity studio. The real celebrities were people like *Coronation Street's* Elsie Tanner (Pat Phoenix), who with her young colleague, Lucille (Jennifer Moss) opened the Oldmeldrum Sports one year. When invited from Grampian to present prizes, I was delighted to meet them both. But while Elsie's astronomical fee was "the spik o the county", Being 'staff, no fee' I had to be content with a free cup of tea!

Sixty years on, my abiding memory of Grampian is of what a congenial place it was. Technicians and broadcasters, studio staff, management and office personnel, we were a happy crew on the Good Ship Grampian, which served its area well and provided a variety of local broadcasting which is simply not seen today. Nowadays, if you want to hear a Scots song, you have to sing it yourself!

The debt our family owes to Grampian

By Fiona Kennedy

In 1955 a joyful 28-year-old Calum Kennedy stood on the platform of the historic Music Hall in Aberdeen and received the highest accolade in the Gaelic cultural and music world, the National Mod Gold Medal, from Her Majesty the Queen, with Princess Margaret in attendance. My mother Anne had won the coveted Gold Medal two years before him and was proudly looking on from the wings, preparing to come on stage to present a bouquet of flowers to Queen Elizabeth.

Little did my father know at that time that winning the Mod gold medal would be a pivotal moment which would change his life forever - thoughts of his career as a cost accountant would quickly fade and become ancient history, while life as a singer on the international stage beckoned.

As a young man from Orisay, on the island of Lewis in the Outer Hebrides, my father's principal audience growing up there was Jessie, the cow, to whom he used to sing outside the family croft to bring her in for milking. A career on stage and television was not on his horizon - television had barely been invented!

Winning the Mod gold medal was the catalyst for my father to enter the World Ballad Championship in Moscow in 1957, which he also won, singing a great Gaelic ballad, beating over 700 competitors. He was presented with another gold medal by President Nikita Khrushchev.

About the same time in far off North East of Scotland, the germ of an idea for a new television station was taking form. Grampian Television was about to come to life and blossom on three-legged television sets in the corners of thousands upon thousands of sitting rooms all over the North. Grampian Television 'the friendliest station' in the United Kingdom was born in 1961.

My father, a dashing young man from the islands was developing quite a name for himself singing in concerts all over

Scotland, following his wins at the Mod and in Moscow. As 'The Golden Voice of the Highlands' he was being offered recording contracts by Beltona, Decca and Pye Records in London. And it wasn't long before he came to the attention of executives and producers at Grampian TV.

Calum's ceilidh

The station's director of programmes, Jim Buchan invited dad to meet him at Queen's Cross for one of the station's famous board room lunches. Jim asked dad to do a series of Scottish traditional music programmes which would be filmed 'live' before an invited studio audience.

And that's how *Calum's Ceilidh* – initially in black and white - came about in the early 60s.

The show was an instant success. Huge audiences across Scotland tuned in weekly to watch this vibrant, family show. From the start they loved the warm informality of my father who sang songs both in English and Gaelic. He hosted with ease and had a lovely rapport with the studio audience which came across naturally to viewers at home. Gifted with a beautiful light tenor voice he was a master of the ballad with songs like Dark Lochnagar, The Road and the miles to Dundee, Land of Heart's Desire and Island Sheiling Song. He seemed equally popular with English-speaking, Doric and

Gaelic native speakers alike.

The series had a house band led by multi-instrumentalist,

musical director and arranger, Alex Sutherland. Alex mainly played accordion on dad's shows, but he was also a tremendous trombonist and jazzer! I also remember the wonderfully-talented and smiley Hebbie Grey on fiddle.

As a child I can remember dad rehearsing at home at the piano, music strewn everywhere, musicians arriving to run over songs - some not leaving for about a week!

Mum provided endless bowls of soup and meals, as the rehearsals often developed into rip-roaring ceilidhs. My sisters and I would often go to sleep upstairs to the strains of dad singing Scottish, Gaelic and Irish songs accompanied by a few drams and much laughter.

In many ways *Calum's Ceilidh* was simply an extension of what went on at our house. This was our normal. My sisters and I didn't know that this wasn't what happened in everyone's homes!

Being the eldest of five daughters, I liked to organise my sisters, Kirsteen, Morag, Morven and Deirdre - all really good singers in their own right - and it was completely natural for us to sing, harmonise and put on our own wee shows as our house was always full of music. So it wasn't too long before we got involved, singing together live in dad's television programmes - a bit like Scotland's Von Trapp family!

From the standpoint of a child, as I was in the 60s, some of my memories are quite vivid about 'the Grampian days'. I remember so many of the people - not least because they were all so friendly - Alan Franchi, Mike Bevan, Tony Bacon, Bob Christie, Tom on camera, Norman the sound man, Colin Mearns who made the scenery, Olive in the Canteen, Peggy at reception, Jimmy Spankie, 'Ginger Peachey' David Bennett, Helen and Jean in make-up and Betty Esslemont in Wardrobe. Grampian was a real family.

I vividly recall the very first time I stepped inside Grampian's granite building at Queens Cross with my father who thought that I was perhaps ready to sing a solo on *Calum's Ceilidh*.

I couldn't have been more excited! We were driven in a taxi to what seemed to me a rather impressive modern entrance. Dad, as always resplendent in his kilt, hopped out of the cab with me in his wake and into reception. Dad charmed everyone he came into contact with. Certainly the ladies at the reception desk seemed delighted to see him and he chatted away ebulliently to them with stories about our journey and how great it was to see them.

Anne Kennedy, Fiona's mother

We were ushered upstairs to the boardroom for lunch with Jim Buchan, whom dad told me was 'the boss of the station', at least in programme terms! That didn't mean too much to me, but he was a really nice gentleman, very friendly, who seemed quite posh! After lunch I was taken downstairs to see the studio.

I imagine most familiar with Grampian remember only too well the long corridor with multiple doors from reception through to the studio at the back of the building. Everyone held these heavy doors open for each other and always stopped for a chat. It took quite a long time to get to the studio!

Once there, it seemed to me a bit like *Dr Who*! Huge 'dalek-like' cameras were gliding across a shiny floor, there were masses of fat cables all over the mock-baronial style set which had an impressive, if scary-looking, lighting rig up above. There was an area for the band with microphones and stands, a central dance floor for the dancers with seating around the edge to cram in the audience.

I felt right at home!

Dad told me that I was to sing The Dark Island in next week's programme. I wore my Albyn School uniform - my Kennedy tartan kilt and dark green woollen twin set. I won't ever forget the feeling of nervousness mixed with excitement as Dad introduced me to the live audience - and then the relief when it all seemed to go well.

Very soon the then powers that were at Grampian suggested that there should be another series *Round at Calum's*, which was very much like our family just singing at home. Mum, dad, four sisters and I sang a wide range of songs every week.

Deirdre, the youngest, captured everyone's hearts as, wonderfully oblivious to the cameras, she would regularly do her own thing - take off her shoes and socks, lie down and sleep in the middle of a song, hide inside the fake chimney, or just wander off! All very natural. And audiences of all ages seemed to love the show which went on to win many awards.

There is no doubt that the popularity of dad, mum and the Kennedy kids on Grampian, the 'UK's friendliest TV station', translated into the many sell-out tours all over Scotland in our family's future musical career.

Happy days indeed!

Views from the fireside
Shona Fromholc

Seventies. Earliest memories for me in the seventies were Friday nights when everything stopped in my household to watch *Round At Calum's*. Out came our special booklet printed as a pullout in a local paper which contained all the songs that Calum sang in his show and we'd sing along, our first karaoke! This show was an invitation into Calum's home where we got to know the girls and the family as well as sharing the songs they sang.

Memories of the seventies also included the competition run by the TV Times magazine in 1973 when winners from each television region were selected to go to the TV studios in Birmingham to visit the set of *Crossroads,* the popular soap of its time. The winner from the Grampian TV area was my mother, Helen Davidson of Turriff. I was lucky enough to accompany her on our first ever flight which was from Aberdeen to Birmingham where we were treated like VIPs for the day. We visited the set at the TV studios, had lunch with all the stars at the Droitwich hotel and enjoyed a trip on 'Vera's boat' along the canals. Noëlle Gordon was especially interested in us as she had relatives from the Grampian area. Larry Grayson breezed in with the producer Reg Watson. Lots of photographs were taken and mother was presented with an ashtray from the *Crossroads* set!

Eighties. My memories of the eighties include my mother's appearance on the show *The Way It Was,* presented by Gerry Davis. Inspired by the ashtray she received after her visit to *Crossroads*, my mother started to collect ashtrays. After trips abroad or to commemorate special occasions friends would gift her ashtrays! My mother was a firm non smoker!

She had a wonderful day at the Grampian studios. A car picked her up from her home and she gave a talk and showed some of her ashtray collection in the programme's 'collectors corner.'

Recently we found the collection in the loft and gave them away to a charity shop, smoking no longer being very PC!

Nineties. During Telethon, which was big in the nineties, children wore blue plastic ears in school and had blue furry gonks stuck to their pencil cases to raise funds for the charity. In 1990, I was teaching at Kinellar school. Our book study was 'The Wizard of Oz' and a parent wrote a script and made costumes for the class to perform a show in the local hall. 'The Wizard of Oz' was performed to a packed-out audience and proceeds were donated to Telethon.

The children were invited to the Grampian studios, one of the parents offered us his bus and the class of witches, muchkins and Dorothy and friends piled into the Grampian studios to present a giant cheque, live on the news. That was our five minutes of television fame.

From OB1 to Obi-Wan

Graham Mcleish
Cameraman/Producer/Director, 1973- 2000

I was always attracted to the behind-the-scenes workings of television. I marvelled, and still do, at the magic of raising a piece of metal (an aerial) up in the air and being able to watch live pictures and sound from around the world and beyond. Even when I gained engineering qualifications and understood how it all worked it made it even more fascinating that someone had thought this all out. I still think television is one of the most amazing inventions ever, and by a Scot as well.

I still have a box of Dinky toys that I, at the age of nine or ten, painted as outside broadcast vehicles with the logos, GTV - not

however for Grampian but Graham Television! I always wanted to be the cameraman who operated the camera on top of the car that drove at speed alongside the horses at the horse racing. This looked extremely exciting - obviously before Health and Safety had been invented.

In 1973 I got a trainee studio cameraman position at Grampian TV. In most television companies training and actually operating a studio camera on all types of programmes would take a number of years. At Grampian you were trained and 'going solo' in a matter of months.

The Aberdeen studios were exciting and buzzing with all types of programmes from light entertainment, arts, religion, news, children's and any others you could think of. Having gone colour only two years earlier there was no Outside Broadcast Unit, but we did manage to do live network church services by stringing all the cables across the road and taking the studio cameras into Rubislaw Parish Church next door. (At that time a colour broadcast camera cost the equivalent of almost half a million pounds in today's money, and your mobile phone actually gives a better picture!)

Graham Mcleish in his studio camera days

Light entertainment music programmes were especially exciting as they were recorded as live with no editing. Traditional Scottish music predominated, but there were also pop/rock music programmes as well. One such was with Scotland's legendary The Sensational Alex Harvey Band. They were so loud that they could be heard all over the building and probably all the way down to Union Street. Music rehearsals were always scheduled to stop for the six o'clock evening news in an adjacent studio. On this occasion, however, the band refused to stop and the news headlines that night were barely heard over Alex Harvey's notoriously risqué performance of 'St Anthony'.

The peak and nadir of my light entertainment camera-operating career probably came within eighteen months of joining the company when world-famous Demis Roussos and his band came from Greece to the Queen's Cross studios. My adrenaline levels (and everyone else's) were through the roof as Demis sang live, and we recorded two programmes containing all of his most popular songs. Unfortunately after the show we were all given four weeks unpaid rest when we went on strike in support of a colleague. He had arranged a viewing in the studio of a pornographic film brought over by one of the band members and was summarily dismissed. Sadly, the Roussos tapes were transmitted only once and then erased. There are only poor VHS copies of these unique Grampian programmes in existence today.

Demis Roussos at Grampian

In 1976 I was promoted to programme director. With my camera experience and a very supportive studio crew I was soon putting my own interpretation and ideas into practice. But I was always aware that I was only a guide to the talents of lots of other people in the large operation of programme production. I still believe that my main job was to be the one who made the decisions. Great ideas are fine, but no one person has all the talents of a production crew to turn ideas into reality. Decision-making is not for everyone. If I got it right the production team was brilliant, if I got it wrong I was an idiot!

In a two-hour live network children's programme Outside Broadcast like *Get Fresh* or *Ghost Train* the most stressful time was the previous day's rehearsals. This was a day of crucial decision-making, telling presenters, cameras, sound, lighting and everybody else what we were doing and working out how we were going to do it. When it came to transmission the next day, if I had done my job properly at rehearsals, then I virtually sat back and allowed the crew and presenters to get on with it. My only further role was to look ahead to what might go wrong and how I would sort it if it did.

In the mid-eighties I was invited to provide input into the design and lay-out of the production gallery of a new Outside Broadcast Unit. My boyhood Dinky dreams were all coming true. Equipment was getting smaller but there was more of it which meant more space for up to eight people in production alone. OB1 when completed with up to seven cameras and 3 video tape machines plus OB2 with 2 cameras (2 VTRs) and Unit 3, a support vehicle, gave Grampian the best Outside Broadcast capabilities of all the regional companies in ITV. The units travelled the whole Grampian area from Gleneagles in the south to St Magnus Cathedral on Orkney. OB1 and 2 brought Harry Secombe and *Highway* to the Highlands, *Telethon* to Dundee, Boy George and The Proclaimers to Aberdeen and Kylie Minogue to Inverness.

At the time of writing, OB1 and Unit 3 are still in action with a large facilities company in Bulgaria which specialises in sport and pop concerts providing up to twelve camera capability from the same original layout. My Dinky OB days growing up in Dundee were clearly not wasted!

In 1987 I was doing a series called *A Touch of Music* with presenter Kay Duncan. Each programme featured musically-talented children and teenagers from around the Grampian area. The quality was very high. One participant was a sixteen year-old boy from Crieff Academy who played Mozart's Horn Concerto Number Four. It was a difficult piece and he made a slight mistake.

We recorded three takes and ran out of our allotted studio time.

As always the studio had to be released for resetting and rehearsals for the live Grampian evening news. Our floor manager came through saying our horn player was insistent that he wanted to do it again. I went onto the studio floor to talk to him and agreed to do one last take. The youth was still unhappy and, as a further final compromise, I said he could choose which take we would use in the programme. I could see he wasn't trying to be awkward, but just determined to be the best he could and frustrated at not achieving this. Eventually I almost had to physically usher the still-protesting lad out of the studio.

I now know it was a good thing he didn't have his light sabre with him at that time to slice me into little pieces. I was talking to a young Obi Wan Kenobi, otherwise known as actor Ewan MacGregor. I still feel chuffed that I helped save him from a career as a second rate French horn player to allow him to go on to save the whole universe from Darth Vader and the death star in *Star Wars*.

I'm not one to believe that our lives are mapped out before us, but where did my obsession with everything televisual come from and at such an early age? Weirdly, apart from my Dinky toys with the GTV logos something else must have been guiding me towards a career with Grampian. Turns out my Dundee grandfather actually taught the young Jimmy Spankie to play the bagpipes before he was ever thinking of becoming the television icon of Grampian continuity.

Grampian Television gave me the best years of my working life. As well as attracting talented TV professionals like my late pal and fellow Dundonian, director Alan Franchi, it also attracted a lot of beautiful girls... including, Allain my wife of over 40 years who agreed to a date after we met at a studio Christmas party! Grampian was a wonderful, magical place where we helped create music, mischief and laughter. For three Dundee lads lucky enough to take the road and the miles to our tinsel town in Aberdeen it really was the equivalent of Mcleish, Franchi and Spankie going to Hollywood!

Much better than a real job

Norman Macleod
Reporter/Presenter, 1987-2021

I joined Grampian Television as a bilingual trainee in 1987. Straight out of college, with limited radio skills, but reasonable fluency in Gaelic and English, I was still very green. However, there was nothing but warmth and encouragement shown towards me among the established staff in Grampian's Queen's Cross newsroom. I remember clearly the words of Alistair Gracie, the Head of News, after showing me to my desk on that first day. "You'll remember this. It certainly beats having a real job." Profound words indeed.

Seated just feet away from John Duncanson and Anne MacKenzie, I really couldn't believe I was there. It was so strange being in the company of household TV names I'd grown up with on my native island of Scalpay.

Not long after joining the station I was sent on a television news-writing course in London run by the inimitable former ITN journalist Sue Lloyd Roberts. She was highly experienced and had a very direct, no-nonsense approach. I was joined on the course by, among others, John Irvine – who had just started with Ulster TV and who is now with ITN – and Anna Walker, who went on to work with ITV, the BBC and Sky. We learned a great deal during that intense but enjoyable week.

On my return to Aberdeen I shadowed the news desk under the watchful eyes of Bill Mackie, Alan Cowie and Bob Kenyon. I was eager to try out my newly-found writing skills but I didn't realise then that only on-the-job experience under time pressures would eventually hone those skills.

When the Gaelic magazine programme *Crann Tara* returned to the TV schedule I was attached to its production team, working alongside Peter MacAulay, Angela MacEachen and Donald John MacDonald. I enjoyed shadowing and learning from these popular professionals and eventually I made appearances on-screen myself. I loved it! I knew then that this was what I wanted to do. I continued to work on Gaelic programming, but regularly crossed over to the news desk to assist when required, working on the highly rated six o'clock news programme *North Tonight*. This was the pattern that I followed during my two year traineeship.

Donald John MacDonald, Norman MacLeod, Angela MacEachern and Peter MacAulay

In 1990 Alistair Gracie asked me to start working under John Duncanson with a view to providing relief-presenting on *North Tonight*. At the age of just 23 I was excited but also daunted at the prospect. With careful guidance and a lot of patience from my editors I made my news-reading debut during the summer of that year. Little did I know then that I'd still be doing the same job some 30 years later.

In 1993 the government allocated funds to produce more Gaelic programmes to help secure the language after recognition by the EU and others that its long-term health was under threat. Funding of around £8m was made available to broadcasters, and as their part of this Grampian elected to provide a daily news service based in Stornoway, backed up by Aberdeen and Inverness.

And so, *Telefios* was launched. Two news bulletins were broadcast each day with a weekly review programme each Saturday. Logistically and technically it was challenging, but *Telefios* soon established itself in the Grampian and STV schedules and was widely viewed not just in the Gaelic heartlands of the Highlands and Islands. Nearly everyone picked up the phrase "Feasgar Math" which means Good Afternoon/Evening. Indeed Gaelic classes were provided at Queen's Cross for those who had more than a passing interest in the language.

Grampian's Stornoway Studios

When there were problems with the line to Stornoway, usually due to the weather, bulletins had to be presented from Aberdeen, often at short notice. It was incredible how quickly and professionally staff could adapt in an emergency situation. I remember on one occasion having to leave my newly-fried fish and chips in the canteen and rush through to the Continuity booth to present the lunchtime bulletin. I think we had less than 10 minutes to prepare.

It always used to amaze me how non Gaelic-speaking staff could follow the scripts by looking out for key words like 'tha' and 'agus'. I recall the normally unflappable director Eileen Doris Bremner swearing out loud during one live broadcast. I was quite shocked as she always appeared so composed and in charge. The more experienced staff reassured me that bursts of profanity were a regular occurrence behind the scenes! The advice was to keep calm and never let it affect the on-screen presentation.

Prince Charles opening Grampian's Stornoway Studios

In 2000 the Gaelic news contract with Grampian and SMG came to an end as efforts continued to establish a dedicated channel. Eventually BBC Alba was launched and I've regularly contributed to the channel over the years.

The change allowed me then to work exclusively with the news desk, leading to various presenting and producing responsibilities. I also took reporting forays into the world of entertainment and the arts. It gave me the opportunity to meet a host of delightful celebrities and some not so-delightful personalities, who shall remain nameless!

I was so excited when I got to meet former *Dr Who* star Jon

Pertwee who was a childhood idol. He was utterly charming and I can still remember that strong gravelly voice. Equally memorable for different reasons was Latina comedian and cabaret star Margarita Pracatan. She was thoroughly bonkers but incredibly entertaining!

During this period I was also fortunate to be able to travel widely at home and abroad. Highlights included eating whale meat with the Faroese national football squad and using my fairly basic French while trying to secure a camera to replace the one an airline had damaged en-route to Brussels!

In 2003 Grampian moved its operations to Craigshaw in West Tullos following the merger with STV. At that time the technology the newsroom had was state of the art. Central to its function was the introduction of desk-top editing. Taking on this new skill was a challenge that all journalists relished. It's true to say the new approach revolutionised the news-gathering operation. What amazed me, having been brought up on the old system, was the speed with which an item could be edited for transmission. Indeed visitors from different parts of the world have come regularly to West Tullos to see the system in operation.

Certainly during the years since the merger the evolution in technology has enhanced news coverage. The digital age now ensures that news is at your fingertips 24/7. But viewers still want to see their news on TV. Recent viewing figures for both North and Central Scotland programmes combined have been phenomenal.

Since 2006 I've been one of the main programme anchors on what is now the STV News at Six (North edition), a duty I share with Andrea Brymer. In 2020 I was fortunate to commemorate three decades since taking those first tentative steps towards the studio hot seat.

Andrea Brymer

Are there many more years to go? Time will tell. But so far it's been an absolute privilege.

Oh, and Alistair Gracie was right. It certainly beats having a real job!

I was in at the start...

Hector Stewart
Programme Director, 1961-1972

The early, formative days of any project are always exciting. Although Grampian Television was in some ways a 'leap of faith' on the part of its shareholders and executives, Independent Television was already proving to be an audience-puller in those parts of the country which had already had the experience of an alternative to the BBC. (There is some truth in the story that what became the Grampian TV area might have been served by 'Scottish Highlands Independent Television' until some street-wise executive realised the acronym initials which would boldly stand out on any vehicle owned by the company!)

For new recruits the four weeks before the station went 'on air' were probably the fastest learning curve of our lives. The studio camera crew had precisely one member with previous experience of broadcasting in any form, and this pattern was repeated throughout most departments. To make sure that we were ready for Opening Night, especially among the Engineering personnel, we had been 'adopted' by ABC Television, one of the network 'majors', who supplied both training personnel and practical assistance. This pattern was also used in the launch of other 'regional' companies around the network.

As the countdown to Opening Night marched relentlessly on, so we began to absorb more of the essentials of our new trades. In my case as a cameraman, for example, I had to learn the proportions of the 'shot' of the human body, the amount of 'head room' to go with the above, so that the tops of heads were not cut off on a properly-adjusted domestic TV, and so on. But the Opening Night was not to be 'talking heads'. Instead we were going to be transmitting a 'live' hour of Scottish entertainment - tartan, kilts, bagpipes, the lot, directed by the only person on the staff who could do so, the Production Controller, James Buchan.

Jim had moved to Aberdeen from BBC Glasgow. In the early 50s long before ITV reached Scotland, he was one of the pioneers of live Outside Broadcasting. Veteran BBC hands claim that Jim was the man who, when rehearsing a live OB from the Forth railway bridge, spotted something on the horizon which, to his mind, spoiled the shot. His P.A. (Production Assistant) was instructed to find out what the blemish was. It turned out to be HMS Ark Royal, moored upstream at Rosyth dockyard. "Shift it!" was Jim's reaction, and the Royal Navy duly obliged by moving the giant

Setting up the studio

aircraft carrier to another location. Such, in those days, was the power of television!

The complexities of a live, one-hour transmission (even in those days!) were quite eye-opening for us 'new boys'. The day rushed by in a blur of rehearsals, technical faults and, finally, the programme itself in the mid-evening. Largely because of Jim Buchan's experience, the whole thing went quite well, but all of us, cast and crew, were reduced to sweaty exhaustion by the end. I discovered that I couldn't loosen my grip on the panning handle (which controlled the direction in which the camera pointed) after we were 'off air' and had to prise my hand open to release it. I didn't realise how much pressure we had been under.

Grampian Television had arrived safely in the North-East of Scotland, and it did not take long until its audience share surpassed that of the BBC, such was the lure of an alternative to the fare provided by the state broadcaster. Looking back on those early years, I'm surprised by the sheer range of programming we created for the region from a tiny production and financial base. Also, it was all live, as videotape for recording programmes had just begun to arrive in

London. However, we were young and (mostly) single, so live programme transmission was usually followed by a mass excursion 'downtown', where adrenaline could be safely dissipated in beer and ten-pin bowling at the ABC Bowl. In my case the latter was particularly satisfying as I imagined a close-up face on every pin!

When the job of News and Current Affairs director came up I applied and was selected for the post. The Grampian area was a remarkably fertile one for stories, both local and national. My first major job after becoming a director was to follow up the loss of the Longhope lifeboat from the island of Hoy in the Orkneys. This was a particularly distressing story, which revolved round the case of a Liberian-registered freighter, 'Irene', which had run out of fuel, in a force 11 storm in the Pentland Skerries and ran aground on the rocks of South Ronaldsay, one of the islands that make up the Orkneys. The lifeboat based on the island of Hoy was launched to look for and rescue survivors. It then vanished without trace for several days, before being found, upside-down with all the crew still strapped in their seats.

Grampian (for the very first time) chartered a light aircraft in order to reach the islands quickly. I had asked the pilot to file a flight plan to Kirkwall (the Orkneys capital) via the search zone, but that had been quickly vetoed by Air Traffic control, so we filed one that took us direct, then diverted into the search area once we were up there. Air Traffic were not best pleased! We ended up 60 feet over the water, with me hanging on to the cameraman's belt as he leaned out of the open aircraft door. But we got the footage of the grounded freighter, and landed in Kirkwall, just at the same time as a BEA flight was disgorging the Scottish National Orchestra, on their annual visit to the islands (this fact would be important later on).

Our hired aircraft flew back to Aberdeen with the footage we had shot so far, and I began to try to find a vessel which could take us to Hoy. Remember, this was the 60s; all film had to be processed before transmission; the nearest point where both of these things could happen was Aberdeen and mobile phones were unheard of. Eventually I struck a deal with the skipper of a 30 foot fishing boat and we set off for Hoy. By now the storm had moderated to a force 9 'severe gale' status and the wave peaks were 'only' around 30 feet. The cameraman and I sat below, with our backs up against the engine room bulkhead, trying to keep warm, while the rest of the crew were up on deck being rather unwell....

We landed on Hoy and made our way to the lifeboat house. Our reporter was Renton Laidlaw (who was later to rise to prominence as one of the best-known commentators on golf on network television) and we filmed several 'colour' pieces for Grampian and the ITV Network before setting off back to the mainland. Our hired plane had returned by that time, so we loaded the remainder of the day's filming and it set off again. It was only then, as the adrenaline began to subside, that our thoughts turned to accommodation for the night. The first thing we discovered, of course, was that the arrival of the Scottish National Orchestra had meant that an already not-very-plentiful supply of hotel rooms was now severely decimated. Eventually, in desperation, we tried the hotel where the survivors of 'Irene' were being billeted. "Are you the gentlemen from independent television?" asked the receptionist. "Yes!" we chorused. "Your rooms are ready" she said as we silently called down blessings on the office in Aberdeen. So, after a quick wash and tidy up, we had a couple in the bar and then a meal, before getting our heads down after a long, fraught and tiring day.

I was sharing a twin room with Renton and we were both sound asleep when we were rudely awakened by thunderous knocking on the door. I unlocked it and in fell Keith Hatfield (a well-known reporter at that time for ITN) clutching 2 bottles of whisky and shouting, "You bastards! You've got our rooms". Needless to say we explained the concept about possession being nine points of the law and the ITN crew staggered off into the night.

Life seemed fairly mundane after such excitement, but I settled down to the day-to-day activities involved in News and Current Affairs. We produced a nightly news programme, *News and Views*, plus several 'strands' including Farming, and one hosted by George Kidd, better known as the world lightweight wrestling champion, who came from Dundee. This was a kind of 'character-based' programme, featuring the real-life stories of people who made their living in the Grampian area, which stretched from the Orkneys and Shetlands in the north to Edinburgh in the south.

Marilyn Gillies had been born without arms – not as a result of Thalidomide, with dreadfully shortened and disfigured limbs, but a 'genetic accident' with no vestige of arms or hands, just totally rounded shoulders. When Ron Thompson, our legendary Dundee-based reported, discovered Marilyn, she was working in the National Cash Register Company in Dundee, using her feet, with her typewriter sat on the Office floor.

You can imagine the audience reaction when we made an item about her for the local programme so when the opportunity came along to make Grampian's first documentary in colour, Marilyn seemed like a natural subject. The problem - what was the best way to use her as a character? We thought long and hard about this and decided that it would be best if we could put her with another character who totally refused to recognise the existence of the word 'handicap'. To our surprise the legless air ace, Group Captain Douglas Bader, agreed to be the second one of *Two of A Kind*.

Bader was with us for only 3 days, and we soon discovered that, although he had aged so gracefully that all the ladies swooned, he was actually a difficult old curmudgeon. However, he turned on the charm with Marilyn, who he obviously admired, and we survived the three days in his company. Marilyn took him driving in her car. She held a full licence – the only modifications to a 'normal' car were the automatic transmission, which was still something of a rarity in the mid 60s, power steering, which she used with a kind of 'door knob' on the steering wheel, around which she clamped her right foot and the fact that things like lights, wipers etc had been remoted to a small panel which she reached with her left foot. I'll never forget the look on the toll booth operator's face as we drove over the Erskine bridge, when a foot came out holding the coins for the toll!

Bader took Marilyn flying in his light plane (property of Shell, for whom he was working at the time!) and they chatted like an old married couple about anything and everything. The major job thereafter was editing the footage into a 45 minute slot, for transmission just after Christmas 1971. The reaction after transmission was quite remarkable. The programme was viewed in 4½ million homes at 10.30 at night, a fact remarkable in itself. It also attracted huge press comment and shoals of letters to Grampian – and Marilyn. More importantly, the programme led directly to Marilyn finding romance – and a husband. (In fact, Eva, my wife and

I, along with several of those who had worked on the programme, were able to attend her wedding.)

I spent eleven happy, fruitful and rewarding years with Grampian in Aberdeen, getting married and having two bonny baby girls before being tempted by the chance to 'spread my wings' in the Midlands of England with ATV. But I will never forget the privilege of being present at the birth of Grampian, the bouncing northern baby which was to contribute so much to ITV and UK television in general.

Isla's Grampian island
Isla St Clair

It was in August 1967 when a telegram from Grampian Television arrived. Addressed to my mother, Zetta, it was from Eddie Joffe, asking if she could provide the singing services of Isla MacDonald (as I was known then) for a programme he was directing called *My Kinda Folk*. My mother, the singer and songwriter, Zetta Sinclair, liked the idea and agreed to the request. But as a painfully-shy fifteen year old at the time I was understandably nervous.

My Kinda Folk was to be presented by Archie Fisher and Alex Campbell, two well-known folk singers. My mother and I both knew Archie quite well, as I'd appeared several times as a guest singer at his Folk Song Club in Kirkcaldy. I confess I'd developed an adolescent crush on Archie and was delighted when he came to sit in the Grampian canteen with my mother and me during a break before the television recording. I was sitting quietly eating a plate of salad while he chatted with my mother. But just as I was about to put a large lettuce leaf in my mouth Archie suddenly turned and put a direct question to me. I was totally flummoxed and began choking on my mouthful of lettuce wishing I could just disappear! This was not the self-assured image I'd wanted to convey to the legendary folk singer.

But worse was to come. The director told my mother he didn't feel my outfit was suitable. I never wore dresses and generally sang in denim jeans but for special occasions I had invested in a grey trouser suit with a pink frilly blouse. I thought this was ideal, but Eddie Joffe didn't agree. He dispatched the pair of us on a hurried shopping spree to the local branch of C & A. Finally, I agreed to a psychedelic patterned knee-length dress with a polo neck collar. I sang a good rendition of *My Bonny Boy,* in front of a tapestry backcloth, and judging by the photographs taken that night, the dress looked pretty good too! Interestingly, when watching the broadcast a couple of weeks later I noticed that during my spot the cutaways to the audience often rested on an attractive young woman with lovely long hair. It was my sister Christine. Clearly, Mr. Joffe was a fan!

My career progressed through the early 70s with many television and radio programmes, folk concerts and festivals. Then in December 1974, came the start of my next memorable period with Grampian. I had just moved to London when director and good friend, Alan Franchi, phoned to ask if I'd be interested in presenting a six-part children's series, working title *Isla's Island,* to be broadcast on Saturday mornings. It would involve me presenting, singing and storytelling with a sidekick glove puppet called Subby, the seal! Would I ever? I promptly headed back north again.

By this time I was known professionally as Isla St Clair and was delighted to be working in Aberdeen where I always felt very much at home. I not only enjoyed making the programmes but also being part of the warm family atmosphere of the studios.

My sidekick, Subby the Seal, was operated by the exceptionally kind and long-suffering Kennedy Thompson, who had to lie on the floor through the recording with his hand operating the glove puppet and telling jokes. Kennedy of course was a newscaster

Kennedy Thompson

at Grampian, but loved being the hand behind Subby.

The permanent set was a sunny desert island where I sat cross-legged on a wooden chest, dressed as a castaway in cut-off jeans and T-shirt, playing my guitar and singing. Before the initial six-week run finished another series was commissioned and then another and another.

Initially the series was directed by Alan Franchi, who was always encouraging and fun to work with. I think most Grampian directors took a turn on the 34 programmes which were made. I got on well with all except one, a cockney, who will remain nameless. The first thing he wanted to do was change our sunny island to a sunset and darken the whole scene. On another occasion, I woke up in the morning of recording with lesions on one side of my face. At first I thought it was chicken pox, but thankfully the spots turned out to be an allergy and the director quite undeterred, simply filmed me entirely in profile.

Generally the format for *Isla's Island* was one of song and jokes shared with Subby, a story, a cartoon and some amusing string puppets called, the Rogies, who used the fast-developing oil industry in the North sea as a backdrop for their adventures. The crew were friendly and accommodating and I got on with all concerned. The only people I rarely saw were the 'high heid yins' (the bosses) who seemed to inhabit another world of which I knew very little. Grampian really had a very happy, relaxed atmosphere in those days with terrific ceilidhs and social gatherings imbued with song, dance and banter in the station's own social club.

During this period I rented a flat in Aberdeen and at some point got the crazy notion of rescuing an Afghan hound, which I named Alfie. Alfie was a beautiful creature but he'd had a bad start in life, including being shot, resulting in pellets in his ears. At first he was quite biddable, but his true nature started to surface when I took him with me to appear on a children's educational series I was making for the BBC concurrent with my work at Grampian. We were filming a beach scene and the plan was to let the dog off the lead and, upon my command Alfie would come bounding back down the beach, coat flying in the wind, and so make stunning shots for the end credits. You've guessed it! The second Alfie was off the lead he must have reached 60 mph before vanishing completely from view.

Next time I was due to film on location, I asked Alan and Jane Franchi if they would feed and walk Alfie while I was away. Things did not go smoothly. Firstly, it took Alan a long time even to get into my flat as Alfie was growling in a very threatening manner. However, Alan persevered, and after some time spent cajoling and bribing he finally managed to collar the dog. Together with Jane they all set off for a good brisk walk which quickly turned into a lengthy marathon run as Alfie managed to slip his collar, before speeding off like Usain Bolt. Poor Alan and Jane were left trailing through the streets of Aberdeen forlornly calling his name. To this day, I'm not quite sure how they got him back again. Needless to say they did not offer another dog-walking service!

On another occasion I took Alfie into the Grampian studios when Jimmy Spankie suddenly appeared. With typical enthusiasm Jimmy got down on all fours to pet the dog. This eye to eye stuff didn't sit well with Alfie, who instantly, and rather ferociously, went for Jimmy. Luckily, no blood was drawn and thankfully Jimmy didn't bear a grudge, otherwise he wouldn't have invited me to share these reminiscences!

On my return from a long tour to the USSR I was asked to take part as a resident singer in two fairly lengthy series of *Welcome to the Ceilidh*, which was presented by comedian Johnnie Beattie. Although my blossoming television career was taking me to London to work on the *Generation Game* with Larry Grayson, I frequently returned to Grampian for one-offs. *Walking Back To Happiness* and *Highway* had unusual and interesting stories to film and I especially remember the episodes on *Forties Charlie* and the *St Clair* ferry.

One performance particularly sticks in my mind. I had travelled up from England, in 1986, to be a guest on a series called, *Ceilidh on the Caledonian*. Various technical problems (including a camera dropped into the canal!) had caused the production to run seriously over time. Unlike the other singers, who were miming to pre-recorded tracks, I was asked to sing live to record, always risky weather-wise in the north of Scotland! With only minutes of recording time left, I was told in no uncertain terms that my song had to be filmed in one take.

Jim McLeod, Stuart Anderson and Johnny Beattie with Isla

I'd decided to sing The Norlan' Wind and luckily for me, the weather remained wonderfully calm. I believe the heightened urgency of the situation focused my performance of what I consider one of the most moving songs I know. The Norlan' Wind embodies my deeply fond feelings, not just for Grampian Television, but for all the fine folk and friends in my native North East Scotland.

I hope to be seeing them all soon when I come North to promote a collection of my mother's songs called 'A Kist of Memories'.

Anybody interested in these unique recordings should contact Isla at islastclair.com

My big break thanks to Spankie
Renton Laidlaw
Reporter, 1968-1970

In my days with the *Edinburgh Evening News* I used to send regular sports stories from the capital to Grampian TV, the last ITV station to go on air. This led to an invitation to take over from time to time the presenting of *Sportscope,* Grampian's weekly sports programme, when Jimmy Spankie, the usual presenter, was unable to do the job because of his other studio commitments as well as such extracurricular jobs as compering beauty contests, opening church fairs, chairing quiz nights etc. He was truly the early face of  Grampian TV and it was my good luck he was such a busy man.

Happily *Sportscope* was recorded on my day off from the paper so it was easy for me to drive up and down for the show and be back in the office in Edinburgh in good time on Saturday to look after the racing pages. Of course I wasn't a stranger to television because Lord Thomson, the owner of the paper also owned Scottish Television, and I was a junior member of the legendary Arthur Montford's *Scotsport* team which included Bob Crampsey and journalist Ian Archer.

It wasn't long before the call came to join Grampian on a full- time basis. What particularly pleased me was that I wasn't invited to join solely to cover sport but as a news reporter joining a team that comprised experienced Dundee-based Ron Thompson, as well as former school teacher Donald MacCormick and Marion White. Donald was our political man and would go on to anchor the *Newsnight* programme on BBC Two. My role was general

Donald MacCormick

reporting and news reading, and Marion more often than not – but not always - looked after the items which required a woman's perspective.

Charles Smith

It was a perfect mix and we all got on well – so well that when Donald and I were together in the studio having a laugh and a chuckle just minutes before transmission our anxious boss, head of news, Charlie Smith, would ask us to stop enjoying ourselves so much because he was finding it off-putting in the production gallery. Charlie, by nature, was up-tight as the minutes were counted down to the start of a serious programme for which he had total responsibility.

He told me early in the relationship, "Let me warn you, son, that for everyone who thinks you are great on TV there are three who simply don't like you." I would have preferred the breakdown to have been 2-2 at worst, but he had made his point in the blunt way a red-top Scottish newspaperman would.

Although Grampian had gone on air in September 1961 and I did not arrive in a full-time capacity until the late 60s I could feel there was still an air of excitement and quiet satisfaction among the staff that the station was providing what the viewers wanted. Everybody was still learning about television and learning quickly with a team of talented young producers and directors brought together by former BBC chief Jim Buchan who, as production controller, was in charge of local programming.

Technology was improving so rapidly that it made the taping of programmes easier but Grampian still did not have the facility, at least not in the beginning, to edit pre-recorded programmes which meant that if anything went wrong it was necessary to go back to the beginning of the show and start all over again. I think this only happened once. That was when the lead singer – whose name escapes me – had a mental block six minutes before the end. He stopped, apologised and did not even think of asking band leader Alex Sutherland what his closing song was supposed to be. It meant starting the show again. The audience had to stay on but there were no complaints. They got twice the usual amount of wine and beer and were the most cheerful guests leaving the studio even though much later than normal!

My own seriously awkward moment came when reading the news one night. Before going to the studio I always checked the pages of the script were in order but, to my utter horror, I noticed after reading the first page on air that the next one was not 2 but 38 then 9. It was a mess.

David Lloyd was our floor manager. It was an apt description that evening because he was literally lying, totally relaxed, on the floor of the tiny cubicle we used for news broadcasts.

I did have a few minutes breathing space because the second item on the news that night was one with sound on film and required the easiest of introductions from me which gave me time to alert David to my problem. He would have to put my script back in order, but not just yet. I was still not out of the woods.

The third item was a film story about the Queen Mother's visit to her home at the Castle of Mey typed on different coloured paper, but there were six film stories that evening. As we were coming desperately close to the end of the sound-on-film piece I plucked out a piece of coloured paper. Was it the right one? Was it Page 3? It was! I threw my script to David who began putting it in order and the news broadcast continued in uneventful fashion. David did a wonderful job that evening and I was totally relaxed again by the time I said "Goodnight" to a viewing public completely unaware of the drama. A few minutes later I popped up again with a cheery 'Good Evening' having made a quick change of jacket and tie to read the Farming News.

Today newsreaders have sophisticated easy-to-follow large print autocues operated on their behalf by someone else in the gallery, but back in the 60s my autocue was a Heath Robinson affair. Items were typed up on pieces of paper sellotaped together and installed on a machine that had a light behind and a magnifying glass in front of them to make them more easily read. To move the roll of paper up I had to use an old Singer Sewing Machine pedal on the floor which if accidentally kicked out of reach meant it was the end of the autocue for that night... unless floor manager David could retrieve it without coming into shot.

One of Grampian's earliest programme directors, Hector Stewart, was interested in golf. We got on very well and devised a stand at the Royal Highland Show at Ingliston one year designed to prove that commentating on golf was not as easy as it appeared to be.

Hector had prepared a three-minute golfing tape giving participants an idea of what they would be seeing before their 'audition'. The difference was that when the members of the public came to try their hand at being Peter Alliss, Hector used the same clip but one on which he could be heard giving instructions and even asking questions of the man at the mike – the same kind of background babble real commentators have to cope with. Everyone messed up their attempt at commentating in what turned out to be one of the most popular show-stoppers that year. Live golf commentary is not as relaxed as it sometimes appears! Hector and I would work later on ITV's golf coverage master-minded by Laurie Higgins of Yorkshire TV

UK and Scottish news were well covered at Grampian with some of the leading politicians, industrialists and personalities from the theatre and cinema all too ready to come north to Aberdeen. Although a small station compared to ATV in the Midlands, Thames TV in London or Yorkshire TV, Grampian had quickly gained a reputation for friendliness, integrity and professionalism in whatever order you like to put them.

Yet local news was still given plenty of air-time too. How were old age pensioners going to get their pensions when they closed the post office in Alford or withdrew the bus service to Inverurie? Why were trains from Aberdeen to Edinburgh no longer stopping at the fast growing commuter coastal town of Portlethen? Was it right that nudists in Turriff should be given the use of the public baths before opening time three days a week?

Sometimes I would be sent off for a week to store up items. At Aviemore I remember that we had been told (by its owner) that his dog could add, subtract, multiply and divide on his command. Was this too good to be true? In rehearsal the dog did bark twice when asked to take 2 away from 4, did bark six times when asked to multiply 3 by 2 but when the cameras rolled the collie was a complete failure. Nerves got the better of him and his arithmetic skills deserted him.

On a visit to Orkney we visited a charming old lady who was an expert on old Scottish songs. She insisted that before the interview every member the crew should have a dram from her late husband's bottle of Highland Park, a malt whisky with an exceptionally high alcohol rating. Our temporary sound recordist from London, paying no heed to our warnings, downed his dram in one big gulp and promptly collapsed. No filming was possible that day. When we returned the next morning we were wisely only offered coffee.

On a more serious note, having to cover one lifeboat disaster was sad enough but two was particularly upsetting. Elsewhere Hector Stewart, has written about the tragedy of the sinking of the Longhope boat in a force 10 gale up in Orkney. The other lifeboat tragedy in my time at Grampian happened at Fraserburgh where the lifeboat turned turtle as it entered the harbour in rough seas. There was only one survivor.

The most poignant moment for me occurred as we were wrapping up after doing a piece for ITN. George Leslie had put his lights out, Gordon Watson was wrapping up his sound equipment in the rain, and on a heavily overcast day it was getting dark much earlier than usual. It was then I felt someone touching my hand. I looked down and there was a little girl with tears in her eyes who asked very politely and very quietly, "Any news of my daddy yet?" "Sorry no", I told her, and she was gone into the dismally bleak night. I still hope her dad was the one survivor.

I was sad then but later delighted when the RNLI commended us and the BBC for our sympathetic coverage of both disasters. BBC Aberdeen's Ron Neil and I were on-screen rivals, but Ron was a regular visitor to Grampian parties as he was married to Isobel Neil, one of the first to sign up for Grampian a month before the launch. She trained as a Production Assistant and ended up working as a senior PA at Thames.

Occasionally top Scottish sportsmen and TV personalities would get together to play Aberdeen FC 'Old Stars' for charity. I was involved when we went to Elgin to play under the lights. On the bus travelling north our team manager told us, regretfully, that one of us would have to be on the bench. I quickly agreed to stand down. I was not a very good footballer and it was beginning to rain heavily. My offer was reluctantly accepted. When we arrived at Elgin, and despite the rain, fans were pouring into Borough Briggs, the Elgin City ground. Jimmy Spankie, our goalkeeper, was busy signing autographs as usual and I was keeping a very low profile. But not for long.

Within a few minutes of the start the Aberdeen left-winger turned on an ankle and was unable to continue. They had nobody on the their bench to take over and suddenly I was the unwanted centre of attention. "Renton can play for us," shouted Aberdeen star Archie Glen whom I knew. It was the worst scenario I could imagine - playing for the professionals! I was not too bad with my right foot, but useless with my left. But minutes later I was running on wearing my Aberdeen strip as proudly as a dyed-in-the-wool Hibs supporter could!

I drifted back to left half, but not before I had closed my eyes and crossed with my right foot to Archie Glen who scored giving goalkeeper Spankie no chance. It was the only highlight of my miserable 84 minutes in the rain. The final whistle could not come quickly enough. We lost but charity was the big winner and the crowd braving the weather had thoroughly enjoyed the evening and the hot pies during the interval.

When it was time to leave Grampian I could look back on two very happy years. Jimmy Spankie had provided accommodation for me in his house just around the corner from the studios which meant I didn't need to travel back home to Edinburgh so often. I had made many long lasting friendships and learned a great deal about TV production.

It all stood me in good stead when I left for the BBC. Unlike that time in Elgin there were plenty of excellent replacements in the newsroom in Bill Mackie and Keith Webster, and new young directors were on hand to fill the gaps when experienced men left.

Summing up I know how lucky I was to have enjoyed my two years at Grampian when it was truly an exciting place to be. My sadness is that the old Grampian survives today only in a skeletal form of that wonderful original.

Bill's Grampian cue

Professor Kirsteen McCue,
Scottish Literature Department, Glasgow University

My Dad's connections with Grampian TV date back to the early years of both the channel and his own career. Born in Allanton near Shotts in 1934, Dad went into the pit aged 14 to train as an electrician. But his wonderfully rich bass voice won him study places at both the Royal Northern College of Music and the Royal Academy of Music in London. He was offered a radio contract with the BBC in Scotland for a new series called *It's a fine thing to sing*. This was undoubtedly a very fine thing! The series offered him the chance to sing songs

Bill McCue

of all kinds, from musicals and operetta to spirituals and Scots songs. And this job also meant that Dad was in Scotland at the time of the foundation of Scottish Opera in 1962.

While we're missing some appointment diaries for the 60s, we do know that the opera was going to Aberdeen from 1965 and that Dad sang in both productions that season, as Nikitich in Mussorgsky's *Boris Godonov* and the Bonze in Puccini's *Madama Butterfly*. In the winters of 1966 and 1967 he was on tour in Canada and the USA with the White Heather Club and Andy Stewart, Jimmy Logan and Jimmy Shand, ensuring that his 'Scots' songs were retaining an important spot in his professional pursuits. But it's the diaries for the summer of 1968, when Dad was involved with several performances at the Edinburgh International Festival, that we begin to note appointments with Grampian TV. Across the following summer Grampian appears more regularly and there is a note of fittings for his 'Gordon trews', which, my Mum recalls, were associated with a new television opportunity at Grampian: "He did not wear the kilt for this, but had new trews made specially"; and the trews were teamed up with a fetching "velvet waistcoat".

Images from an article in 'The Scottish Field' in April 1969 state that Bill was taking up 'screen' for the first time with an independent TV company.

Bill and Calum in fine form

The series was Grampian TV's *McCue's Music* which was first recorded in ten episodes between 21 October and 20 November 1969 and there are various slots in the diary for Grampian throughout December leading up to a pre-recorded Christmas show. The co-presenter was the lovely Anne Linstrum, who my Mum recalls had a fine voice, "She and your Dad got on really well". The winter diary for 1970 notes that Dad had to cancel commitments due to a 'bad throat', but he seems to have been well enough to record an album in Edinburgh on 14 &15 of January 1971 for RCA International. The album cover features a fine image of Dad kilted, but sporting the Grampian-associated velvet waistcoat, standing in front of the ruins of Bothwell Castle (just a walk from the new McCue family residence). There are thirteen Scots songs (from Burns's 'Corn Rigs' to 'The Dark Island') with musical arrangements by Alex Sutherland, the album cover stating that this is 'the real McCUE's MUSIC...the songs of his native land'. So, there's a nice tie in with the Grampian series here! Alex Sutherland was MD for the show, and the house band included Iain Milne on piano, Hebbie Gray on fiddle and Bill Kemp on percussion.

Jim McLeod, Bill and Alex Sutherland

The series continued in the autumn of 1971 and again the following year. Mum, who never attended the recordings, as she was stuck at home with two very small children, remembers the show as "an after-dinner cabaret" with Dad as singer and master-of-ceremonies. There were guests who were interviewed in between the songs. Mum's memory that many viewers thought the set (designed by Eric Mollart) was a *real* restaurant is endorsed by some of the press cuttings about the show that Dad kept. His diaries don't always mention the guests, but press clippings list Dickie Henderson and Kenny Lynch in 1971 and Frank Carson, Marion Davies and Sheena Southern the following year. In 1973 Dad seems to have taken part in a Grampian panel show, alongside Una McLean and Jimmy Logan, but there are no *McCue's Music* episodes listed. He toured in the Grampian TV area with a live show of the same name in 1974 and there are other connections with Grampian in his diaries right through the mid-70s, including a show of gospel songs and the Hogmanay show for 1975.

Undoubtedly *McCue's Music* gave Bill a brilliant opportunity, early in his career, to ensure that the 'songs of his native land' were at the centre of his professional life. His natural abilities as an interviewer would also come in handy later on with the BBC. Although a proud son of Lanarkshire, Dad's close love of Aberdeen stayed right through his life, and one of his final professional gigs was with the BBC SSO at the Music Hall in the winter of 1998, when he narrated The Snowman at their Christmas show. He always loved the silver city and the audiences in the North East, revelling in his regular visits to His Majesty's and always enjoying his 'digs' with the Shirreffs in Gray Street. My mum also recalls lovely times with Jim and Nan Buchan, with whom my folks retained a lovely friendship for many years. Jim, of course, was controller of programmes when Bill got his first break with Grampian in 1968.

Reporting from the road and the miles

Alan Saunders
Reporter, 1970-2000

The Dundee studio was set up in 1965, five years before I joined Grampian TV, in a most unusual location in what looked like a shop under the Angus Hotel in the city centre. Behind the unlikely exterior was a studio and offices for a secretary, two reporters, a cameraman and a sound recordist.

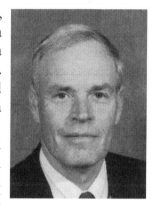

The legendary Dundee journalist Ron Thompson directed operations, with Jean Milne the office secretary, Malcolm Campbell on camera and Neil McMillan on sound. I joined the team as a TV novice from the Sunday Express where I had covered sport. The Dundee team handled news and sport throughout Tayside, Fife and Perthshire. In the early days the aim was to get filmed stories on to the 3pm train to Aberdeen so that the material could be edited in time for the news at 6pm. If the train was missed it meant a drive north to Aberdeen for whoever was handling the story to deliver the cans of film straight upstairs to the film editors.

With two successful football teams in Dundee there was no shortage of sport. Dundee United under manager, Jim McLean did very well to reach the final of the UEFA cup, losing out to Gothenburg in that final. While many journalists crossed swords with the mercurial Jim McLean I have to say I was never one of them. After the Gothenburg defeat I managed to have a private word with the deeply-disappointed manager. To my surprise he confided that I was the only journalist he had never banned from Tannadice. Praise indeed! In the run up to the final Grampian crews had followed United on the winning trail to a number of European countries. And for a regional TV company we were certainly no strangers to international travel. I remember taking a Grampian crew to Japan to film World Gold Medallist Liz McColgan winning the Tokyo Marathon.

Ron Thompson, Neil MacMillan, Malcolm Campbell in action

The big change in the Dundee operation came with the introduction of ENG - electronic news gathering. Again, Grampian showed their ambition to be among the first masters of the new technology by sending members of staff to the United States to see how it worked. It meant stories were covered on tape and fed electronically up the line to Aberdeen, allowing a much later deadline for Tayside stories.

The news programme changed in the summer months giving the chance for more feature type stories, with Ron interviewing local characters like Dick McTaggart and wrestler, George Kidd as well as air ace, Sir Douglas Bader, with whom he later made a documentary. As a big fan I particularly remember interviewing Sammy Davis Junior in Edinburgh at the launch of his autobiography.

Among the many lighter highlights of my career was an exclusive I came upon when interviewing the Perthshire wrestler, Andy Robbins. Andy, it transpired, had found a bear which he was teaching to wrestle. Hercules became an immediate hit with wrestling fans.

Andy was a burly character, but the bear was even burlier. Such a bond grew up between wrestler and bear that neither seriously injured the other in bouts. The fans absolutely loved it and Hercules became an international superstar in many TV commercials and programmes. The world's favourite bear made world-wide headlines when he disappeared during a shoot on Benbecula. TV crews piled in from around the globe, including one from Grampian. Hercules was eventually found safe and carried on living with Andy and his wife, Maggie, until he sadly passed away in 2001.

Building of the Tay road bridge

But there were also more dynamic stories. The Timex dispute saw us filming violence on the picket lines and the eventual closure of Dundee's watch-making factory with the loss of hundreds of jobs. A Dundee crew also filmed the Dunblane school killings. Thomas Hamilton took the lives of sixteen children before killing himself.

There was never a rational reason given for his actions which remain a dark mystery to this day.

Alan interviewing artist James McIntosh Patrick

By this time we had a new cameraman in Henry McCubbin, Grampian's Dundee operation had moved into a mansion house in Albany Road, Broughty Ferry. My long-time sidekick and mentor, Ron Thompson (now MBE) decided to hang up his mic and Craig Millar joined us from The Scotsman. There was a final office move to the Customs House in Dock Street, but having completed 30 years reporting on events from Dundee and Tayside, I decided to retire in 2000.

Like others I have nothing but good to say about Grampian. It did a remarkable job covering such a big area and in Dundee we were never left feeling that we were junior partners in any way.

Spankie Doodles 1
Jimmy Spankie

Jim Buchan fixed it for me

My first audition for Grampian was in the Marryat Hall, Dundee. On camera I interviewed another hopeful, was interviewed by the same person, then read some news stories; all under the watchful eyes and ears of Jim Buchan, the Production Controller and his P.A. Maggie Barr. Jim then interviewed me about my life generally, at the end of which he invited me to Aberdeen to do it all again. I did.

Then the bad news - all announcers posts were filled. I was kept on a reserve list. A month later the phone rang. "If you're still interested please come to Aberdeen for one more test." I did. The camera malfunctioned. One hour later on we went. Success! Position offered and accepted! Some years later I was told that the camera 'problem' at my final audition was a 'hoax', My reaction to the delay was assessed as part of my audition!

The last Monday of October 1961 at 10am I reported for duty. At 6.30 that evening I interviewed a delightful young man about a 50 megaton bomb which had been detonated. In deepest Russia, I seem to remember. My interviewee was Sinclair Forbes, a physics student at Aberdeen University's Marischall College. The detonation had been picked up by the University's equipment.

The live programme was called *News and Views* and after it was over Jim Buchan said, "Not too bad, but try not to stick out your tongue every ten seconds, and don't say 'I see' after every answer."

The next day, in Jim Buchan's office, some guidelines to consider.
INTERVIEWING:-
Do as much research about the subject/person as you can.
Questions should be concise, to the point and as far as possible arise from the previous answer.
SCRIPT-WRITING:-
Make it easy for your viewers to understand what you're saying.
Use colloquial, everyday language. You're telling a story NOT issuing an edict.

I remember being asked to write a sentence including the word 'THAT.' I wrote as follows, 'I hope that you're enjoying your day.' Jim helpfully pointed out that eight or nine times out of ten you can omit the word 'that' and it actually improves your sentence. Among the many things (that) I learned from Jim Buchan that was a tip (that) I never forgot!

Just a second

A relevant phrase if ever I heard one. In all forms of broadcasting seconds are important. Particularly so in commercial broadcasting because advertisers pay for air time - by THE SECOND

In news reading one second equals three words (or two words and a full stop). Our news bulletins were read from a very small studio which had a remotely controlled camera. The engineer responsible for the picture would say to me via talk back "Jim would you please adopt your news reading position?" Accordingly I would straighten my shoulders, make sure my tie was neat, comb my hair, fasten or unfasten my jacket, depending on how good a fit the jacket was and raise my eyebrows as if to say "how's that?"

To which he would often respond with "Thanks Jim. That's the best possible picture I can obtain with the available material."

I never took off my jacket because I hadn't ironed the sleeves or the back of my shirt.

News reading was usually straightforward. During rehearsals each paragraph was timed to a second and added up to the allotted overall time - including, of course, 2 seconds for each page turn over.

If news reading was NOT straight forward it was because there was a piece of film to insert. Each piece of film had a 7 second leader on it before the actual film began. Therefore I counted back 21 words from the last word immediately before the film began. Three words per second for 7 seconds equals 21 words. When I read THAT word the machine with the film began and as I read the 21 words the film leader ran its course and when I finished my words I was electronically faded from the screen and the film appeared. Not a lot of room for error!!

Tapping into how the other half live

How much do you know – or think you know about your other half? One of our programmes in the mid-60s was called *Mr and Mrs*. I was asked to present it and the lovely Samantha Lee assisted. The idea was to find out how much husbands knew about their wives and vice versa. All done by question and answer.

Unlike most quiz-style programmes it was a good idea to meet the contestants before recording so that I could try to decide who the 'characters' were – those I could chat up and get a response from during recording.

Circumstances dictated that the couples stood very close to each other and I had a few letters from viewers claiming that some individuals tried to cheat, maybe by tapping their partners. I was unaware of any potential 'tappers', but I was taken aback by a character from a North East farm. I don't remember why I asked him to sing a couple of verses from the 'Nicky Tams' bothy ballad. He passed the two verse mark without seemingly pausing for breath.

The programme was tightly timed so it caused more than a little concern when he sang on – and on – and on. The floor manager waved frantically for me to stop him but he almost deliberately seemed to be avoiding my eye. Eventually I managed to signal to his wife who stopped him with a swift dig in the ribs. It looked to me as though that had not been the first time he had been the recipient of a bruised rib!

But the episode reminded me of a hilarious 'tapping' story told to me by that marvellous broadcaster, Donny B. Macleod. In his Grampian days Donny was apparently doing a studio interview with the legendary air ace, Douglas Bader. Donny took Bader through the drill for live interviews which under no circumstances could over-run. "When I get the wind-up signal from the floor manager I'll start to nod more quickly" Donny explained, "but if you don't take this cue I'll tap you gently on the ankle with my foot to remind you that we are nearly out of time. OK?"

Came the interview's ending with Donny nodding furiously and Bader still in full flow. A gentle tap on the ankle was needed. No reaction. Donny kicked harder. Still no reaction - apart from a dull metallic clang. And then it dawned on the horrified interviewer.

Douglas Bader had lost both legs in an air accident. His ankles were artificial and had no feeling!

Way north of Watford

Jeremy Taylor

Head of Production, Programming Planning and Presentation Aberdeen, 1970-1974

All this starts in my last days at Pitman's College in London, learning shorthand and typing, when I was interviewed by one of Monty's staff officers, Col Denis Hamilton DSO. He was the Editor of the Kemsley Newspaper Group and I won a place on their journalist training scheme. Should I go to the *Aberdeen Press and Journal* or the *Western Mail* in Cardiff? Well, Cardiff was 168 miles from London and Aberdeen was 545 miles from London so it would be cheaper to travel home to see my family if I went to Wales. Little did I know that ten years later I would end up first in Edinburgh with Grampian Television and later in Aberdeen.

Flying into Turnhouse airport I was met by Dougie, resplendent in chauffeur's cap with a shiny peak, and a rather sporty Rover 2000 TC. The Rover and other cars crop up later in my memories of Grampian.

Arriving at the tiny Grampian Studio in Edinburgh, nestled in the valley between the Canongate and Carlton Hill, was quite a shock after six years with ITV in London on *This Week* travelling the world as a researcher and producer. I walked into the reception area to meet my new team. As I went into my office the receptionist said, "Good morning, Mr Taylor" as I walked past. No one had ever called me Mr Taylor at the 'Western Mail' or on *This Week*. Later I asked her why not "Good morning Jeremy"? – she said, "Mr McCall insisted on this form of greeting." David McCall, my predecessor, was an Aberdonian accountant, and I was a roving journalist. Clearly times were changing.

Grampian Edinburgh was like Dundee, an outpost of the Aberdeen television empire. We were making programmes both for transmission on air and for the Edinburgh University/Grampian Television service. What a contrast. The programmes for the audience in the North East of Scotland were mainly entertainment: *Bothy Nichts*, *Round at Calum's* and *McCue's Music*. Programme directors, Gordon Thompson and Tony Harrison took this contrast in their stride. Very popular with the studio crew and the audience was a series of *Katie Stewart Cooks* where the *Times* Cookery Correspondent made delicious recipes. After the recording the crew ate well.

For the University the programmes were made for television as a teaching aid. Cameras would be used in teaching dentistry and medicine to reach the parts that other students could not reach except by crowding each other out. There was a lot of committee work involved in this project and the patrician John Gillingham, professor of neuro-surgery, was a masterful chairman of our joint liaison committee.

Grampian's Edinburgh studio

One of the nicest people I remember was Edinburgh artist and impresario, Ricky Demarco. We set up a loan plan for Scottish artists. Ricky would select pictures by contemporary artists and we would exhibit them in our studios in Edinburgh and Aberdeen on a rolling contract. In a small way this, I think, helped to make the workplace more convivial.

In 1969 I had to apply to the Lord Chamberlain for a performance licence for *Bothy Nichts*. It took some time and a little explanation to get it. However it was well worth it since it was one of the first truly Scottish performances at the Edinburgh International Festival. It was a sell-out every night, locally appreciated, and for those visiting the festival from far and wide it was an amazing experience. This, and other broadcast programmes benefited from the fact that the studio was in the converted old Lady Haigh Poppy Factory with atmospheric workshops which, when used as a backdrop, enhanced the atmosphere of these studio-based programmes.

One hazard which I had not foreseen was the 4am call from Edinburgh City Police. Being a small studio we had an alarm system tied into police HQ. I had to jump out of bed, put on whatever clothes were at hand and speed off to the studio to meet the police. Usually the alarm had been set off by someone, a little the worse for wear, leaning against the door. However, on a busy night one policeman would make sure you reset the alarm; and so home to bed. But on a slack night there might be three patrol cars, and the dog handler's van waiting at the kerbside. Then a studio tour was necessary, a check on equipment and of course an examination of the drinks cabinet. This might last an hour or more, so when the phone went in the early hours I always hoped for a busy night on the force.

Grampian's managing director, David Windlesham, helped us to obtain some high profile interviews. The Duke of Edinburgh was interviewed by Ludovic Kennedy about his views on education just as Prince Charles had finished at Gordonstoun and was about to start at Trinity College, Cambridge where 'RAB' Butler, former Conservative education minister, chancellor and foreign secretary, was Master.

Captain (later Sir) Iain Tennant, the chairman of Grampian Television, might have also had a hand in setting up this interview since he had acted *in loco parentis* for the Duke and the Queen while Charles was at Gordonstoun. Iain Tennant was the perfect chairman, informed, interested, at ease with everyone and a truly Scottish gentleman and polymath.

Ted Heath, Conservative prime minister was also a visitor to the studio for an interview in the days before the SNP was a power in the land, and the Tories had 23 MPs sitting in Westminster for Scottish seats.

In the end, however, after obtaining the necessary audience penetration for Edinburgh to be in 'overlap' with STV, it became uneconomic to keep the old poppy factory studio going. Then the broadcasting authority allocated the new transmitter on the Fife coast opposite Edinburgh to STV. So Grampian was forced to retreat to its stronghold in the North East. All the staff from Edinburgh were relocated to other parts of the ITV network, the BBC and to Grampian in Aberdeen without any redundancies. I moved from Edinburgh, a cool city, where radio was still referred to as the wireless, and some still saw television as the work of the devil, so the journey up to Aberdeen in 1970 was in some ways a

Sir Iain Tennant

welcome relief. Aberdeen was much more friendly than Edinburgh. Happy times at Queen's Cross lay ahead.

Leaving the tiny studio in Edinburgh, with 25 staff and moving to Aberdeen with about 100 was liberating. I took on the role of Head of Production, Programme Planning and Presentation, which meant that I was in charge of all programmes for the station except for news and local programmes. News was under the firm hand of Charles Smith, and local programmes were the fiefdom of the mercurial James Buchan.

Charles Smith told me that those sitting in London had no idea of the size of Scotland. ITN requested a story from Grampian about Shetland and expected it for their six o'clock bulletin. Not possible. But, said ITN, Shetland is only 40 miles east of Aberdeen in the North Sea. Charles pointed out that Shetland was in a 'box' on their map and in fact the island was over 200 miles north of Aberdeen.

Jim Buchan was famed around the ITV network for a local programme that featured as Number One in the local Top Ten ratings whenever a series was transmitted. *Bothy Nichts*, was a truly Doric experience. ATV network, the Midlands ITV contractor, asked after the programme, since if it was number one in North East Scotland, perhaps it might be number one in the Midlands. A tape was sent to Birmingham but when previewed their programme planners were none the wiser!

Also, on a more serious note, Grampian at this time were the leaders of all broadcasters, both ITV and the BBC, by making the hugely successful *Living and Growing* schools programme on sex education under the guidance of Elizabeth Garrett, Jim Buchan's Head of Education Programmes. Grampian was also the first ITV company to show the hugely successful US pre-school programme, *Sesame Street*. Little Aberdonians were familiar with Big Bird, Oscar the Grouch and Miss Piggy well ahead of little Londoners.

Somewhat strange was the scene in Aberdeen when the studios were transformed, usually to an interior of a baronial hall, for the traditional Hogmanay programme, often recorded at the end of the summer depending on the availability of top Scottish and sometimes international stars.

I recall engaging Bernadette de Loriol, speakerene, from ORTF the French national TV service, to come to Aberdeen for the first week of 1973 to share in-vision continuity announcing with our own team of announcers, led by the delightful and friendly Jimmy Spankie. This was to celebrate the UK joining the EEC on January 1, 1973 and, incidentally the Auld Alliance of 1295 between France and Scotland. For the 1972 Hogmanay Show principal guests were Seda Aznavour, daughter of French heart-throb, Charles, and German singer/composer Oliver Freytag. There was also a specially-composed 'Fanfare for Europe' from the Gordon Highlanders.

When Ted Heath won the 1970 General Election rumbles were felt by us in far away North East Scotland after the last results were in on Friday June 19th. David Windlesham, a Conservative member of the House of Lords, was the managing director of Grampian. I told Alex Mair, the general manager, that David would not be with us if he was appointed to a ministerial post by Ted Heath. Alex thought he would have to honour his contract with Grampian which had some time to go. But David was made Minister of State for the Northern Ireland Office and started work for the government on Monday June 22, leaving the road clear for Alex Mair to become the company's new chief executive.

Alex was famed for his reputation as a canny Aberdonian accountant throughout the ITV network. So, with only 1.6% of the ITV advertising revenue, Grampian, under Alex became the steady hand on the tiller of ITV's finances. He was the chairman of the ITV finance committee. One of my later colleagues, long after I left Grampian, told me that Alex scared all the bosses around the ITV Network with his dexterous use of the slide rule.

Alex Mair

At the start I mentioned that I would return to cars. Ward Thomas, the founding managing director of Grampian, had been a war-time bomber pilot and later a successful racing car driver. So the Rover 2000 TC in British Racing Green was the right image for him. When I was in Edinburgh sometimes the Rover would go into the garage for longish visits and then Ward's Mini Cooper S would come down from Aberdeen. With its steel studded ice tyres and massive power unit it was a challenge to drive and useless for picking up guests from the airport. Another memorable car was the Saab driven by shop steward for the ACTT, Ron Barton. Tony Elkins, kept his Rover 3 Litre in the company garage all winter and then took it out in the summer months for picnics by the river Dee. Cars told you a lot about people in those days!

Film technician, Fred McLeod, worked in the dark recesses of Grampian and then at weekends, and on summer evenings he took to the hills to make his 16mm master work *Culloden* with perhaps only 10 extras to represent the thousands who took part in the notorious 1746 battle. I never did find out if he completed it. Perhaps it lies in a Scottish cultural archive.

Perhaps the strangest mission I undertook when Head of Presentation at Aberdeen was a visit to the Lord Lyon King of Arms at New Register House in Edinburgh. Grampian had included the cross of St Andrew, the Saltire, in its monochrome logo on air. The introduction of colour TV at Aberdeen meant that for the first time we were using the Saltire in true white and blue on air. We decided that we needed to get the permission of the Lord Lyon for this use of the Scottish flag. I set off to Edinburgh not very confident about getting this permission. I foresaw trouble as the youngster of television met up with the ancient office of the Lord Lyon. As it turned out it was a very friendly meeting and the Lord Lyon was quite happy to see the national flag shown on ITV in the North East of Scotland on a very regular basis.

What was it like living and working in Aberdeen? Living in this close-knit community where everyone knew everyone else took some re-adjustment. But it was fun and friendships flourished both with colleagues and with neighbours. Maybe living three minutes walk from work was not too good an idea. I did miss the break time of a commute. I shall never forget the three day long Hogmanay parties, the icy cold winters and the friendliness generally shown towards us as a family living in a strange land. It was an enriching experience, even if sometimes the predominant culture suggested that the world began and ended in Stonehaven.

On a bright cold November morning in 1974, with Christie, James aged 7 and Polly aged 3 we drove out to Dyce Airport and boarded the Air Anglia flight for Leeds/Bradford airport.

There was a thin layer of ice on the inside of the little rectangular windows, and slowly it melted as the two Pratt and Whitney 1,100 hp radial engines coughed into life. We trundled down the runway and the tail wheel left the tarmac, the front wheels under each wing followed suit, and we were airborne.

The Dakota flew at a comfortable 5,000 feet and the views of the Tay Bridge, the Forth Bridge and Edinburgh were fantastic in the morning sunlight. Over the Borders and descent into Leeds and the start of a new Chapter for me with Yorkshire Television. It was farewell Grampian after a fantastic six years.

Highland focus

Isabel Fraser
Inverness Reporter, 1984 - 1995

"Hello and welcome to the Grampian Television studio for the Highlands and Islands."

Lights, sound, camera, action: the team when the office opened was four-strong. I was the reporter, Steve Horrocks the cameraman, no longer with with film but with this new thing called electronic newsgathering: Palvinder Jagpal was the sound engineer and Alasdair Macpherson the lighting sparks. Gaelic output had its own dedicated reporter as part of the team.

Isabel with the Inverness team

This was June 29th, 1984. For more than a quarter of a century, commercial TV had been 'a licence to print money', as Lord Roy Thomson had said of STV. From Glasgow, it was carried on wavelengths stretching north into Lochaber and even including the

Isle of Barra. Yet for most Highlanders and Islanders, we were lumped in with Grampian, a distant mountain range of which we knew little, but the nightly news taught us more. We learned about Grampian Regional Council and Health Board, and the latest team news from Pittodrie, but we rarely reciprocated. 'The Press and Journal' told us daily that we were 'North men and North women'.

Opening an Inverness office planted a flag in a vast new territory. The studio was located on Huntly Street, one of the most conspicuous sites on the banks of the River Ness, between Hector Russell the kiltmaker and Fraser the undertaker. There, it was impossible for the Highlands and Islands Development Board to ignore us. We were equidistant between the law courts and the council. It was handy for the Gellions and the Phoenix bar - vital resources for journalistic research. The Eden Court Theatre had opened only eight years previously, bringing national touring companies and international arts. And fewer than ten years before that, the boundary lines of ancient county councils had been erased. There was a new power base in the north: Highland Regional Council, carrying the new-found confidence as if a parliament of the Gaidhealtachd.

Starting with the Hydro Board, and stepping up in 1966 with the Highlands and Islands Development Board, such institutions of Highland identity and economic development were being created. At the same time, the infrastructure of the Moray Firth area was being put in place, uniting communities with sleek bridges; symbols of Highland modernity and connectedness, named after Kessock, and the Cromarty and Dornoch firths. The new A9 road was being opened up in stages, with magnificent sweeps through Perthshire, Badenoch and Strathspey, replacing tortured dog-leg turns under rail bridges and through Highland villages. New industries were under construction too - fabricating vast oil platform jackets at Nigg, Ardersier and Loch Kishorn, and farming salmon in west coast sea lochs. We highlighted older industries and crafts threatened with extinction, such as Harris tweed, and fed the monstrous news appetite for sightings from Drumnadrochit and Castle Urquhart.

What was still building - intangible but no less important - was confidence in the Highlands among Highlanders themselves. That was the other essential ingredient to reverse the narrative of decline and depopulation. The media played an honourable part, Grampian Television included. We were there to reflect Highland stories back to viewers, giving Highlanders legitimacy and permission to feel proud of who they were and what they were achieving. As a Highlander, from Rosemarkie on the Black Isle, I felt strongly that the region's many social and cultural nuances should be accurately and respectfully reflected.

Much of what we covered was the staple fare of an evening news programme; council elections and political disputes, winter weather, mountain rescues, fishing boat sinkings; High Court murder cases and sheriff court battles over land rights. We covered the difficulties in providing health services to remote communities or even the new Raigmore Hospital: multiple deprivation in Easter Ross; the rise eventually to national status of the 'Staggies' of Ross County, and the forced, reluctant merger of Inverness's footballing Thistle with its Caledonian. There were Camanachd Cup finals and the National Mods. For a young journalist, the variety of stories made this a world-class job; the annual Lairg sheep sale, the Black Isle Show, big cat sightings in Moray, royal visits, new ski centres opening, the activities and occasional crashes at RAF bases, Lossiemouth and Kinloss, including controversies about low flying, touring actors appearing at Eden Court, occasionally a feature film crew on location, and visits to France to commemorate war and mark European peace.

Political party conferences came to Inverness, where the journalistic cliche of a 'ring of steel' was thrown around Eden Court to protect an in-bound prime minister. In summer, the news schedule was softened, as we went on tour, to bring people the colour and culture of the region.

We captured the rise of new political stars from crofting stock, such as Charles Kennedy; incomers who made the Highlands their own, including Winnie Ewing: and we marked the departure of clan chief war heroes, Lord Fraser of Lovat and Cameron of Lochiel. While local politics shifted from the landed gentry to professional politicians, from independents towards party labels, we were witnessing an end to feudal clan deference and a renewed assertion of land rights. A recurring theme was the tension between conservationists, demanding better protection of nature, versus the pressure for development, and particularly housing. The Assynt crofters' buy-out of their land was one of those stories that had national and international reach: so too the Braer tanker grounding on Shetland, the Orkney child-abuse scandal, and the nuclear waste shaft at Dounreay. The Skye bridge brought huge bills owed to Bank of America, 'the highest tolls in Europe' and a wily protest movement that tied the prosecutors in knots.

The area was vast, often compared to that of Belgium. To cover it for TV now requires as little as a mobile phone, a 4G signal and some editing know-how. It wasn't always so easy. Before pagers and mobile phones, we had a car-phone for communication with our news desk in Aberdeen. But often, we had to find a red phone box, with a ready supply of 10 pence pieces. Footage was sent down a dedicated telecom line from Inverness to Aberdeen. Unable to edit at the Huntly Street studio, we hoped that our editing instructions were sufficiently clear for the craft editors at Queens Cross to work their wizardry. They were, usually.

As the face of Grampian in the Highlands, there was community outreach and charity work to be done. On one occasion, the whole team had dressed up in panto costumes and we were on our way to a charity event, when a call came through diverting us to Ardersier fabrication yard for the announcement of a major contract. The American oil executive looked a little surprised to be interviewed by Prince Charming, filmed by two tramps and a clown.

Working for Grampian TV in the Highlands was sometimes challenging, often fun, always rewarding, but never just a job.

No Cannes-do!

Graham Mcleish
Producer/Director, 1973-2000

On a dreich Monday morning at Aberdeen airport we climbed the Trident aircraft's steps for the 6am 'redeye' flight to Heathrow. There was a palpable air of excitement for all the film crew as we were on our way to a dream week of dazzling sunshine at the 1979 Cannes Film Festival. However my expectations of a glamorous week hobnobbing with our programme's lined-up stars of Joan Collins, Simon MacCorkindale, David Essex and Jenny Agutter, were soon to evaporate in an operational nightmare. I was on my first trip abroad with Grampian's ITV network movie review programme *The Electric Theatre Show.*

For those under fifty this was at a time of no mobile phones, no internet and no cash machines. Re-arranging equipment or dealing with other emergencies during an international festival without modern communications would have been almost impossible. It seemed sensible to take along an amount of emergency cash, or 'float', split between me and the production assistant. As far as the Grampian bosses were concerned my reputation as a director depended in part on how efficient the week's filming went without having to touch the 'float'.

Our producer was a freelance on contract for the programme series. He had worked in the film industry for many years and had good contacts. To say he was a mercurial character would be an understatement. However, he was a good producer and I got on well with him most of the time. He would regale the crew with stories and gossip about the big screen icons he had met - Sylvester Stallone, Lisa Minnelli, Burt Lancaster, Sophia Loren, Robert Mitchum, Richard Attenborough to name just a few. But he was also subject to extreme mood swings and there were many in Grampian, including myself at times, who would have happily murdered him!

Most of our filming would take place at the fabulous seafront five star Hotel Majestic Barriere right across from the glamorous Palais de Festivals. But we weren't staying there. Instead we were billeted in a glorified motel in the suburbs of Nice 20 miles away. For our first night we wanted to experience a restaurant in the

Cannes Festival atmosphere itself. Since the places along the sea front were prohibitively expensive I thought we should find a less expensive restaurant set back from the sea front. As soon as we'd sat down two attractive young women appeared at the table. Our producer immediately launched into his movie exploits, some exaggerated, others clearly imagined, while the girls feigned awe and giggled at his dreadful jokes.

PA Helen Straine, Graham Mcleish, Cameraman Malcolm Campbell, Sound recordist Ino Visser and camera assistant Pete Moran enjoying a much calmer and cheaper meal another night.

It was soon apparent that these were no hopeful starlets but professional escorts, quite possibly in cahoots with the restaurant itself or some local underworld organisation, hired to con wealthy festival visitors into spending more than they intended. Our honey-trapped producer's ego was bubbling over faster than the endless bottles of champagne he was ordering for the growing number of freeloaders suddenly attracted to our table. The meal was mediocre, the service worse, stretching over two hours with the string of bottles down at the producer's end of the table being instantly replaced.

Eventually it was time to go and I said he'd better settle his bill, whereupon our bubbly-infused producer/raconteur announced he had no money and staggered out of the restaurant with his two giggling faux admirers in tow. I was immediately surrounded by three burly members from the kitchen, each with one hand concealed about their person clearly threatening my impending harm! I was then presented with the bill - or more accurately, with one end of the bill. The other end was still being printed out of the machine like an unravelling toilet roll!

While a meal for myself and the crew could be charged to the programme budget, alcohol was strictly not chargeable. Our PA, Helen Straine, had a company credit card but that was only to be used for emergencies. I felt that preventing my threatened demise by the heavies might have been a justifiable emergency, but there was no guarantee that the Grampian accounts department would see it that way. There was no way out. I was forced to settle with cash - mentally relieved that the heavies had left my person intact, but physically and literally relieved of the entire week's filming cash 'float'. Worse, the crew and I had to use our own cash to top up the bill. We were left absolutely skint and now had to face a week's filming at the most expensive event in France with absolutely no cash in hand!

To my absolute surprise next morning who should be waiting to greet us at breakfast but my boss, Bob Christie, Grampian's Production Controller. He had decided to pop down to Cannes to see how the filming was going. Never had a boss been more welcome. Even more so, the company cheque book that accompanied him!

One of the events we'd arranged to film was the publicity launch of a major entertainment conglomerate who owned movie studios in the UK. Their place in the industry had been waning for years and this was their big push to get back to the top. They were releasing four films at the festival and had hired a whole floor of the prestigious Carlton Hotel for the launch. It was an impressive room with grand marble pillars, but filming was going to be difficult due to the contrast between the dark luxurious décor and the Cannes sunshine streaming through the windows.

The saving grace was the heavy velour curtains which would prevent any exterior light intruding and effectively 'blackout' the room. But this meant we had to totally light the whole event. Our lighting cameraman gave his instructions to a freelance electrician we'd hired as to where to place the lamps for our shots as well as generally lighting the whole room. I decided the rest of the crew would go out and film some of the general Cannes Festival atmosphere on the seafront outside the hotel and leave the electrician to set up the lighting.

What I hadn't noticed was the freely-available hospitality food and drinks table, complete with strawberry dipping chocolate fountain fondue and groaning with as many rare and expensive brandies, gins and malt whiskies as you could imagine. Our electrician didn't seem to have an alcohol problem as such, but when we arrived back from our exterior shots he was extremely cheery and "Cannes wus chust brill-yant!". The immediate panic regarding the lighting rig was relieved since all the lamps and stands necessary for filming had been erected. We proceeded to rig the rest of our filming equipment and await the arrival of the festival media and the organisation's bigwigs.

When they arrived it was quickly obvious that the 'bigwigs' had more in common with our inebriated electrician than with their company's big launch. Eventually I got them to take their seats, sat in a row on low-raised rostrum between the marble pillars slurping their dripping chocolate-covered strawberries and sipping their brandies and champagne. They looked for all the world like a mix of retired pinstriped sumo wrestlers - their levels of hierarchy displayed not by the size of their bellies but the size of the expensive cigars they were puffing on with blue-hazed waving gestures.

We closed the last of the velour curtains covering the entrance and turned on our filming lighting... the back lights, side lights and finally the main key lights. Suddenly there was a low thud and the place went pitch black. We had blown out the whole floor's electrical circuits. There was a short period of eerie silence in the total blackness with the surreal sight of around 20 firefly-like cigars brightly glowing from shocked intakes of breath. The silence only lasted a few moments until the fireflies began dancing around tracking our sumo cigar suckers starting to panic in all directions as they and their cigars crashed into each other, the marble pillars and off the raised rostrum and onto the floor.

One crashed headlong onto the drinks table knocking the chocolate fountain over himself including the small alcohol burner that melted the chocolate. His jacket came alive with small trails of blue flames which started flowing beautifully around the floor where the spilt burner alcohol was still ignited. In the darkness our briefly flaming sumo made a ghostly image of a giant Christmas pudding. Thankfully the flames extinguished in an instant and he was completely unharmed, although very chocolatey and sticky. Suddenly the pitch darkness was broken at the doorway by a bright shaft of light (which you knew you shouldn't look at but everyone did) which burnt a black and white image of two running human images on to the back of everyone's retinas.

The image will stay with me forever. Our inebriated electrician was running for his life out into the dazzling Cannes sunlight immediately followed by our cameraman, howling oaths and clearly intent on murder. The velour curtains closed again and we were back into our pit of darkness. We subsequently found out that our electrician had rigged all the lights as asked but had only tested them individually. When we started filming and turned them all on at the same time we had overloaded the hotel's circuits and blown the floor's main fuses. We eventually completed the filming after an Oscar-winning performance of grovelling on my part.

It was a memorable baptism of fire (literally) as a rookie programme director. We arrived back on the last flight on a still dreich Friday night at Aberdeen airport, penniless, exhausted, mentally bruised and battered. But we had two programme's worth of good material – and I had lived to direct another day!

'Black Water – Bright Hope'

Ted Brocklebank

Reporter/ Head of News and Current Affairs, 1970-1986

It's given to few of us to be present at the making of history. And history was the last thing on my mind that evening in October 1970 just a week after I'd joined Grampian TV in Aberdeen as a news reporter. I was about to go home when Bill Mackie, the deputy news chief, stuck his head round the door. "Fancy grabbing a taxi and heading out to Dyce airfield?" Apparently a British Petroleum spokesperson was arriving in a helicopter from something called an oil rig drilling in the North Sea and would be making an announcement. Clearly, it was nothing my rookie status couldn't handle and not important enough to justify overtime for a film crew.

When the cab reached the ramshackle group of portakabins around the single storey terminal building that was later to become Aberdeen International Airport there were already about a dozen journalists milling around – local journos representing the main Scottish media as well as a handful of Fleet Street hacks flown up especially for the announcement. Something bigger than expected was clearly afoot.

Soon we heard the thump, thump of an incoming helicopter rotor. The chopper landed and we gathered round as a burly character wearing a hard hat and US redwing workboots clambered down. With all the flourish of a magician pulling a rabbit from his hat he produced what looked like a horse radish sauce jar containing flat Guinness. "This, gentlemen, is North Sea Oil", he announced. By next morning news of the dramatic discovery of oil in vast quantities under the seabed off the Scottish coast had flashed around the world and Aberdonians were waking up to the prospect of their granite city becoming a boom town.

For the next 25 years at Grampian, firstly as a reporter, then Head of News & Current Affairs and finally heading up an award-winning documentary department, oil was a constant and lucrative backdrop to the economy of my adopted city as well as a rich source of stories for Grampian. But in the early years the wealth it created set the city and region apart as well as allowing Grampian, the ITV station that served the North and East of Scotland, to punch way above its weight at the network table. I remain forever in the debt of Bill Mackie, our deputy head of news, for sending me out to Dyce on that dark October night half a century ago, although I have a sneaking suspicion that he wouldn't have despatched such a novice if he'd realised the significance of what BP were about to announce. In the event, at the start of a new career in TV journalism, it gave me a foothold on the bottom rung of what turned out to be Britain's biggest 'feel-good' story of the 20th century.

In the decade before the discovery of North Sea Oil Grampian had already forged an enviable reputation for current affairs. Charles Smith, a former deputy editor of the Sunday Mail, brought a keen news sense and inspired leadership to his role as Head of News & Current Affairs. He also had a shrewd eye for journalistic talent. Among his early appointees Donny B Macleod, Donald MacCormick and Renton Laidlaw all went on to succeed as network anchors, Renton as an internationally-renowned golf pundit. While Charlie's team was building a reputation for news coverage over the vast GTV transmission area with programmes like *Grampian Week, Points North* and *Country Focus,* Jim Buchan his counterpart as light entertainment controller was pushing up the ratings with essentially local programmes like *Calum's Ceilidh, Bothy Nichts* and *Ingle Neuk.*

Ever-competitive Charlie waged unrelenting warfare with the affable Jim for air-time and facilities as they both vied to position Grampian programmes in the local Top Ten, a vital requirement to win advertisers to the new station. Charlie referred to Jim, a likeable ex BBC producer, as 'J the B'. Charlie, slim as a pencil with an intense blue gaze and Clark Gable moustache, constantly warned his team to keep our distance from 'the song and dance people'. I recall Jim coming back from holiday sporting an admittedly straggly beard. Charlie couldn't wait to summon me to his office. "Have you seen J the B, son?" (he referred to all male staff as 'son' no matter their age). "What do you think of the beard?" I stammered a suitable reply. "Aye," retorted Charlie with a look of deepest suspicion, "but what does it mean?"

I owed much to Charlie Smith as we expanded our news output on the back of Grampian's growing financial security which was fuelled by the region's soaring oil economy. I became a kind of unofficial oil correspondent filming reports from Shetland and Orkney in the far north, twin landfalls for the richest offshore oilfields, and from Easter and Wester Ross where the broad inlets and deep sea lochs were ideal for building production platforms.

Bill Mackie, Charles Smith, Ted Brocklebank and programme director Alan Burrell with the BAFTA award for 'What Price Oil'

After co-presenting a BAFTA-winning studio debate called *What Price Oil?* featuring key industry figures, Charlie generously fixed it with chief executive, Alex Mair, for me to join a business mission to Houston, the world's oil capital. If the Dyce press call had opened my eyes to the very existence of crude oil, Houston alerted me to its importance in a global and political context.

Apart from Charlie himself, a keen TV interrogator, our in-vision reporting team included Colin MacKay, a convivial and knowledgeable political correspondent, Alistair Gracie, a future head of department, of whom more later, and in Dundee the popular Ron Thompson and Alan Saunders. Heading up the editorial production team was Charlie's assistant, Bill Mackie, a former award-winning journalist with the Press & Journal, from whom I learned much. News editor was Keith Webster with Jen Malcolm as his assistant.

Patsy Briggs produced *Country Focus*, presented by local vet, Hugh Kay. The Aberdeen team was completed by Charlie's secretary, Judith Robertson, a shrewd weather vane on the state of the boss' ongoing feud with 'J the B'! Jean Milne was PA to Ron and Alan in Dundee. Our Aberdeen-based current affairs director was Hector Stewart, a former cameraman, and later, after Hector moved on, Alan 'Curly' Burrell.

Grampian's transmission area was the biggest in the ITV network. Apart from oil the fishing industry was a constant source of stories. My first report for ITN was filmed at Peterhead harbour from where an inebriated local fisherman had absconded with his skipper's trawler. Singlehandedly he sailed the vessel half-way to Norway before the coastguards apprehended him. The Cod War with Iceland and Ted Heath signing up to the EU's Common Fisheries Policy were huge stories for us in the early 70s. The Cod War actually worked to the advantage of the North East since the big deep sea trawlers that fished Icelandic waters came mainly from Hull and Grimsby. With the collapse of these ports Aberdeen and Peterhead were to become the UK's leading fishery and processing centres. But for the next half century the CFP would turn out to be an ongoing disaster for the North East with dozens of local ports closing and fishermen thrown on the dole. Somehow Peterhead and Fraserburgh survived but with vastly reduced fleets.

Grampian was also first port of call for ITN when, as happened regularly, climbers got into trouble on the mountains. I recall covering the tragic loss of five children from an Edinburgh school who froze to death in a blizzard on the Cairngorm plateau. The small helicopter which spirited our film crew through atrocious weather conditions to Aviemore later helped airlift some of the children's bodies to Rescue HQ at Glenmore Lodge. It was an unforgettably tragic sight. But the Cairngorms, the Hebrides and the Northern Isles were also wonderfully scenic backdrops for outdoor filming. With the help of gifted naturalists like Adam Watson, Dick Balharry, Desmond Nethersole Thompson and Roy Dennis, Grampian film crews charted the return of the ospreys to Speyside, the snowy owls to Fetlar in Shetland and the re-introduction of sea eagles to the west coast. No area in Britain had the diversity of scenery and wild-life Grampian TV was lucky enough to include in its transmission area.

By the early 70s Grampian was reaching an audience of over a million and employing more than 200 staff. On the technical front, and despite being smaller than most ITV companies, Grampian more than kept up with the latest innovations in television technology. Its first colour programme, the 1972 Hogmanay Show, was quickly followed by the networked documentary, *Two Of A Kind,* shot in colour and featuring Ron Thompson in conversation with Dundee's Marilyn Gillies, who had been born without arms and hands.

Here tribute must be paid to Alex Mair, the company's canny chief executive, who wisely used Grampian's growing economic clout to argue with his network colleagues for more coverage on ITV about the major economic developments being played out in his company's back yard. Because of my familiarity with the oil scene I'd made a number of local documentaries showing how the new wealth was affecting different parts of our viewing area. These mini-docs included *Flare Up at Shetland, Cinderella from the Sea* and *A Place in the Sun.* But not everywhere welcomed the new industry with open arms. In 1973 I was asked to start working on a network documentary contrasting the success and brashness of boom-town Aberdeen, with oil's impact on more vulnerable places like Wester Ross and Skye. The result was *Black Water – Bright Hope*, directed by Bernd Schulze, formerly one of the company's most talented film editors. I'd been impressed by an early film Bernd made about North East Scotland called *Land of Plenty* and lobbied Charlie Smith to give him his chance on a network documentary.

Buoyed by the success of *Black Water* Grampian pitched another oil documentary at the ITV network. This time we called it *A Tale of Two Cities*, comparing as it did the oil boom cities of Houston, Texas and Aberdeen, Scotland. Once again it was directed with verve and chutzpah by Bernd Schulze and shot by Grampian crews. It won the award in 1974 as Scotland's best TV documentary of the year.

Meanwhile the restrictions of film meant footage shot in the Dundee or Inverness areas had to be driven or sent by train to Aberdeen to be processed. Realistically, since there were no live links between the outlying studios and Aberdeen's Queen's Cross, this meant that news stories happening after 1500 hours didn't make that night's bulletin. Dundee was the second largest city in our area and Grampian was keen to raise its profile on Tayside.

A TALE OF TWO CITIES

Aberdeen, Scotland.

Houston, Texas.

A Grampian Television Production

Ron Thompson, a native Dundonian, came up with the idea of a weekly show profiling characters and stories from the Fife and Tayside areas, *Thompson at Teatime*. The well-known Dundee artist, James Mackintosh Patrick, boxing gold medallist Dick McTaggart, and champion wrestler, George Kidd, made regular appearances. It was an immediate success and featured regularly in the local Top Ten ratings. Alan Saunders, another Dundonian, was given the job of presenting a weekly sports programme, *Sports Call*. It was recorded in Aberdeen but it was the best that could be achieved until a live link was established with Dundee.

'How you gonna keep 'em down on the farm after they've seen Paree' was a World War 1 song that highlighted the problems faced by American country boys coming home after experiencing European city life. I felt something of this after my first five years with Grampian. Apart from reporting for the nightly news and sharing the presenting of the magazine programme, *Grampian Week*, I'd particularly enjoyed the creative challenge of producing two well-received network documentaries. But I understood that others in our current affairs team also deserved recognition. It seemed unlikely that there would be similar documentary opportunities in the

101

immediate future.

I had made the short leet for a new BBC appointment, that of UK Energy Correspondent based in Scotland. In the event I was pipped for the job by Michael Buerck. But my disappointment was short-lived. The London-based PR Consultants, Charles Barker, had formed an alliance with leading Aberdeen advertising agents, Mearns & Gill. A telephone call from Graham Mearns offered a substantial salary increase and a company car as chief exec of the new organisation. I knew that my first love was television and I had it written into the new contract that I was to be allowed to free-lance as a broadcaster. But something told me that I had to learn to run my own show. Graham's offer was too good to turn down, but in the event my time as a PR executive was to be short-lived.

On April 22, 1977, less than a year after I left Grampian, the North Sea suffered its biggest-ever oil spill when a blow-out preventer failed on the Phillips Bravo platform in Norway's Ekofisk field. Dermot McQuarrie who had been recruited as my replacement from BBC Aberdeen was the reporter on Grampian's network documentary entitled *Blow Out At Bravo*. The oil and gas flow was eventually capped by the legendary Red Adair whom I'd interviewed in Houston for *A Tale of Two Cities*. Given my commitment to the ongoing oil story it was galling to be missing out on what was the biggest offshore disaster since the start of the boom.

But a much more personal disaster had stunned Grampian just a week before the Bravo blow-out when Charlie Smith, the company's inspirational current affairs supremo, died while golfing at Banchory. Charlie had a history of heart disease but he seemed so fit no one thought it remotely life-threatening. To my total surprise I got a phone call from Alex Mair. Did I want to "throw my hat in the ring" as Charlie's possible successor. Did I ever! Within a matter of weeks I was back at Grampian about to take on the biggest challenge of my career – filling the boots of one of the best journalists of his generation.

There was little time to ponder the scale of the challenge. In my absence plans had been pressing ahead, master-minded by head of engineering Alex Ramsay, for Grampian to be the first British regional TV company to replace 16mm film cameras with Electronic News Gathering (ENG) video cameras for news coverage. It made sense for such a diverse area as Grampian's, stretching from Shetland in the North to Tayside in the south to feed stories electronically from all points into Queen's Cross. No more trains and boats and planes carrying cans of unprocessed film. Alastair Beaton, Grampian's PR chief, and a good pal, joined me on a fact-finding mission to see the new technology in action in the USA. We visited Atlanta, San Francisco, Boston, St Louis and New Orleans and returned to Aberdeen suitably impressed with the speed and flexibility of ENG. News crews typically consisted of a cameraman and reporter. The establishment of links from Dundee and then Inverness also made it possible for local presenters to appear live in news bulletins. We decided to extend *Grampian Today* from three to five nights a week, with regular inserts from Dundee and Inverness making it sensible for a change of title to *North Tonight*.

We next equipped an OB van initially with studio equipment. Later, among other 'firsts' Grampian was the first UK station to transmit a news story direct from a North Sea oil rig using ENG technology. Selina Scott, who later enjoyed huge network success with ITN and the BBC, was the reporter. With family connections to the Aberdeen-based Scott kilt-making company, Selina was one of my first appointments on returning as current affairs chief. She was an obvious and popular choice as co-presenter of the re-vamped *North Tonight*. Alistair Yates, Ron Thompson and John Duncanson shared presenting duties. But a nightly news magazine needed a rapid beefing up of reporting and editorial staff. Among the new recruits were Joan Ingram, Alan Cowie and Bob Kenyon. Bill Mackenzie had earlier been head-hunted from the Scottish Liberal Party as our new political correspondent when Colin MacKay moved to STV. We re-vamped the monthly *Points North* as *Crossfire* and screened it weekly while parliament was in session. Isabel Fraser joined as our Inverness-based reporter. Alan Saunders and Frank Gilfeather, a sports-mad fellow Dundonian and member of a well-known local boxing family, handled sports stories from all over the north in *Sports Call* and *Sportscope*.

It was a period of tremendous change and it wasn't without personnel problems. As Charlie's successor I'd been brought back over the heads of colleagues arguably higher in the department's former pecking order. Under the new regime Bill Mackie, Alistair

Gracie and Bob Kenyon became programme editors alternating as producers of *North Tonight*, with Bob also producing *Country Focus*, now presented by former Liberal MP, Jim Davidson.

But I had an additional role in mind for Bob whose mother's people came from Harris. It had always seemed to me that Grampian couldn't really call itself the station for the Highlands and Islands if we didn't also produce a news service in Gaelic. With Bob's local knowledge we recruited Angus Peter Campbell and Maggie Cunningham as free-lance presenters of a weekly Gaelic current affairs show called *Crann Tara* (Fiery Cross), later to be expanded as *Seachd Laithean* (Seven Days). We could have had few more distinguished anchors. Angus Peter from South Uist joined our permanent staff and went on to become one of the foremost Gaelic writers of his generation. Maggie from Scalpay was destined as a future Controller of BBC Scotland. Anne Mackenzie from Point in Lewis joined the presenting team straight from University, and she would go on to become an award-winning BBC political anchor. Later, with programme funding provided by the Tory government via the CTG (Comataidh Telebhisein Gaidlig) Grampian would appoint Alan MacDonald from Eriskay as its Head of Gaelic. But I have little doubt that our early recognition of the need for Gaelic current affairs, the successful documentary series *The Blood Is Strong* (of which more later) and Grampian's pledge to establish a studio base in Stornoway (eventually opened by HRH Prince Charles in 1990) were key ingredients in the campaign for a separate Gaelic TV Channel.

As Grampian moved into the 1980s Bill Mackie took time off to study for a university degree and Alistair Gracie became my deputy. With the departure of Selina Scott to ITN and the recruitment of Anna Soubry, later to become one of Theresa May's fiercest backbench Brexit critics, the department enjoyed a period of stability, with the flagship *North Tonight* regularly topping the local TV charts.

Apart from our regular run of programmes we also produced one-off studio specials. Land use in the Highlands was a big topic especially with the oil industry commandeering sea lochs and adjoining land to build their production platforms. We called one of these shows *Grounds For Change*. It featured a studio audience including Brian Wilson, the radical editor of the West Highland Free

Press, who went on to become a Minister in Tony Blair's Labour Government, along with landowners like Lord Burton of Dochfour. The programme was lively and informative. It also marked the only time I was ever pressurised from above about our current affairs coverage. Iain Tennant, the company chairman and himself a Highland landowner, invited me for lunch. He'd had a phone call from Michael (Lord) Burton criticising our 'biased treatment' of the land-use issue. I defended our coverage and the balance of the studio mix. Iain was all apologies about even raising the matter, but the message was clear. A local TV station like Grampian always had to look over its shoulder at its shareholders, board members and power-brokers in the region. As Lord Lieutenant of Moray, chairman of Gordonstoun School board of governors and Glenlivet Glen Grant Distillers, Iain (later Sir Iain) Tennant was an arch power-broker in the North. No matter how sugar-coated, I got the message!

It was time to start looking outwards again at network programming. We had produced a number of local documentaries, notably Bob Kenyon's *Commando* in the wake of the Falklands War, *Picnic at Whitehill* about the Forbes Magazine founder from Aberdeenshire, and the *A9 Mystery*, Alistair Gracie's film about the disappearance of Inverness woman, Renee MacRae and her son. Others I recall from this time include Alan Cowie's film about the tiny Byre Theatre in St Andrews entitled *Please keep Your feet Off The Stage*. A native St Andrean myself I got Ron Thompson to make a documentary about the artist, Jurek Putter, a former schoolmate of mine at Madras College, which we called *City Out of Time*.

But a letter from Bjorn Nilssen, a documentary producer from NRK, the Norwegian state broadcaster, was to re-kindle my own dormant love of film making. Why didn't the two TV companies on opposite sides of the North Sea's richest oilfields join forces to make a TV series about oil? Not just North Sea oil, but world oil? The scale of the ambition was breathtaking, but we would need a network channel to screen the series and pay for it. Carol Haslam, the commissioning editor at Channel Four, was supportive but concerned about the scale of the project and our lack of experience as producers at network level. It took Alex Mair's personal intervention with the head of Channel Four, Jeremy Isaacs, to secure the funding. Bjorn and I were to be co-producers with Mick Csaky, a

Channel Four veteran, as director. We chose Anthony Sampson, author of the much-praised world oil history, *The Seven Sisters*, as programme consultant.

Ted, Carol Haslam, Jeremy Isaacs, Anthony Sampson and Bjorn Nilssen.

Our initial plan was for seven episodes but this was later extended to eight. The series, entitled simply *OIL*, was a critical as well as financial success for both companies and for Channel Four when it was screened in 1986. It won a coveted Norwegian Amanda award as best TV documentary series of the year and sold in some fifty countries worldwide, including PBS in the USA. It was two years in the making and consolidated Grampian's growing reputation for quality documentaries. It also posed big decisions for me personally. While I'd relished the task of re-building Charlie Smith's news and current affairs department along with all the personnel headaches, recruitment of new talent, technical innovations and studio expansions this had involved, at heart I was a programme maker. Alistair Gracie had been a capable deputy while I had been filming around the world. I had a number of offers to go independent, mainly from London. But I was loth to leave Scotland.

Alex Mair again came to the rescue. Why didn't I set up a documentary and features department within Grampian aimed at securing network productions from ITV and Channel Four? Grampian would give me job security and I'd retain executive status. The clincher was that I'd have a free hand to make the kind of documentaries reflecting our area that I wanted to produce. It sounded like a dream job. And so it proved.

Where's my statue?

Alistair Watt
Senior Cameraman, 1975 - 2018

As a born and bred Aberdonian I started my TV cameraman's career the wrong way round - I trained in the London Weekend TV studios with a diet of big drama, situation comedy, outside broadcasts etc. I was learning my camera skills from very talented people, but I was a very small fish in a very big pond. I think it might have been a Grampian cameraman, John Radley also ex LWT, who mentioned to the Personnel people at Queen's Cross that I might be worth

contacting to see if I would leave the smoke and return home to work.

So that's how two months later I found myself pointing a studio camera at a stuffed seal ('Subby the Seal' operated by Kennedy Thomson) on Isla St Clair's desert island set and then at two string puppets. The puppeteers were above us on a rig having an argument on the motivation of why one, 'tattie bogle', would be motivated to walk that way across the miniature set. It was a far cry from tracking a big camera crane within a huge ballroom or castle set.

However, although a mega distance in studio size and type of production, it was just what I needed to progress my camera skills level. Grampian had the Philips Camera, a very clever three tube colour one instead of four tubes. The only trouble was that the Dutch design engineer had not thought of putting a tilting viewfinder on the camera. So if you were shooting a Mike Bevan light entertainment show he would want a whole song done on one camera. Thus you couldn't see in the viewfinder as you started to track behind the seated audience and round the singer into a close up then pull out at end for the wide shot.

Although this was mid 70s I still covered football using two Marconi black and white cameras. The outside broadcast unit was made from a horsebox type trailer (affectionately nicknamed 'the Porta-loo' by the crew) towed by a hired Landrover. Later we took the colour cameras from the studio out after the Friday evening news programme was over. I remember we did a recorded network church service with a black and white VTR modified to record colour. Unfortunately while we could record colour we couldn't replay in colour. It was only when we got the tape back to Aberdeen we realised there had been a disaster. Someone in the horse box had slammed the door which, unknown to us, had turned the colour images to black and white. The whole travelling circus had to retrace to a remote church hundreds of miles away, request the minister, choir, readers and congregation to return and re-run the whole church service to record the entire four camera O/B again.

Tracking a 'Mole' camera crane

At LWT I would never have been introduced to Googie Withers or Gordon Jackson as the new cameraman, but at Grampian the crew were always introduced and became personal friends with many artists. I was very fortunate to work with many celebrities over my career, even Royalty including being presented to the Queen mother, dining at Buckingham Palace and spending a week on a

Hebridean island with Prince Charles. But I'll never forget the programme *Gunfire at Gleneagles* and filming clay pigeon shooting at Gleneagles Hotel with Gene Hackman, Harrison Ford and Sean Connery to name just three.

Although spectacular that wasn't why I'll remember this particular production. Under the direction of Alan Franchi I'd just started to film an interview with the legendary Hollywood director, Steven Spielberg. The camera was already rolling but Alan decided he wanted the shot lower, so I knelt down. It was a very hot day and I soon became dramatically aware that from my knee up the trouser stitches were pinging undone going upwards fast towards my crotch. It began to get worryingly cold. Luckily TV's Sarah Kennedy had some safety pins and did her best to surgically close the gap. I certainly didn't want to go down in movie history as the cameraman who flashed at Steven Spielberg!

Strapped into 'Steadycam' harness

I have to say the skill of Grampian crews was of a network level. I was told when I became a senior camera person and had to interview for new camera people, "We don't care how much it costs to get them up for an interview, but we want the best." Most were the very best. With the arrival in the late 70s of small electronic portable recorders and ENG (electronic news gathering) cameras I was very lucky to be taken out of the studio to set up this hitherto unknown technology for the UK. BBC and ITV had no agreement with TV technicians and thus could not use it, whereas Grampian, incredibly, had negotiated a deal to allow every member of staff to use it. But at that time no other staff cameraman in the network knew how the gear worked. I thus had the honour to be the first cameraperson in the UK to regularly use and train others from different broadcast companies in ENG. (As granddaddy to all who came after me where is my statue?)

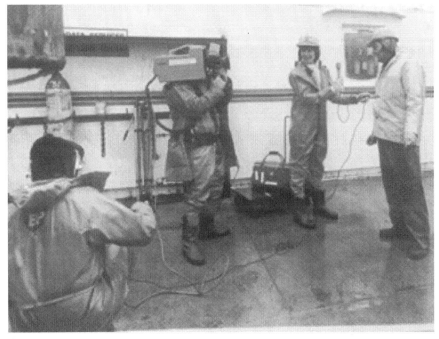

Tony Langton, Alistair Watt and Selina Scott on a North Sea oil rig

I well remember the new-found freedom of not having an umbilical cable attached to the wall or outside broadcast unit, but instead connected to a poor engineer carrying a heavy recorder who had to follow my footsteps everywhere. We did the first-ever recording from an oil rig from the North Sea with Selina Scott with amazing quality. The camera was not the easiest to work with as the slightest over-exposure turned the picture into a green blob and caused the viewfinder to go negative. I'm sure this enormously helped my future single camera career as it meant every shot had to be perfectly exposed. It opened great freedom for me to work on the 1988 Olympics with my old company LWT, to work in Seoul, South Korea. I went on to work on many network documentaries with Ted Brocklebank. I worked on news and travel shows, as lighting cameraman on kids shows, network dramas etc, with great directors and producers who became firm friends.

The thing about Grampian TV was that one week I would be in studio on light entertainment, next week on news gathering or a network kids show, or outside broadcasts, all using different camera skills. I worked with some really skilled people with a great 'can do' attitude who never let a network production or director down. Those were the days indeed.

Go north, young man

Colin MacKay
Reporter/Presenter, 1970-73

I was working as a reporter for Border Television when Jim Buchan, Grampian's Controller of Programmes wrote to me saying he had enjoyed my contribution to the Carlisle-based company's coverage of the 1970 General Election. Would I consider auditioning for a presenter/reporter job in Aberdeen? I would also be presenting the monthly political programme.

I thought long and hard about it. I was young, single and wanting to get on – and the voices were saying "Go south, young man". I looked at the ITV transmission map to see what sort of patch I would be working in. For a native Glaswegian it was a bit daunting. I had never been to Aberdeen or Dundee or Inverness. Maybe southwards was the way.

Then the name of one of the transmitters, Mounteagle, leapt out at me. I was sold. This was a whole part of my native country I had to get to know. There weren't many eagles in the West End of Glasgow. All these years later I know I made the right decision. The North East and the Highlands and Islands proved a wonderful place to work. The sheer diversity of the franchise area – the rich farming land of the Mearns, the spectacular open spaces of the Highlands, and the bustling communities in the cities and towns – was a constant source of inspiration to me.

Points North was the monthly politics programme, featuring local MPs. I joined the company in September and was soon into the routine of recording the programme at midday on the Friday, followed by the guests – always in the Aberdeen studio – joining myself, the Controller of News (Charlie Smith) and other executives for a first-class lunch in the boardroom, before the guests made their often very long journeys back to their constituencies for the regular round of Friday surgeries followed by constituency functions.

And after the 1970 general election what a cross-party assembly of political talent we had, all representing seats in the

Grampian transmission area. Former Prime Minister Sir Alec Douglas-Home (Perthshire) ; a former leader of the Liberal Party, Jo Grimond (Orkney and Shetland); the Secretary of State for Scotland, Gordon Campbell (Moray); Alick Buchanan-Smith and Jock Bruce-Gardyne who held the two Angus seats, both ministers in Conservative Governments; Labour's George Thomson (Dundee), a former Foreign Office minister and editor of the Dandy (not at the same time); a new arrival, Donald Stewart (Western Isles) of the SNP, who was to lead the party at Westminster for many years; Russell Johnston (Inverness), later a most effective Leader of the Scottish Liberals; Lt-Col Colin Mitchell (West Aberdeen); and Willie Hamilton, Labour's man in West Fife.

The latter two were great characters. Colin Mitchell had been commanding officer of the 1st Battalion, the Argyll and Sutherland Highlanders, during the Aden emergency. He resigned from the Army in 1968 over the decision to disband his regiment. He could be prickly in interviews, but you could see the qualities that clearly inspired his men in the field. Willie Hamilton, a man of impeccable manners, was the scourge of the right-wing press because of his criticisms of the Royal Family – but, as he said to me once, "It's not them so much as the courtiers fawning all about them".

Two memories of those times come back to me in particular. I recall the genial Donald Stewart arriving at Queen's Cross. As we chatted and went towards the studio, I realised that there was something vaguely out of the ordinary that I couldn't quite put my finger on. Then I realised it was a smell, a rather strong smell – of fish.

At that time, Aberdeen was bustling with fishing boats in the harbour and the smell of fish was not unknown. But emanating from a Member of Parliament? Sensing my curiosity, Donald revealed that, at one point in his long journey that morning, he had missed a connection, and cadged a lift for many miles in a fish lorry. The smell was still there in the studio during the recording. When told, the other MPs sympathised with the vagaries of transport difficulties in their often vast constituencies – some of the biggest in the UK.

On another occasion – not *Points North* this time, but a party conference – the then Leader of the Liberal Party, Jeremy Thorpe, was coming to us in Aberdeen from his Aviemore conference in a helicopter. We got a phone call from our people at the conference to confirm that Thorpe had left. It was a case now of waiting – and waiting and waiting. Not long before transmission we learned that the pilot had radioed from a hilltop that they'd had to force-land because some protective plastic strips on the helicopter blades had started to shred: the pilot asked if any of his passengers had a pen-knife, so he could cut the plastic off. Jeremy duly obliged, and the knife in question was apparently gold-plated, as one might expect with him. They got airborne and duly arrived in time for the programme.

But it wasn't all politics. Reporters contributed to a splendid little series called *Viewfinder*: the guest arrived the night before, you joined them in their hotel and had dinner with them, and then met up again in the morning at the studios. I remember one in particular – Jimmy Reid.

Jimmy Reid, along with Jimmy Airlie, ran a famous campaign in the shipyards of the Upper Clyde, which were facing liquidation in the early70s – but instead of a walk-out they vowed to stay at work. Jimmy made a memorable speech to his fellow workers, "We are not going to strike. We are not even having a sit-in strike. Nobody and nothing will come in and nothing will go out without our permission. And there will be no hooliganism, there will be no vandalism, there will be no bevvying because the world is watching us, and it is our responsibility to conduct ourselves with responsibility, and with dignity, and with maturity." The world's press was bemused by

Jimmy Reid

'bevvying' but all Glaswegians recognised the reference to drink.

Jimmy had been a member of the Communist Party of Great Britain, so it came as something of a surprise to me when he revealed in the interview that his first job had been in a Glasgow stockbrokers' office. This struck me as out of character for a man thought of as a firebrand of the Left, but he didn't think so, and found it surprising that I was surprised. I later came to realise that he was a man of wide and deep erudition who would never pigeon-hole people and could not be assumed to hold traditional views.

Jimmy was always entertaining, wearing his wide-reading lightly. This was perhaps best exemplified in his belief of the need for equality in these words of his on looking at a block of high-rise flats, "Behind every one of these windows is somebody who might be a horse-jumping champion, a formula one racing champion, a yachtsman of great degree, but he'll never know because he'll never step on a yacht or formula one car - he'll never get the chance."

Another series we all contributed to was called *People We Meet*. If folk were in town, and perhaps doing a short interview about something else, they would be asked if they would like to contribute to the programme. We usually aimed for an edited length of anything from ten to thirty minutes. On one occasion, I did a double interview – with Jimmy Edwards, best remembered for the radio series *The Glums* and the TV series *Whacko!*, and the actor and scriptwriter Eric Sykes. They were appearing in a farce, *Big Bad Mouse*, at His Majesty's Theatre in Aberdeen. The interview was an anarchic riot – Edwards was loud, booming, slightly irascible; and Sykes was quite the opposite – quiet, thoughtful and cerebral (he arrived early for the interview and sat in a corner of our office successfully completing The Times crossword).

My colleague Ted Brocklebank went to see the play a couple of days before I did, and in the office the following day he demonstrated how Edwards answered the phone by banging the end of the handset so that it leapt off the cradle into his other hand. Ted did this rather expertly and we all had a go at doing it. The sight of four journalists apparently trying to wreck company property is one that is still with me half a century later. I'm not sure our boss, Charlie Smith approved!

I have had the enormous privilege of working as a broadcaster, mostly in Scotland, for 54 years – or over 60 years, if you count my time doing *Children's Hour* on the Scottish Home Service (now Radio Scotland) from the age of 15 until I went to university. For two decades I worked for STV as political editor and later

Westminster lobby correspondent. I joined BBC Radio Scotland in 1992 and still work a couple of days a week at Pacific quay.

But in semi-retirement I still recall Charlie Smith, a Glasgow man like myself, telling me that Aberdeen was a terrific place to bring up a family. Marriage and family were to come after I left Grampian. However, now a proud grandfather, I often reflect that, had I been married while in Aberdeen, I would have thought many times before being tempted to go elsewhere. The quality of the schools and medical services struck me as being of the highest class. Likewise the quality of people I worked with at Grampian's Queen's Cross studios.

North East folk speak as they find which means that they may on occasion be almost unnervingly direct. But once they think you might be a 'sort of OK' person, they are as warm-hearted and generous as any I have ever met. The Grampian I knew may be no more, but I for one am glad – and I am sure it is so for many – that I decided to sign up to three happy, fulfilling years at a company which served its diverse communities so faithfully and so well for so long.

Spankie Doodles 2
Jimmy Spankie

'Mr Grampian' Alan Franchi

In the 60s there weren't many Grampian staff from the Dundee area. Franchi and Spankie were. So Alan and I had a special bond which was strengthened when we discovered we had both taken part in the world of amateur drama in the Dundee area. Our surnames sounded similar which occasionally led to confusion, particularly when reception put telephone calls through to the staff restaurant. If we were both there we'd arrive together at the extension not quite sure for whom the 'phone rang. If the Krankies were around we were usually both wrong!

Confusing? Certainly was!

Alan, who was never short of female company, eventually asked the lovely Sarah-Jane McKenzie, of BBC Scotland fame, to marry him. Sarah-Jane said "Yes" It took Alan a while to recover from the shock! From that day, for a month or two, the words 'wedding' and 'marriage' were missing from Alan's vocabulary. However, he made a good recovery and did me the honour of asking me to be his Best Man.

Alan was a huge part of Grampian. How fortunate I was to have worked with him on a number of programmes. Please note I 'worked WITH him' Not 'FOR him'. He was a team player with the ability to bring out the best from his crew. He was courteous, ready to smile, gentle, a straight talker who loved discussions. From a front of camera perspective he was a delight.

Alan's stag night, handcuffed and chained to a stage weight by studio floor managers Chris Kay and Kerr Paterson

However, he was a stickler for ensuring his shots were EXACTLY what he wanted. He also had a way of stretching rehearsal time to the limit – and considerably beyond. Rehearsing a Christmas show he was unhappy with the tree decorations. His crew had to strip and redecorate the tree until their frustration nearly spilled over. Then a pregnant lady appeared and sat down where she would be seen on camera

No way, thought Alan. So he said to his Floor Manager through earphones, "Please ask that pregnant lady to move three seats back. Tell her she'll have a better view of the show." Whereupon a member of the crew said quietly to Alan, "You do realise that when you began rehearsals that lady wasn't pregnant."

My pal Al

No appreciation of the Grampian years would be complete without paying tribute to Alastair Beaton. Al was that rare combination, an intellectual who also understood the tastes and loyalties of ordinary people when it came to television. With parents from Lewis and Skye Al was a highlander at heart, with all the lucidity and poetry of the breed. But he was also a first class journalist with a keen news sense which was perfectly adapted to the new medium he found himself in.

Alastair Beaton

Trained as a wordsmith by DC Thomson in Dundee Al had earlier seen national service in Korea, so there was little to faze him about the challenge he took on as Charlie Smith's news editor and de facto deputy. Later, he would become the station's PR chief and finally head of presentation, which included the station announcers, in which role he was technically my departmental boss. But titles meant little to Al. And as bachelors many's the adventure we shared together. We were the closest of pals until his untimely death in 2010.

In the early days we had a Sales Team sited in London's Piccadilly. When dear Alastair was Charlie's deputy on the news desk (and unmarried) he somehow began to have long telephone conversations with one of the sales team's female staff, name sadly forgotten if ever known. Anyway the upshot of their conversations was a date! In fact a double date! The girl would bring a friend for me when next we were in town. Oh the excitement! A double date in London. Still my beating heart indeed!

Came the appointed evening and time at the Piccadilly Hotel. Alastair and I arrived early - well you would, wouldn't you? We had never seen either girl before nor them us. We placed ourselves behind a large pillar from which we could see the front door. Can you picture the scene?

Two country cousins (albeit well-scrubbed) looking closely – nay scrupulously examining every female entering the hotel.

Alastair 'What about this couple?'

Me 'I don't think so – I reckon both our dates will be more attractive! Here's another two.'

Alastair 'Oh goodness, I hope not. Move around the pillar a little. The next two look promising!'

Me 'Promising what? I speculated to myself, horrified. If they come towards us, walk quickly towards the Gents!'

This charade lasted about half an hour until Alastair, trying to keep his emotions in check, said confidently – 'that's them!' 'By this time I HAD to go to the Gents, but he was spot-on. They were stunning, attractive and good-looking, and as it transpired, intelligent with it. Good conversationalists. AND as our wallets were later to discover, expert at sinking whisky.

We said to ourselves – 'Great they are on the whisky, but we're from the place they make the stuff – we'll show them!' Well it was actually they who showed us!

After some nine doubles, more drinks at the theatre, it was on to a swanky place to eat. Afterwards, simply for a change – 'something to drink girls?' When we emerged from the restaurant the last we saw of our dates was them disappearing in an alcoholic fog and a taxi! Alastair clung on to me to prevent me falling – or maybe it was the other way round! What on earth did we see at the theatre? And what were the girls' names? Al couldn't remember. I didn't ever know. We didn't have the cost of a taxi back to the hotel between us.

Al eventually went on to marry his beautiful PR assistant, Kay, and they produced four lovely kids. Occasionally, when we shared a couple of drams in later years he would recall our Piccadilly night of shame. Me? I preferred not to dwell on youthful ignominy. And particularly not on the subsequent talks I had with my bank manager!

Finally, I must make mention of Jim McLeod, a Grampian regular, with his band in programmes like *Cairngorm Ski Night* and *The Jim McLeod Show*. Jim and his boys were a delight to work with, musically talented with well-developed senses of humour. Sadly Jim is no longer with us, the only surviving member of that band is John Sinton.

Jim McLeod at the piano, with his band

An Englishman abroad in Grampian land

Roger Pearce
Vision Engineer, 1979-1982

I was delighted to get an interview with Grampian Television for a Vision Engineer vacancy in 1979. When I went for my interview with Alex Ramsay in London I don't think I could have accurately pinpointed Aberdeen on a map, so I was relieved he didn't ask me to. I was chuffed to get a job offer and, after a long drive in my old mini, I arrived with all my worldly possessions and no money just before the ACTT Union strike in 1979. This was a potential end to my short career but, in a wonderfully humane gesture, Grampian ACTT allowed a few of us non-member 'newbies' to cross the picket line.

Alistair Watt, Roger Pearce and Mike Taylor in vision control

The strike seemed to go on forever so we had to be creative in finding 'work' to do. After all there were only so many equipment manuals to read during the ten week hiatus. When it was over and the crews returned there were a lot of complaints about strange scuff marks on the studio floor. We did not let on that it was where we had set up our indoor badminton court.

I really enjoyed the mix of programmes we produced, and I received great tuition in the art of vision control from Ron Turner and Mike Taylor. I made the big mistake early on of concentrating too much on Selina Scott's camera during *North Tonight* and was relegated to doing camera rehearsals for a month or so!

RCA handheld cameras were a generation ahead in terms of size and quality and it was hard to believe that they would be reliable enough to operate in the harsh news environment of northern Scotland. But they were, and ENG soon replaced film in location news around the world.

Church service with Roger and an IVC 7000

The studio and OB cameras needed a lot of care and attention in those days. The studio cameras were first generation colour units from Philips, with whom I was an apprentice engineer, and they were showing their age. The OB cameras (IVC 7000) were particularly needy. We covered most sports with three cameras, mainly because that was all we could get working at one time.

It was a wonderful immersion in Scottish culture for me, and I loved it. I tried hard with the Doric but apart from "fit like" I struggled. Coming from the land of pubs the toughest cultural shock was understanding Scottish bars and whisky in particular. I was initially banned from buying whisky in the Grampian social club. The nameless barman said it would be wasted on me. However, he agreed to teach me how to appreciate a wee dram or two and we spent some weeks going through the bottles on the back wall gantry. He finally allowed me to choose my own tipple so I ordered a Glenmorangie, but stupidly added, "Can you put some blackcurrant in it?" as a joke, which got me banned from the cratur again.

I never got used to the local customs. I am sure there was no real need for me to dress up as a woman on my stag night. Yes, there are photos to prove it. I also remember marching around Queens Cross behind piper and studio supervisor, Fred Morrison, but I can't remember why? It felt good anyway.

We produced a lot of great entertainment shows and most of them had a large element of wonderful live music. It was a huge privilege to work on Andy Stewart's last series and I loved doing *The Entertainers*. I never understood *Fiddle and Box* but I'm sure that a dram or two would have helped. Our crews were not only full of great people but they were an impressive production unit. I got so much from working with them. The professional standards I learnt at Grampian allowed me to hold my head high anywhere after I moved on.

On-screen highlights? Billy Connolly on *North Tonight*, and an American Country and Western singer, Joe Sun, on *The Entertainers*. His band seemed to get more and more drunk throughout the day, but they somehow played better at each rehearsal and it was an awesome recording.

The one that got away? World War Two air ace Douglas Bader, who had appeared in an earlier Grampian documentary, was booked for a studio interview but sadly passed away the week before.

As a football fan it was also great to get the chance to cover the game in Scotland and to understand the true passion of both players and supporters. I quickly learnt it could be scary for all concerned if Rangers or Celtic were involved. We covered the Dundee v Celtic game on the last day of the season, and Celtic lost, giving the title to Aberdeen. As they left the ground the Celtic fans tried to rock the Grampian OB van over while we were still recording. An interestingly Scottish experience!

I lived in a tenement flat two floors above Aberdeen and Scotland midfielder Alex McLeish, but the only time I got to talk to him was when he complained that my toilet overflow was dripping and it was keeping him awake at night. I worked with him 30 years later at ITV Sport and we had a good laugh about it. The other thing I remember about covering outdoor sport was the cold, and having to carry a hairdryer in the tool kit to defrost our lenses.

I regard my time in Aberdeen with Grampian TV as the highlight of my career. Not only did we make some amazing TV, we had some great times along the way. Grampian was a model regional TV service as it was totally immersed in the culture and people of the area. I enjoyed every minute of my time in the North East where I brushed across some fantastic people and had the privilege of calling Scotland my home if only for a wee while.

How do you say that in Gaelic?

Angus Peter Campbell
Reporter, Presenter, Producer, 1976 - 1985

Gaelic broadcasting in Scotland began on Sunday 2nd December 1923 with a 15 minute religious address by Reverend John Bain, recorded in the High United Free Church in Aberdeen. Two weeks later, a recital of Gaelic songs was broadcast, though it set a familiar historic pattern by being introduced and linked in English.

The first regular programme was singer Neil MacLean's *Sgeulachdan agus Òrain (Stories and Songs)*, again broadcast from the BBC's studio in Aberdeen, and in 1939 a weekly Gaelic news review was launched. By then the BBC had established a Gaelic Department, with Ballachullish man Hugh MacPhee appointed to run it in 1935. It was the 60s before television made its incursion.

Commercial television didn't arrive in Scotland until the 50s. Scottish ITV began broadcasting on 31st August 1957, with Grampian Television, serving the North-East of Scotland, launched in the Spring of 1960. I arrived there some seventeen years later to help establish the first-ever regular Gaelic service on commercial television in Scotland. It's something.

I wasn't fully aware of the politics behind it at the time, though I am now. When the Canadian-born British media proprietor Roy Thomson was given the franchise to run the commercial television station in central Scotland he was quoted as saying it was "a licence to print money.' And he was right, for those boom years through the 60s, 70s and 80s saw an exponential rise in advertising, which made enormous profits for the three Scottish companies at the time – Grampian, STV and Border TV.

Gaelic wasn't financially profitable, but it was part of the contract when the franchise was being renewed. Often the best life-giving things come out of necessity. So, as far as I am aware, I was hired to produce and front the first-ever regular Gaelic independent television broadcasting in Scotland. I can't fully remember how I got the job. I must have seen an advert somewhere and applied and travelled through to Aberdeen and put on my best suit and my best shirt and my best tie and my best accent and did a screen-test and, lights camera action, cue Angus Peter, there I was as a News Presenter in Mrs MacGillicudy's kitchen in Auchterless. If not Auchtermore.

Maggie Cunningham and Angus Peter Campbell

And I enjoyed every single moment. I produced and presented a weekly news programme *Crann Tara* which then changed to *Seachd Làithean* over and above working as an English-language reporter and presenter, before being promoted to Programme Editor, on the daily news programme *North Tonight*.

I have such fond memories of those I worked with. My newsroom colleagues, the late John Duncanson and the legendary political reporter Bill MacKenzie and gentleman Ron Thompson, one of our Dundee-based reporters. And Alan Saunders, who worked for us down there, and in Aberdeen itself, the fantastic fun team of

Alan Cowie and Frank Gilfeather and Bob Kenyon and Selina Scott and Joan Ingram and Anna Soubry and Anne MacKenzie and the late Alistair Yates, and Isabel Fraser who worked for us over in Inverness.

And our bosses, the senior editors Bill Mackie and the late Alistair Gracie, not to mention the Big Blond Boss himself, Ted Brocklebank, who gave me the job in the first place. I have much to be forgiven for myself, so I have no problem in forgiving both Ted and Anna for later unfurling their Tory flags on the pirate ship called Conservatism! I always valued the complete editorial freedom we were given as news journalists: no superior ever told us what to say.

There were so many others within and outwith the News Department who made my time at Grampian TV a delight. Hazel Deans, the kindest quine I've met, who rescued me from many an escapade, and Peggy at reception, and dear Mrs Gray in personnel, and all the PAs and the film and sound and editing crews (thank you Ian 'Sparky' Murray, and Barbara Dickie, and Pete and Terry and all the rest) and those who directed operations from upstairs, such as Bob Christie and Donald Waters, who were always personally gracious and kind to me, despite my follies.

Oh, and I don't want to forget those special announcers who added such *joi de vivre* to the station – David 'Ginger Peachy Goodnight' Bennett and the late, dignified Kennedy Thompson. And we even had a PR department, with the late Mike McLintock sometimes despatching us to open the Monymusk Vegetable Show as a special treat. And characters like Chris Kay, coming to work dressed as Yasser Arafat...

I learned a great deal during my years at Grampian and – of course – would do it all so much better, more calmly, now with hindsight. More soberly, you might say. Though that might have removed most of the fun. Looking back on it now some 40 years later, we were all so very young. Just kids really, knowing next to nothing.

As a professional writer, I owe a huge debt to my days in the newsroom. Prior to Grampian, I had learned some of my trade at the 'West Highland Free Press' and at BBC Radio Highland (as it was then), but the speed and precision learned working in a busy newsroom with a daily programme has been invaluable to me as an author. I learned to write quickly and accurately. If a thirty-second voice-over is required, it's required instantly, not when the muse comes. Get the facts right, and tell them well.

As for Gaelic broadcasting, these were generous days. We had a very good budget, and it was no problem to ask someone from Barra, for example, to fly up to Aberdeen (via Glasgow, or Stornoway and Inverness) to take part in the programme. I think we covered the enormous geographic area with honesty and integrity. Which was tough, because in many ways I was a one-man Gaelic band with the help of freelancers (Angela MacEachern, Peter MacAulay, Maggie Cunningham, the late Hector MacDonald – Aimsir Eachainn – and my good friend, the late Chris Dillon) 'competing' with a whole Gaelic Department at the BBC in Glasgow. We held our own and broke several stories, which is always the small ambition of a news journalist.

I realise news programmes are meant to be politically neutral, but I was never ashamed of promoting and therefore supporting the 'Keep Nato Out' campaign in their efforts to stop the development of a NATO base in Stornoway. How could any 'neutral journalist' resist the charms and arguments of the great bàrd, Murchadh MacPhàrlain as he, and others, campaigned succesfully against the military expansion?

One of my favourite recordings was doing a profile with Professor Donald MacLeod, then Principal of the Free Church in Edinburgh, during which that great scholar and theologian was seen singing 'A Pheigi a' Ghràidh,' with his gracious wife accompanying him on piano. The programme went out very late in the Gàidhealtachd, and lit up the place. Talking of lighting up the place, one of my lasting memories is being with the crew at Corgarff when electricity final reached the area. It was quite moving being in a place only 30 miles or so from the 'oil capital of Europe', as Aberdeen was known at the time, which was only then getting connected to the national grid. I remember the faces of the local men and women being like the faces of my father's people in Eriskay.

I also had the job of voicing the hugely successful *Blood is Strong* series for Grampian/Channel 4, including asking the great Sorley MacLean over to Aberdeen to record his wonderful poem 'Gaoir na h-Eorpa' ('The Cry of Europe'). He arrived by train, with his book 'Reothairt is Contraigh' in his tweed-jacket pocket and once in the recording booth pulled it out and read it in that wonderful mythic voice of his. I came to know him well and I miss him terribly. As I miss the legendary Dr John MacInnes whom I interviewed (which is to say listened to) many times. I could have listened to, and learned from him, forever.

Angus Peter, Sorley MacLean, Ted Brocklebank and Bernd Schulze

I've always believed that it was a great mistake that the Grampian TV I knew was then profitably swallowed up, by the bigger whale of SMG, and lost much of its identity. The only journalism that matters is that which is rooted in the local community it serves and helps articulate. Once that is removed it becomes colonial. Media has become much more global since then, with the 'licence to print money' now online, where we can all run our own stations from our sitting-rooms if we want, serving the multinationals that run the web.

Though that will not replace the dynamism and the adrenaline and the fun of everyone working together in the one room, in that one special building at Queen's Cross. They were remarkable days, which I recall with great fondness, past regret and continuing delight for the lovely people who made it all worthwhile. It was like a sudden flash photograph which has never faded.

In search of the Gaelic Monkees

Graham Mcleish

Producer/Director

In the 70s very few at Grampian spoke or could even understand the Gaelic language. I had been newly promoted to programme director and given the children's Gaelic series *Cuir Car* to produce and direct. There had been a previous series of *Cuir Car* (Turn Around) presented by the Gaelic Mod medallist Margaret, and brother Donnie MacLeod (Dotaman in a later broadcast life). But Margaret didn't want to present another series.

Cuir Car had been a sort of Gaelic *Playschool* for young kids but it was difficult to keep their interest as they got older. As for teenagers it was of course 'uncool' to show interest in anything your parents or grandparents did! I needed to find a programme format that would win over the 'I'm bored!' teenage kids from the Gàidhealtachd and beyond.

Mike Bevan, a fellow programme director, had just given a Gaelic band a spot on one of his English-speaking light entertainment shows. I could see at rehearsals that these lads were certainly attracting the attention of girls on the production crew. For them the Gaelic music with beefed-up drums and soaring electric guitars was 'cool'. Where teenage girls go, teenage boys would inevitably follow, I reasoned. My musical magnet to the Gaelic language for the youth of Gaeldom had been found! The band's name? RUNRIG!

My planned programme format would be from more than a decade earlier where they would get involved in hammed up sketches and story lines while featuring their songs and tunes throughout. I never told Runrig that I initially saw them as a kind of Gaelic Monkees (the US TV series that created a band in the wake of the Beatles). But whereas the Monkees were totally manufactured and their material mostly written by other people, Runrig were self-made, very much in control of what they wanted to achieve. More important, they wrote and played their own original and special brand of music.

If the band had known what I had in store for them they'd probably have staked me out naked in a machair somewhere in peak midgie season! And my enthusiasm for this Gaelic-language programme format using Runrig as the new *Cuir Car* presenters wasn't shared by everyone. Indeed, the programme's Gaelic adviser and script writer who'd worked on the previous series wasn't keen at all. He was afraid my concept of the band's zany sketches and pop/rock music was a bit too much of a change and we should try to persuade Margaret and Donnie to do it again with a more traditional presentation.

Filming the opening titles at Portree harbour

Years later I learned from Tom Morton's book *Going Home, The Runrig Story* that my decision to use them as presenters of *Cuir Car* got the band through an eighteen month period when they were on their financial uppers. If I remember correctly the band got £350 (about £1,800 today) between the five members, per programme, plus expenses. Those expenses were definitely needed on the first day's recording when I had to authorise a new pair of jeans for one band member when, on the way down from Portree in their battered old transit van, he ripped the backside out of the only pair he had!

You can still see the programme's opening titles on YouTube, with the band members getting into their van and leaving Portree to catch the ferry to the mainland. These opening titles were three times as long as normal because I felt it was important to show where the band came from – the islands of North Uist and Skye. At that time it was said more people in mainland Scotland had been to the island of Majorca than to the island of Skye!

Donnie, Rory, Calum and Malcolm enthusiastically picked up the daft situations and scenarios I gave them, ranging from Malcolm dressed in armour fighting a dragon, to Calum, Rory and Donnie flying in and falling out of a hot air balloon. Blair was rather less keen. This was all shot against chromakey back screen projection, as our budget wouldn't stretch to anything outwith the studio. The programmes were fun to make and the band members were always willing to ham up some crazy sketch. Their only condition was that we would always treat their music seriously. Grampian studio bosses agreed to honour this and Runrig were the first musicians in the station's history to be given days of studio time pre-recording all the songs to be used in the series. Not even the Demis Roussos band were given that kind of treatment!

I don't think Grampian or Runrig ever imagined the potential impact *Cuir Car* might have on the band's future. It was certainly a lucky break for Grampian to get them at that time with the new Gaelic language fund in the offing. The band simply needed the money to survive the next eighteen months and I needed a successful programme as a rookie director.

Their meteoric rise in popularity started happening during or close after the transmission of the programmes. Few bands got this type of television exposure at such a crucial time in their development. The Monkees shot to fame from their TV series which lasted eighteen months and they went on to sell over seventy-five million records worldwide. Runrig's series of *Cuir Car* had exactly the same duration. The internet hadn't been invented, there were no computers, no tablets or mobile phones. There were only three TV channels, BBC1, BBC2 and ITV (locally Grampian or STV). There was no satellite television, no breakfast television. There wasn't even Channel Four. It's often said that to succeed you need good timing and lucky breaks. There are thousands of talented musicians and song writers who never make it big. For success lots of things have to come together at the right time. Grampian's *Cuir Car* series was lucky to be screened at the right time and to be able to include Runrig's explosive and ground-breaking 'Highland Connection' songs and music before they had even recorded them for the album. The opening titles music for both *Cuir Car* series, 'What time', was a special shorter version from that album.

Top UK bands did do guest spots on Saturday morning children's television series like *Tiswas* and *Swop Shop*. The reasoning was that these young viewers would then go out and buy the bands' records. By the time Runrig's second series was being screened on Grampian and STV in 1979 we knew people were watching because the commercial breaks were full. Avertisers don't pay good money unless they know they have big audiences watching. It was around this time that the band had their greatest popular success to date at the Stornoway Mod Fringe. In November of that year this gave them the confidence for the first time to hire and sell out the 900-seat Eden Court Theatre in Inverness. This generated banner headlines in the *Press and Journal* of 'Beatlemania for Runrig'.

So, did Grampian's *Cuir Car* Gaelic Monkees allow Runrig to survive until they found future fame and fortune? I'll leave others to decide.

Blow out at Bravo
Dermot McQuarrie
Reporter, 1977 – 78

Saturday April 22, 1977, seems a long time ago now, yet when I walk along the beaches of Fort Lauderdale in Florida where I now call home and look out across the calm waters of the Atlantic, there are days when I'm taken back to that windy trip over the North Sea in a small plane en route to report on the first blow-out on a North Sea oil platform.

Changed days as I feel the warmth of the sun every day, even in winter. And while my career in television took me to work in countries as diverse as Italy, Egypt, Hungary, Poland, the Czech Republic, Sweden and eventually to the United States, I look back on my time at Grampian with great pride. It was there under the tutelage of Charlie Smith where I developed my craft as a television journalist. I went on to become a producer/director at STV and was later invited to join Fox in the USA to run their newly-acquired Spanish language sports channels. This, mainly thanks to a spell in Gibraltar, where I'd learned Spanish. My temporary contract lasted eighteen years. I ended up as Senior Vice President of Production and Programming and am now happily retired in Florida. Yet, over cocktails of an evening, my thoughts still stray back to these halcyon days at Queen's Cross, Aberdeen.

January 1977 – a newcomer to Grampian I was usually first in to the Newsroom and would get the coffee machine started. A little later in would come Charlie, "Morning Son", and before helping himself to a cup he'd swing an imaginary golf club. "7 Iron Charlie?" I'd inquire. "No Son, 5 iron, watch the position of the feet." It has to be said that this was the daily routine and I never got the right club once!

Charlie was an amazing man to work for and as a mentor. Always approachable even after I damaged his company car which I'd been loaned to cover a story in Tain, "Sorry Charlie, but I slid off the road on the ice and scratched your car." "That's what insurance is for, Son, Get it washed and then we'll get it round to the garage and see what needs to be done".

Grampian would not have been Grampian without the colleagues and long-time friends I made there. Bill Mackie, Charlie's deputy, who stepped temporarily in to the role when Charlie suddenly died, Alistair Gracie, taken from us far too young, Bob Kenyon and Jennifer Malcolm on the News Desk; Bill McKenzie and Alan Cowie with whom I shared an office, and of course Selina Scott who joined us just before I departed for Scottish Television in Glasgow. It was a great group of people to work with.

The Bravo blow-out

So back to Blow-Out at Bravo, a routine maintenance on the Ekofisk Bravo platform led to the North Sea's oil field's first major disaster on April 22, 1977. Safety valves had been removed and not replaced during maintenance, and the well spiraled out of control. The platform was evacuated immediately, but soon combined oil and gas was spewing out of the drill hole. For an entire week, the platform sprayed oil and gas into the middle of the North Sea.

I had been up all night with our 2 year old son Jonathan pacing the floor in an effort to get the child to sleep. In those days there was no overnight television so I turned on the radio. Around 4am reports started coming in that there had been a blow-out on an oil platform in the North Sea. Initially scant information, but by 6am it was confirmed that the blow-out had occurred on the Bravo Platform in the Ekofisk oilfield in the Norwegian sector of the North Sea.

There was no weekend news at Grampian in those days so I called the duty news intake editor at ITN in London. The conversation went like this:

Dermot "There's been a blow out on an oil platform in the North Sea and oil is spewing out of it".

ITN "Can you get a crew and a plane and get out there?"

Dermot "Sure can"

On putting the phone down I thought "Where the heck am I going to get a crew and a plane at this hour?"

I had the telephone number of an Aircraft Charter Company, and thank goodness they were open even at that time. The plane would be ready in an hour. It was a small plane so only room for the pilot, myself and a cameraman.

I tried the two Grampian staff cameramen both of whom were out of town. I then telephoned a freelance cameraman – Mike Herd who lived near Grampian. I told him, "Mike, I don't care what you are doing today, there's been a blow out in the North Sea and we are going in a plane in an hour." "Give me 15 minutes and I'll be there" replied Mike.

So, Mike and I got together at Queen's Cross, loaded up the gear and set off to Aberdeen Airport. I'd called Bill Mackie and asked him to get everything organised for our return. I reckoned we would be back around 3pm and at that time the film would have to be processed and then edited.

It was a bumpy flight over the North Sea, but as we came out of the clouds we saw the Bravo Platform with oil spewing out of its top. What a sight! The pilot was surprised to find that there wasn't a flight exclusion zone around the platform (well not yet!) so he took the opportunity to overfly the platform from all angles including tipping the wing over and coming straight down on top of the platform! The only problem was that the G Force was such that Mike's camera nearly flew out of his hands and I heard him shout, "I can't bloody film like that."

So after a few passes over the Platform somebody came on the radio yelling at us to "get the hell out of there". A No Fly Zone was installed due to the possibility of the oil going on fire. So it was homeward bound. A Grampian car met us at the airport and whisked the film away to the developing labs. Back at Queen's Cross I got on the phone to ITN to be told that I could have 55 seconds for my report in the early evening news... and it would be Live! For TV scripts we speak at approximately 180 words a minute – I got well over 200 words into that 55 seconds!

So we had the lead story on the early news and I delivered my 55 second report over the shots of the platform and the oil spewing out. Almost as soon as it finished the phone rang and it was ITN. "Great stuff Dermot! You have a World Exclusive! 168 countries were hooked in to the broadcast. If you'd f****d that up, the whole world would have known." The next day it was 'rinse and repeat' this time in a slightly larger plane and with Ino Visser the sound recordist.

Just as we were leaving Queen's Cross, Alex Mair the Chief Executive arrived – I believe to collect his Sunday papers. He said he'd seen the Saturday broadcasts and asked whether we had enough material for a documentary? I said, "Well, we have the opening titles, but all the action is now in Stavanger in Norway." "I'm going to contact the network and I'll TELL them we are making a documentary about this and it HAS to air on ITV." said Alex. And sure enough he did. Monday morning we were all called in to Alex's office and told to make arrangements to go immediately to Norway.

We arrived at Stavanger Airport the next day in to a massive media circus. Every TV and newspaper from around the world was there. Internationally recognised reporters such as Bernard Nossiter from the Washington Post and squads of reporters from the British press as well as BBC, ITV, ABC, NBC, CBS plus Asian crews. And there was wee Grampian right in the middle with them!

Phillips Petroleum who owned the Ekofisk Oil Field held a press conference at 12 noon (local) and 12 midnight (local), the late one for the benefit of the US audiences. Questions were fired at the Press Officer who, hour by hour, was having the energy sucked out of him. Then at the midnight press conference on Day 3 he announced, "We discovered that the Blow Out preventer had been put on upside down". In a flash somebody called out "Would you say that was a mistake?" "Yes" replied the now stunned Press Officer.

Earlier in the day Phillips announced that they had contracted the Red Adair Wild Well company to come and try to cap the well. So into Stavanger arrived two of Adair's top men, Boots Hansen and Coots Hatterberg. It was those two who discovered that the blow out preventer had been installed upside down.

A day later the famous Red Adair himself flew in on a private jet to be met by the media scrum, "Are you here to cap the well Red?" "Nope, I'm just here to hold Boots and Coots' hands!" Of course, within a few hours of his arrival the well was capped. The media circus was over. Red, Boots and Coots were the heroes of the day!

We arrived back in Aberdeen and began the process of editing the documentary. My colleague Alan Cowie voiced the program and *Blow Out at Bravo* went out on ITV throughout the UK.

The programme was very well received and question were raised the House of Commons about how prepared the UK was to cope with a similar blow-out. It wasn't! Plans were made to build a special ship and store the necessary equipment all under the supervision of Red Adair, but nothing came of it and the Oil Industry still relies on its supply ships as fire engines.

Blow Out at Bravo was nominated for a BAFTA Best Actuality Award and Elkan Allen the then Sunday Times TV critic wrote 'Grampian should win, but as it was the Queen's Jubilee, no doubt the prize would go to the ceremony at the Abbey.' It did. Heck they had 25 years to prepare for that!

I retired to Florida in 2014 and can now walk in the sun almost all year round. But occasionally I think back to what Charlie Smith's wife, Margaret, confided at his funeral. She took my hand in hers and said, "Charlie had great plans for you, Dermot."

I sometimes wonder how my life would have been different had he lived.

The researcher's tale

Clare Gimingham
Programme Researcher, 1982-1993

When I arrived at GTV in 1982 I kept being told I had missed the best days. That I couldn't believe as it was all so fantastic. I had a ball.

It was a very exciting world and the production department became like a family. It was hard work with strange hours and lots of travelling and I think that when you work like that your colleagues become so much more than co-workers. Under the watchful eye and care of Marian Hepworth I found my feet quite quickly.

As Programme Researcher much of my travelling was done on my own. I would fill in a CIG (Can I go form) and head off on a recce, lucky enough to travel not only all over the UK but also Finland, Sweden and Denmark. I did have the odd moment when travelling alone when I was anxious or uneasy and often lonely but that was more than made up for when I set off with a crew to do the filming. I was keen to join in with all the community at GTV had to offer and became involved with the Union and of course the Social Club which was a hugely important part of my life at GTV. There were so many memorable evenings there and some of which I have little memory.

The 25th anniversary party was held there and we decorated the club with silver (from milk bottle tops). I loved the Christmas parties we ran for children of staff, I loved the Burns Suppers, but the best night out of all was the crew night out in December. I had a few enjoyable years as the chairperson of the club with some great and hard-working committee members. It was at the wedding of the Social Club Secretary, Avril Luke,that I met my husband to be. We had our wedding reception in the club!

Programme highlights are many but some call for special mention.

A Working Faith was the first religious series sold to Channel 4 by GTV. Using my background of a degree in Divinity, I worked closely with Michael Steele on this series of six programmes. They were transmitted on C4 at tea-time on a Saturday just before *Brookside*, which was an amazing slot for a religious programme. I received a bottle of Grampian TV whisky from Alex Mair for my part in that. ITV's *Highway* led to wonderful trips with Alan Franchi and Harry Secombe who used to call me 'Clare de Goon'.

Another highlight was a studio show called *A Personal View* which allowed me to meet and work closely with a huge list of 'weel kent' faces including Norman St John-Stevas, Len Murray, David Steel, Richard Baker, Terry Waite and many others and led to a lifelong friendship with Bruce Kent. Other 'names' I was lucky to meet were, Kylie Minogue, Frank Bruno, Kate Adie and Hannah Gordon but so often the most amazing people we met and worked with were the folk 'on the street'.

There were many notable one-offs such as the live Network Church Service we held in a ship-building yard and the documentary on Billy Graham's visit to Pittodrie. Some of the memories are not so good, as the 80s saw a number of disasters including the explosion on Piper Alpha and the Lockerbie tragedy. Early morning of the Piper Alpha disaster, I was called at home and told to come in. We were to go live with the ITV network programme *The Time the Place*. I was to be on an open line to London to take instructions. It was exciting and awful at the same time. At that point I did not know that a close school friend had died in the tragedy.

I think it is a great shame that Grampian Television no longer exists. It provided a wonderful service and fantastic programming and is greatly missed.

Far's Jimmy?
Bernd Schulze
Film Editor/Director, 1965-91

It was something of a life-changer when Director of Programmes Jim Buchan asked me up for a month's trial as news and current affairs film editor at Grampian Television in April 1965. It was in response to a letter I sent to TV stations and film companies asking for a job. It was the only reply I got and it came in the form of a telegram asking me to attend an interview in London. I was 23.

Since I didn't drop the centre out of a roll of film, as other hopefuls had done before me and my splices didn't come apart on live transmission, I lasted the month, and as Alastair Beaton in the News Room remarked in that droll way of his, I didn't get my P45.

The editing equipment was basic. At the window end of my 7 x 10 *doocot* was the editing bench taking in the width of the room constructed from Handy Angle and white Formica top plus a high round stool with a back support. A simple Zeiss Moviescop viewer with a geared winder and film reel at either end, a film splicer, a little bottle of film cement and a film timer was about it. You simply wound the film through the flickering 3 x 4 inch screen of the Movescop by hand at a steady 25 frames per second.

The film arrived in negative form after processing. To edit mute film you marked the 'in and out' position of the scene in the Moviescop with a yellow wax pencil, cut it with small brass scissors and hung it on one of the many pegs on a narrow vertical board above the desk and flopped the rest of the shot into a cotton lined trough below. The scenes were then spiced together and the running time noted, viewed, approved and transmitted on a telecine machine, which reversed the negative to a positive image.

You needed keen eyesight and a decisive mind to work against the clock. Often film arrived after processing with minutes to spare before going on air.

There was a sliding door to an adjacent editing room, the domain of Roy Smith, who had been with Grampian since its inauguration in 1961. He had a motorised editing machine as well as a bench like mine and cut important stuff like *Grampian Week*.

Marion Ritchie, Roy Smith and Bernd Shulze in Roy's editing room.

I got adept at cutting 30 second clips for *Grampian News* and sound stories for *Sportscope*, and in my first week edited an Easter documentary *He is Risen*, directed by the ambitious young TV Director, Adrian Malone. "If you can do this you'll do anything" was his parting shot as he left me to match the film to music he had specially chosen. The trouble was that the music was to be dropped in from the sound studio in the gallery when the programme was to be recorded on video tape. Trying to edit to music was near impossible. I resorted to a stop watch to time the musical phrases where film edits had to match and I needed to get the hang of the motorised editing machine in Roy's room to get the synchronisation perfect with the music on the record player. No wonder that Adrian was worried. Jim Buchan had given him a special budget to hire a talented freelance cameraman to work on the complicated craning shots and smooth zooming he had in mind to match the elegiac 'Adagio for Strings' by Samuel Barber and Mascagni's spine-tingling 'Easter Hymn' from 'Cavalleria Rusticana'.

Adrian had got Lesley Blair, from Grampian's *Romper Room* to pretend to be Holy Mary, or was it Mary Magdalene, as she collapsed at the end of long camera moves among a host of daffodils in a desperate sense of mourning for the Good Friday sequence against the strains of that Adagio. Later she would dance with joy to the uplifting cadences of the Easter Hymn on Balmedie Beach after he was risen. It was my first triumph against the odds. Adrian was chuffed that the film flowed perfectly with the mood of the music. Soon afterwards he left Grampian to direct the ground-breaking series for BBC 2 presented by Dr. Jacob Bronowski – *The Ascent of Man*.

Eddie Joffe, one of the other programme directors (later to become Lesley's husband) presented me with something resembling a bundle of knitting with his series *Animal Heritage*. I separated the jumble of footage into ordered sequences where I could lay my hands on them more easily. One of the highlights of the series was a fight between mice, drawn on still captions and given dramatic movement by tilts and crash zooms and clever editing.

The secret of news film footage was that it had to look zippy and brief, often no longer than 30 seconds. Each shot ran for three or four seconds and even less, and you made sure that the last shot had a bit extra left on the end to come out on. You didn't want any blank when coming back in vision to the newscaster on transmission.

Sound interviews were more complex. The news assistant or reporter listened through the interview with me and selected the sections to be used. I then decided where and when appropriate overlay was required to illustrate what was being said or to cover a jump cut, and this was edited on a separate reel, with a countdown leader. It was exacting work. Timings in and out of overlay were called out by the production assistant sitting next to the director in the gallery during transmission. For years after I left Grampian I remained attuned to news interviews and sensing when enough was said.

The light-hearted *Wednesday People* became popular with Grampian viewers fulfilling the remit of regional television to feature local interest and culture. It was fronted by star reporters like June Shields, Ron Thompson and Jimmy Spankie who sought out the canny, the curious and the cranky folk of the North East to tell their stories. There was 'the witch of Kiltarlity' who cast spells, a wizened old countryman who could tell the weather and warned of 'teuchit' storms, advising viewers to "hap yer hurdies", and a Mynah bird in deepest Buchan that called out "Far's Jimmy? Gie him a dram". Clearly, it had previous experience of Mr. Spankie's drouth!

It was during this time that I learned to appreciate the rich doric tongue, still spoken with relish by country folk and indeed by some in the Grampian film department. It was important when handing film reels to the telecine department that the splices wouldn't come apart during transmission and that the film would be free of any specks of dust. I used to run the film through my left thumb and middle finger to test the strength of every splice at a fair speed. The film was then rewound back to the start through a soft selvyt cloth impregnated with lighter fuel to ensure a clean transit. The film department's Fred McLeod guarded the selvyts as if they were gold. I used to help myself to several in one go and can still hear big Fred's strident Buchan tones – "Foo mony's he awa wi noo?"

The quality of news footage shot by 'stringers', local freelance cameramen, was variable! Jimmy Primrose Smith, based in Aberdeen worked to the maxim – 'never mind the quality, feel the width'. His news instincts were excellent and he often scooped the BBC opposition with exclusive but often unusable footage. He'd look over my shoulder in the cutting room when I was searching for anything he'd shot in focus. "You've got plenty there" was his usual parting shot as he left me trying to assemble a short clip that we could air.

Ron Thompson, the reporter based in Dundee, worked well with cameraman, Malcolm Campbell, to produce inventive longer stories, often quirky in nature. One item about a glamorous auction at Gleneagles of a Bugatti that fetched £10,000 seemed a bit thin to me. There wasn't enough of it to hold interest for the time intended, and I suggested to Ron that he might broaden the story to include our general fascination for cars, from new showroom models to old bangers that might need a push to get out the auction shed. I suggested using library footage of car crashes when things got out of control and proposed a natty wardrobe for his to-camera appearance.

He and Malcolm rose to it splendidly. It turned out to be one of the liveliest 25 minute films that Grampian had done so far, with the title of 'BANGERS – not the kind you eat.' It ended dramatically with Ron getting out of an old Austin A30, a crane with a grab crashed down onto it, picked it up and dropped it into a compactor, neatly squashing it into a solid cube. "Well, the management have given me a nice sporty alternative," Ron said to camera as he whipped out a pair of cycle trouser clips and rode off on a bike.

I applied for staff programme director jobs when they came up, but was regularly turned down. So I decided to fulfil a long held ambition to make a film on my own about the music of the Norwegian composer Edvard Grieg, whose Gregg ancestors hailed from Fraserburgh. I bought a second hand Mini, found Jamie, a university student in Aberdeen who had passed his driving test to join me on location in Norway, persuaded Jim Buchan to give me a fortnight's holiday in late May 1968, and set about editing during evenings and at weekends the material I had shot in 16mm Ektachrome.

It all came together miraculously. Evelyn Hood, a journalist and writer from Perthshire who had collaborated on major Grampian documentaries and programmes agreed to write the script, my best chum John Thomson who processed film and took publicity photographs at Grampian helped with the stills from the Grieg archive, Sandy Massie in the graphics department mounted them and designed the title cards which cameraman Gordon Watson helped me shoot. Roy Smith gave me sage advice on how to cut 'The Hall of the Mountain King' sequence from Peer Gynt – throw it all up in the air and see how it comes down. Tom Fleming, the TV voice-over on state occasions, narrated the commentary which was recorded by Sandy Craib in the sound department. The film sound track was mixed together on a quiet Sunday in the dubbing studio of Yorkshire TV in Leeds.

The Aberdeen premiere was held at the Cosmo cinema in

Diamond Street in the presence of Aberdeen's Lord Provost and others who had contributed. Among those attending was Ron Neil, who was later to move from BBC Aberdeen to London. He suggested that I take *GRIEG* for an audition to the BBC, and it got a *S*unday Evening slot on BBC2 in 1971 following a documentary about the Norwegian adventurer Thor Heyerdahl. It was later shown by the Canadian Broadcasting Corporation in their *World of Music* series, and over time I managed to recoup the production costs with further international transmissions.

I decided to go free-lance, but couldn't resist returning to Aberdeen as an independent film-maker for the Clydesdale Bank to create my own film tribute celebrating the folk of the hard North East knuckle of Scotland who'd made a success of things long before the coming of North Sea oil. Grampian's Bill Mackie wrote the script and *Land of Plenty* gained my first documentary award. This was followed by a filmic pæon of praise for Glasgow and Strathclyde, which helped kick-start the commercial and cultural regeneration of Glasgow. Both films were narrated by Tom Fleming with uplifting sound tracks by Beethoven and Brahms. I had found my métier in matching music to film and this was to be my trademark, coupled with an eye for quality camerawork and elegant editing.

Out of the blue Alex Mair, Grampian's Chief Executive, phoned to ask whether I'd like to direct *Black Water - Bright Hope* for Grampian. Ted Brocklebank was to be the reporter and producer of this prestigious hour-long documentary for the ITV network featuring the coming of oil to Scotland, something on which Ted had become a bit of an expert.

With Malcolm Campbell and Grampian camera teams working on far-flung locations along the West Coast of Scotland and North to Shetland, with special praise for Roy Smith in the cutting room, an astonishingly dramatic documentary emerged. On location at Loch Kishorn Ted and I shared digs in a B&B owned by Howard Jules, a retired schoolteacher and his wife. They treated us to a selection of his extensive classical record collection at the end of a day's filming. "I bet you won't know what this is and who wrote it?" Howard tested me as he lowered the needle onto a mystery LP. My ears pricked up as I recalled a historic BBC documentary about the

Churchills which had featured this very piece of music. "Symphony No 3 by Camille Saint-Saens, known as the Organ Symphony," I said triumphantly. This, I knew there and then, would be the uplifting accompaniment to what we were trying to achieve in portraying the oil drama unfolding in Scotland.

For Ted, more accustomed to writing over news footage, working with these cadences was a revelation. I would time sections precisely where music was to be faded down for commentary, and this technique gave the words an extraordinary punctuation which produced a powerful interplay between music and commentary. The film was cut to match the rhythm of the music and also of the phrasing of the commentary. When the final sound track was dubbed by Mike Billings, with whom I had worked on my own independent films, the result was sensational.

My work as director involved bringing the various aspects of film-making together, the quality of the camerawork, the placing of commentary and dialogue and sound effects along with the music during the editing phase, and all the while imagining how it would sound together in the end. That is why a film is born in the dubbing studio.

"When do we get to hear the commentary?" Charles Smith, our Executive Producer, would ask anxiously as we watched in the darkened recording studio with its large screen and dynamic speakers. I explained that laying down the sound tracks for film is different from the procedure in a television gallery where you get to hear everything first go. Still no commentary. For Charlie WORDS were KING in film-making.

As the majesty of Saint-Saens swept through the studio, there was still no commentary and I had to calm Charlie. "It will all come together in the final mix," I reassured him. I believed we were bringing together a sound and visual experience for television that promised something out of the ordinary, even by network standards. It was the first time that I was able to combine the talents of television journalism with my instinct for quality documentary production. Little Grampian would shine with the best of them, I felt sure.

With Ted's commentary the full sound track now came alive. Charlie moved visibly in his big leather armchair. Film editor, Roy

Smith looked relieved that there were no holes in the sound tracks and that everything was in perfect synch. We had a triumph on our hands. Ted's script, his handling of the complex storyline and the honing and pacing of his commentary in the cutting room now came into its own. We made a perfect team. It was to be our first success.

It was nearly midnight when the phone rang yet again. *Black Water* had finished its transmission on the ITV network and the phone had been ringing almost constantly since the Grampian logo faded to black. This time it was Charles Smith. "I thought you'd call me," he began, perked up with pride and a stiff dram or two. I told him I couldn't get off the phone for well-wishers. He was cock-a-hoop. *Black Water – Bright Hope* was for Grampian and for Charlie as the news chief a defining moment. Willie Hunter, the Glasgow Herald's TV critic described it as 'maybe the best documentary ever made about ordinary people anywhere'.

Black Water led to a second collaboration with Ted and Grampian, following up on the oil story by comparing Aberdeen with Houston in *A Tale of Two Cities,* a network ITV documentary devised and produced by Ted. As with *Black Water*, a great deal of planning and research was put into selecting contributors for the storyline in locations around Texas and Scotland's North East. My job was to direct the camera team filming the entrepreneurs and experts who had created Houston as a centre for oil know-how and contrast them with the fledgling oil men of Aberdeen who were learning fast and flexing their muscles for a slice of the action - and proving that they were no pushovers.

Ted's talent was to find these people and discover what made them tick. It made for rumbustious television, written and presented with his laconic flair and chutzpah. I made sure the pictures matched Ted's energy and vision and ensured that the sound- track swept viewers off their feet. I had Sibelius as my ally with his first symphony, some foot-tapping hillbilly banjos and Texan soul music coming out of juke boxes in Houston's Fourth Ward that touched the heartstrings.

My abiding memory of Houston was of a large neon light flashing over a congested six lane highway proclaiming 'Our Girls are Totally Nude', and back in Aberdeenshire, feeling like Peter Pan, as the camera helicopter swept low up and over the craggy sea cliffs of Cruden Bay to reveal my favourite beauty spot, the dramatic ruins of Slains Castle. This experience of directing helicopter movements with a pilot used to smooth and steady camera revelations stood me in good stead for my independent North Sea films which were the pinnacle of my life as a film maker, winning many documentary awards over a decade spanning the mid seventies and eighties.

In 1986 Ted was to contact me again about directing a series of three one hour Grampian documentaries for Channel 4 about the Gaelic diaspora entitled *The Blood is Strong.* Ours was proving to be a rewarding partnership, not least in the discovery of a hitherto unknown Gaelic folk/rock group called Capercaillie who created the haunting music for the series and rose to stardom in the process. We lived with them in an Edinburgh recording studio for two weeks while I helped them create a

Charlie McKerron, Karen Matheson and Donald Shaw of Capercaillie

bigger, more dynamic sound with additional instruments and exotic synthesisers that produced weird and wonderful effects. The LP of the music for the series established Capercaillie on the concert and stadium circuit and won a platinum disc for sales in the process.

While filming in Stornoway for the series, I had watched schoolchildren in their lunch hour ordering deep fried Mars Bars and chips at takeaways. I had heard on the news that Scotland was once again the worst country in the world for heart disease. I mentioned this to Ted and that led to our next documentary together for Channel Four, entitled *Scotland the Grave.* Our diligent researcher, Imogen

Foulkes, tracked down a man who had just died of a heart attack in his early forties and permission was given by the family to allow filming at the graveside of his burial. It was a deeply moving opening to the film. The priest intoned the funeral rites, the many young mourners wept grief-stricken, and as the coffin was being lowered into the grave up came the chilling blast of 'O Fortuna' from 'Carmina Burana' with the opening titles.

I was in tears putting this sequence together with video editor Charlie Main. It was a wake-up call to Scotland. Change your eating habits. We filmed the young enjoying a good time in night clubs, smoking and drinking hard, on crowded football terraces chomping on bridies and we were given access to the coronary ward at Ninewells Hospital in Dundee talking to survivors or strokes and heart attacks.

We flew to Finland to find out how a national heart awareness campaign there had reduced the incidence of heart disease. From Stanford University researchers we learnt of the dangers of smoking linked to heart disease and the benefit of a heart-healthy diet coupled with exercise. It was a hard-hitting timely programme, narrated by Bill Paterson. It won a BMA award for Grampian and myself.

For my swansong in television Ted and I flew to the Outer Hebrides in the autumn of 1991 in the company of Selina Scott, who had persuaded the Prince of Wales to spend a few days on the island of Berneray to join in the simple life of a close-knit crofting community. Grampian was given privileged access to film this private visit of Prince Charles for an ITV documentary to record his impressions. It was moving to hear his concern for the islanders with his genuine interest in farming and fishing, discovering at first-hand the hardships of making a living in these outer reaches of his realm. Charles touched every one with his easy banter and he wasn't afraid to muck in and get his hands dirty, be it dipping sheep, digging for potatoes or fishing for lobsters and crabs.

I was impressed by the way he would pick out a member of the TV team for a one to one chat on the walk back to base at the end of the day's filming. When it was my turn he was curious about the role of music in programme-making. Once again, Capercaillie came up trumps with their wonderful recording of Gaelic music and song for *A Prince among Islands*. It was a fitting and rewarding finale to my career as a television director.

Prince Charles aboard the Berneray Isle

Shooting the breeze with Jackie

Mark Lynch
Rigger/Scene crew, 1981-1989

It was a glorious June morning when John McAdam, Ron Whichelow and myself set about surveying the site at the luxury Gleneagles hotel to lay our OB camera, sound and vision cables in a safe fashion. A magnificent Ford Escort Cabriolet (a loaner from Ford to racing ace, Jackie Stewart) was parked in our cable run line. John said, "We're going to have to get that moved".

Ten minutes later the man himself was marching towards us from the hotel, calling out instructions to his following entourage. It was clear Jackie had no intention of moving the car himself, so I piped up, "Mr Stewart, could I possibly have this vehicle moved slightly so we can get our equipment through safely?" Without changing stride and continuing to bark out orders to his troops Jackie removed the keys from his pockets and skilfully tossed them in my direction from 20 feet. Getting to move his classy-looking car a few yards made me the envy of the whole crew and was a great start to Grampian's OB recording of *Gunfire At Gleneagles*.

That afternoon I was sent around the grounds to tidy up and make safe any cables before we finished for that day. I was approached by what I thought might be a tourist, possibly American. The smartly-dressed, diminutive man asked me if I could explain what was going on (referring to the OB vans). I gave him a rundown of what was due to happen over the next few days. He thanked me just as a beautifully-attired lady and two companions called him over. The two companions were instantly recognisable as Princess Anne and Captain Mark Phillips. I realised very quickly that I had just had a conversation with King Hussein of Jordan, and the lady who had called him over, sporting the biggest diamond ring I have ever seen, was his wife, Queen Noor.

By the following afternoon the Clay Pigeon Shoot was well

into practice-mode, with the Celebrity contingent getting some first-hand tuition and the Royals having the chance to get their 'eyes-in'.

There was raised seating behind the shooters so the general public got great views of the clay shots appearing after 'pull' was heard, then the bang. Lots hit the targets, producing puffs of charcoal grey powder, but there were lots of misses too. The crowd was treated to a great afternoon with celebrities like Harrison Ford, Steven Spielberg, Billy Connolly and a very pregnant Pamela Stephenson milling around.

As the afternoon progressed most of the Royals and celebrities had had their fill. But one lone 'celeb' seemed determined to stay until he actually hit a clay. The lone shooter was a very short chap, mounted on an old-fashioned fruit crate, dressed in the tweed and matching bonnet which was later to find fame in sketches like 'Four Candles' with Ronnie Barker. But 'pull' after 'pull' Ronnie Corbett was getting no nearer hitting the targets. Unbeknown to poor Ronnie the crowd behind him had grown in size. Nobody wanted to leave until he had scored a 'hit'.

Around 5pm he finally did hit something - well more of a wing, a slight deviation in the clay's flightpath and the smallest of puffs. But the sudden outburst of cheering and clapping as this happened came as a complete surprise to Ronnie who had been oblivious to the growing crowd. But then that trademark grin appeared. His wife, sitting in the bay with him was in hysterics. I thought Ronnie was going to turn the gun on her but soon he was laughing louder than anybody.

But while we were waiting for Ronnie to find his target one of the Gleneagles ground staff got chatting and asked what the crew was doing that evening. I said we were hoping to get eighteen holes of golf in after a quick something to eat. He asked which of the Gleneagles courses we planned to play on. I explained that I would have to take out a second mortgage to afford the fees and we would probably be playing locally.

"Rubbish man" he responded. I don't know who he was but he signed a chit for me, John McAdam and Ron Whichelow to play the famous Queen's course. One hell of an experience. Unfortunately the heavens opened on the sixth hole. John said it might ease, but it only got worse. The best soaking I have ever enjoyed.

To Dundee to cover a midweek football match when United were flying high.

John McAdam, Bob Reid and myself arrived early at Tannadice to set the cables and camera and sound gear. Interviews before, during and at the end of the match were to be done. So, we had a few 'flats', tables and chairs to set once the usual OB gear was in.

We had not long started laying the cable runs when the rest of the crew arrived all at once. This was a little unusual as they would all have to wait until their equipment was set, rather than arrive when it was all in and ready for erecting and testing.

The Set Designer - we'll call him Andy - also arrived at this time and was hanging around the OB tender, prompting John McAdam to say, "You're all going to have to get out of our way so we can get on with our side of things. Andy, we won't get to your side until near lunchtime. How about making yourself useful and nipping down to the shop at the bottom of the street to get me a *Daily Record* ?"

At that Bob Reid said he wanted a pack of Silk Cut fags and then somebody else wanted a bottle of ale and so on and so on.

Andy said he'd need to write all this down. Patting his chest shirt pocket he groaned, "I've left my specs in the car". I came to the rescue and offered to write everybody's orders down on the foolscap book we always kept in the tender. Something like this;

20 Silk Cut (Bob Reid)

1 bottle of Lemonade (Gordon Reid)

1 Daily Record (John McAdam)

2 Packets of Golden Wonder Crisps…and so on

Then, as a laugh I put down a few sundry items at the bottom of the list.

Ten minutes later Andy arrived back with the goodies and a face like thunder. "What's wrong with you?" asked John.

Andy looked straight at me and said "Ha Bloody Ha!"

All eyes were now turning to me for an explanation. "When I wrote the list up I added a couple of extra things on at the bottom." Like what? "One packet of condoms and six dirty magazines", I confessed. The whole crew fell about at this with the notable exception of Andy who was not in a forgiving mood. So, what had gone wrong?

"When I got served I realised I'd still left my specs in the car", he explained later. "So I gave the list to the young lass serving. She said that'll be £12.95 and we don't sell 'those' magazines, and you'll need to go to the chemist for the other things."

This still cracks me up to this day, although I'm not sure if Andy ever saw the funny side!

Views from the Fireside
Memories of 'the Grampian'
Peter Mitchell
Aberdeen Journals, 1972-2009

Here's a brainteaser. What do a
newspaper's rugby pundit with a naturalist
father who was also a minister and a luxury
Caribbean cruise have in common? Easy. It's
Grampian TV's original Queens Cross
headquarters, with the city's handsome
Queen's Road a hop, skip and a jump away.

Smack in the middle of World War
Two, my twin sister, Jill, and I were born at
55a, Queens Road, gloriously named the
Rubislaw Memorial Maternity Pavilion, I
believe. The pinkish building is today part of the Chester Hotel, but
to date there is no plaque on the wall to indicate its previous life. Nor
indeed the fact that Jill and I were born there!

Our poor rather petite mum, Mora, had to bedrest for weeks
before she was delivered of her twins, thanks to the awesome skills
of Professor Dugald Baird, later knighted for his services to
obstetrics and gynaecology. Guess who has Baird as a middle name?
PAB Mitchell.

Mora was originally from Appin in Argyllshire, where her dad,
the Rev Charles Macdonald, from Tiree, was minister and took
services in both English and Gaelic. He kept moving his large family
east because of his asthma, first to Enzie, near Buckie, then to
Ardallie, near Ellon.

Meanwhile, my dad Robin, son of an Edinburgh minister, the
Rev David Mitchell, became another man of the cloth and had his
first parish at Rathen, near Fraserburgh, where you can find in the
local graveyard the headstones of the ancestors of Norwegian
composer, Edvard Grieg. They were, you've guessed, Greigs and of
North-East farming stock.

Buchan Presbytery ministers enjoyed the occasional social
gathering and at one of these harmonies at Ardallie, as dad scoffed
mum's delicious scones and jam, romance blossomed, he claimed.

They got engaged at the Bog of Ardallie, honest, and married at the West Church of St Nicholas in Aberdeen in 1934.

Already an authority on birdlife and the flora and fauna of the Aberdeenshire countryside, dad augmented his meagre stipend with articles on nature. After a move to East Lothian and the West Church in Haddington, he hit the jackpot by becoming chairman of a live BBC Scotland children's programme at the Edinburgh studios called *Nature Scrapbook*.

There followed stints as minister in the Fife parish of Kilconquhar and Colinsburgh and at Maryculter from 1964 to 1971. Now at last we get to the Grampian TV connection. Dad was invited to chair a nature programme under the watchful eye of producer Alan Franchi. It was an experience both cherished as they held each other in high regard.

Moving on, what is my rugby link to Grampian TV? After cutting my teeth as a journalist on the Highland News in Inverness, being promoted to editor of the Caithness Courier in Thurso in 1970 (that was promotion? – ed), I then joined the Press and Journal in 1972. I began as a feature writer, then reporter, then became night news sub-editor in March 1975. It took some effort to adjust to starting work at teatime, but it was portrayed as a necessary evil to acquire the production experience that might one day secure promotion to the editor's chair. "Try it for six months," I was told. I staggered off the subs' table 26 years later!

However, as a keen member of Aberdeenshire Rugby Club, indeed captain of the 3rd XV, an opportunity arose later in 1975 to take on the mantle of the P&J's rugby writer. It was a 'no-brainer' and come January 1976, I was forced to drag myself to Murrayfield to write about Scotland's game against France.

The double life lasted until 1985, and included Scotland's famous Grand Slam in 1984, a feat first achieved way back in 1925. And here's where Grampian TV, in the shape of its lean, mean boxer and sports commentator, Frank Gilfeather, came calling, "Can you come in to do live chats on the eve of Scotland games?" I was asked.

Easy peasy, I thought, having done a bit of public speaking. Not true, as it turned out. Actually, I never lived down my first appearance. Nothing prepares you for how nervous you feel talking in front of a TV camera. Apparently, as I waxed lyrical about

Scotland's forthcoming chances my left shoulder twitched uncontrollably. I had to go straight on to work at the paper after the live programme. "You were great," laughed colleagues, shuddering their shoulders in unison.

So where does a Caribbean cruise connect to the Grampian studios? Fast forward to 1998 when my lovely girlfriend, Irene, later my wife, and I decided in a mad moment to audition at Grampian for a place in a quiz show produced by STV, who had taken over the Queens Cross station in 1995. Somehow we managed to win a slot on *The Passport Quiz* on November 27, 1998.

The STV host that day was DJ Bryan Burnett, who hailed from Aberdeen. But he didn't do us any favours, honest. We were up against two other pairs and somehow managed to triumph. We hadn't given any thought to what the prize for winning might be, perhaps a long weekend in Wick. A week in Thurso? However, it turned out we were playing for the star prize, a two-week Caribbean cruise. Wow!

We had to wait until the last month of the century for our trip out of Southampton, and on our return saw in the new century as bronzed and fit as we have never been since. Thank you Grampian TV, for playing your part in our great adventure and for reaching out faithfully over 40 years to the far-flung corners of my beloved North of Scotland.

From the back-end staggers to 'Commando'
Bob Kenyon
Researcher/Producer, 1974-1997

It was hardly the most auspicious start
to my career in broadcasting when I arrived at
Grampian Television's Queen's Cross studios
in January 1974 from Aberdeen Journals. I
was employed as a researcher/news assistant,
but on arrival there was no spare desk for me
and I was located a small table in the office of
Charles Smith, the Head of News and Current
Affairs, who, for at least the first two weeks,
called me Benion.

I didn't realise that one of my roles
would be to research and produce the station's farming programme
Country Focus and in addition to getting to grips with mastitis in
cows, back-end staggers, swine fever and the Green pound, I had to
develop an ear for the Doric tongue in deepest Aberdeenshire and
realise that loonies were not how I had once perceived them. Vet
Hugh Kay and presenter James Davidson, the chief executive of the
Royal Highland Agricultural Society, were the on-screen talent and
superb company in the green room following shows.

The company had offices in Aberdeen and Dundee in the early
70s, and news in the outer regions was covered by stringers
(freelance cameramen) Brian Peach in Inverness, Bill Lucas in
Lewis and others giving us coverage in the outer reaches of an
extensive television region. Jimmy Primrose-Smith was the local
stringer in Aberdeen. These days there are instant pictures of
broadcast quality pictures from mobile phones, but in that dim and
distant past when film was the medium of news coverage, it was
often a wonder that events reached the screen in time. A driver had to
pick up film from the Inverness or Dundee train, arriving at ten past
five, drive it to the studio, we would run it through our film lab,
hoping that there was an image on the exposed film, then edit the
required length before lacing it on a telecine machine. If it was mute
film we then had to specify to the sound department which effects
were required to run with it.

Crann Tara, (Fiery Cross) was one of Scotland's first Gaelic current affairs programmes. I produced it, and the main reporters and presenters in the early days were Angus Peter Campbell, the award-winning Gaelic author. Maggie Cunningham, who went on to become Controller of BBC Scotland, and Peter Macaulay, the well-known Gaelic broadcaster. They were later joined by Martin Macdonald, giving his take on political matters, Chris Dillon, with a unique sideways look at life in the Highlands, the late Donald John Macdonald, who was to become Head of STV North. With Norman MacLeod, currently one of the leading TV news presenters in Scotland, it was a stellar line-up.

One of the main strengths of the programme was rooting out original stories. It is fair to say that the programme took a left-wing slant on Highland and Island issues, but given the political persuasion of the Gaidhealtachd we felt this was justifiably representative of the area. It was also one of the programmes which gave aspiring musicians their television debuts. I recall Donald Shaw, of Capercaille, contacting me and asking if they could record a slot. He obviously knew that our budget was tight because he said they could sleep in their transit van.

The recording, directed by Graham Mcleish, was highly successful, providing material for several programmes, but more importantly it brought them to the attention of Ted Brocklebank, who was looking for original Gaelic music for the multi-award winning *Blood is Strong* series.

The North East of Scotland has always had a great affinity with the sea. It was an area rich in fishing success and tragedy, long before oil exploration changed the harbours and the economy of the area, but in 1991 the harbour was transformed to an era when sail ruled the sea. The Tall Ships race, with crews and vessels from around the globe berthed in Aberdeen for four days of fun and festivities. *North Tonight*, the nightly news programme, ran live broadcasts from the ships.

More than 300,000 visitors thronged the harbour streets with a variety of musicians and characters there to greet them, before they were able to steep themselves in the city's nautical past. The event was such a success, and the demand for memories so great, that Grampian asked me to produce a commercial video of the event, which sold around 10,000 copies.

The Tall Ships visiting Aberdeen

The longest project I worked on was a programme called *Commando*. Initially we were commissioned to make a half-hour profile of Simon Fraser, Lord Lovat, to mark his 70th birthday in 1981. Lord Lovat was one of the founding leaders of Commando units formed during World War Two and described by Churchill as 'the mildest-mannered man that ever scuttled ship or slit a throat.' He was certainly one of the most charismatic characters I ever came across. When our TV crew visited him at Beaufort Castle near Beauly, he opened a bottle of whisky, poured us all drinks, threw away the top saying, 'We never put the top back on the bottle here.'

Before we finished filming with him the SAS were involved in ending the Iranian Embassy siege in London in May 1980 and it was decided we should include material about the Special Air Services, started by Lovat's cousin Bill Stirling. We sat for two days in London waiting for Stirling to give a rare interview. (Unfortunately, years later in a clean out of Grampian's library the film went missing).

The programme took another turn when the Falklands War started in 1982 and 45 Commando from Arbroath were in action. We waited for their victorious return to their Angus base before completing the programme.

Beaufort Castle, former clan seat of the Frasers

Our flamboyant director, Chris Kay, mostly kept in control by his production assistant Barbara Dickie, was in a helicopter shooting aerials of Beaufort Castle when he spotted Lord Lovat on the lawn. He instructed the helicopter to land, much to the surprise and delight of his lordship who introduced the crew to his guests and promptly gave them all another large whisky.

Spankie Doodles 3
Jimmy Spankie

My Camanachd shame
Grampian traditionally sponsored a Shinty Tournament organised by the Camanachd Association. For the early rounds it was divided into areas with the first final held in Inverness at the Bucht Park. Who better to present the Cup and medals than *SPORTSCOPE*'s host? I can tell you – as one who didn't know a caman from a caber - almost anyone else! The game was won by Newtonmore. I seem to remember their opponents were Kyles Athletic, and like all Shinty encounters it was a tough battle with no prisoners taken.

The game had barely started when I realised both teams were fielding 12 players. TWELVE PLAYERS! How dare they? If eleven was enough for football and hockey why did they need twelve? With me I had the Cup and ELEVEN Medals!

How well had I done my homework! Zero out of ten. Of

course I could have blamed my pal, Alastair Beaton. Why hadn't he told me? After all, despite his giant intellect he was really a teuchter at heart. And he was the one who'd fixed it for me to do this presentation. But typically when I needed him most Al wasn't there.

During the match I cried a little to try to relieve the tension. Didn't really work and I soaked my one and only handkerchief as I spent the afternoon plotting my revenge on the whole Beaton clan. At full time the players came up to the grandstand to receive their hardware. The spectators - perhaps eight or nine hundred - gathered at the edge of the pitch facing the presentation area. Before any one said anything an elderly male spectator shouted 'What did you think of the game Mr Spankie?' He was vaguely familiar. Almost certainly one of Beaton's cousins from Newtonmore. I could cheerfully have throttled him. Using my knowledge of football and as many sporting cliches as I could muster I stumbled through all the team positions. When I finished and happily realised I didn't have to go to the toilet after all, there was something of a hiatus.

It took only seconds to explain my medal predicament to the winning captain. He gave me a toothy grin (he had lost one in the match) and said 'Just pretend to give one to me.' What a gentleman. He did receive one the following week! As for Al Beaton, I knew what I was going to do with the caman the winning team presented me with!

Me and Innes (capable) Wright

Lenzie has a quiet calm about it as though it's happy to be eight miles away from the hustle and bustle of Scotland's largest city, Glasgow.

It's a summer's evening. All is quiet on Longmuirhead Road. A garden gate opens and in steps a young man. He's called Innes Wright and he comes from Aboyne in Aberdeenshire. He rings the door bell and an attractive slim young lady appears.

'Hello Janette, 'I've brought you some flowers'.

'How thoughtful of you' says a beaming Janette. 'I'll just put my clubs away and put the flowers in water.' She's talking about the golf clubs with which she's been practising in the back garden.

Janette Robertson was one of Scotland's most accomplished golfers. A Scottish and British internationalist and Curtis Cup player,

Janette also enjoyed many successful tours particularly the five weeks she spent in Australia and New Zealand. However she met her match in Innes Wright whom she married a year after he delivered that bunch of flowers, "It wasn't till the following morning that I realised he'd picked them from my own garden," she recalls. 'That was typical of Innes'.

No matter his success on the golf course nor as the professional at Aboyne Golf Club, Innes became a Grampian TV favourite via a Friday evening fifteen minute live programme called *Grampian Golf*.

Innes was a TV 'natural'. Few people come over naturally on television. Talking to a camera is not a natural way of conversing. Perhaps the most telling thing you could say about Innes was that the camera liked him. For a year he took me and our TV audience through every golf shot in the book with clarity and humour. It was easy for me as programme presenter. I introduced Innes, asked a couple of questions then kept out of sight until it was time to say "Good Bye, folks".

Jimmy Spankie with Innes Wright

But there was one occasion when, inadvertently, I nearly 'corpsed' him. He'd just finished explaining how to approach the

168

green through a strong cross wind when out of the blue I asked, 'Are you troubled with wind, Innes"?

Our studio was meant to be sound-proof but I could hear the howls of laughter from the control room!

Innes handled it like the consummate 'pro' he was! 'No I simply adjust my stance'.

Transfixed by telly and Spankie and Franchi!

Joan Ingram

Reporter, 1983-2000

I was five years old when the black and white TV arrived in our council house in Myrtlefield, Aviemore. More specifically, Jimmy Spankie arrived and he transfixed me the way youngsters are now hooked on *Teletubbies* or *Peppa Pig*. Eighteen years later, still starstruck, I walked through the door of the Grampian studios to work as a reporter. The people who had masterminded *Bothy Nichts* and other such wonders of my childhood; Alan Franchi, and Alec Sutherland (Grampian's musical director who led one of the most successful Scottish Dance Bands) would stop for a chat in the corridor. Even Jimmy Spankie!

Alan Franchi produced great programmes because he had great affinity for people. He once said to me that at that time, in the early 80s almost all our viewers were never more than one generation away from the land, and that's what made the GTV connection so strong; the sense of identity and community and shared culture.

The photos along the walls of the corridors at the Queens Cross studios showed the likes of John Duncanson, Bill MacKenzie and Alan Cowie. I would eventually join them.

In many ways television was still a man's world. When I was hired women were not allowed to wear trousers to work, and a memory that still jars was being addressed by a senior executive as a 'dolly bird'! Sports reporting was an occupation women had yet to enter. On Fridays, Alan Saunders would arrive up from Dundee to do two things - place an accumulator bet along with Bob Kenyon on the horse races for that day - and put together the weekend sports preview, both high concentration activities. One afternoon in particular Alan was under a lot of pressure as he tried to put his 'goals' together for North Tonight. The horses were coming in, all in the right order, but this must have coincided with a newsroom shortage of men. So I was dispatched to Pittodrie to interview Alex

Ferguson. I'd never done a football interview before and wasn't sure what to ask, but the questions I was given were not very challenging. I needn't have worried. Alex Ferguson took me aside before the interview and told me exactly what to ask, including a signing he was about to make, and a team change. When I got back to the newsroom they were very impressed with my incisive questioning, my relaxed and communicative interviewee and my 'big scoop'.

A couple of weeks later, faith in my footballing knowledge led me to be asked to present a portion of the Friday sports round up. I confidently misread the autocue and said Alec Sutherland had named his squad for Saturday! By the time I got back to the newsroom, a viewer had rung in to say, "Don't blame the lassie, her mind was on the dancing not the football." My gaff probably set back the cause of women football reporters for – oh, at least a fortnight!

Grampian viewers were very loyal as if the station was part of them. Sometimes too much so. One day a package arrived containing women's tops. The gentleman who sent it wrote a note to me explaining he would love to see me wearing his dead wife's blouses on *North Tonight*. It sort of freaked me out. They were clearly last worn around VE day, and the sweat stains showed it had been a good night! I sent them back with a short note saying they didn't fit. Now, looking back, I switch between thinking this was a very creepy thing to do, or alternatively an incredibly grief-stricken way of trying to keep a treasured memory alive. Still, I'm glad she was a much bigger size than me.

I had 17 years amazing years being part of a newsroom where pride and professionalism shone through. We proved ourselves fit to meet any journalism challenge as well as anywhere in the network.

In the early hours of 7th July 1988 I remember being awakened by the sound of multiple helicopters flying overhead into Aberdeen Royal Infirmary. I barely had time to gather my thoughts when minutes later the phone rang and I was called into work. Over the next few days Grampian news teams led the world in the coverage of the Piper Alpha tragedy and the loss of 167 men. There were stories of tragedy and heroism, first-hand memories of those who were lost and those who were saved, and the men and women who saved them. The corporate responsibility and the health and safety narrative was for a later date. Ably led by Alistair Gracie Grampian's entire team did their job with compassion and humanity. I am proud to have been part of it.

My life-long love affair with Grampian TV has endured for more than half a century, as it has for so many colleagues fortunate enough to know the place and its people. The annual reunion of staff is still a highlight of my calendar. It's like a return to these heady days in the social club at the back of the tram shed, but we now have many more absent friends sadly, and us 'young girls' are not nearly so young.

Grampian's quiz queen
Evelyn Hood

Within a few months of Grampian opening in September 1961 someone came up with the idea that viewers would be enticed to switch to the new ITV station serving the North of Scotland if a programme could be devised featuring local folk. Thus was created the first of Grampian's quizzes, *A' the Airts* – a quiz on Scotland and the Scots, pitting family teams of three against each other in a series of programmes, with a major prize of £600 of household goods or a Morris Minor car.

In November 1963 my brother Iain persuaded me and my husband Angus to form a team. We did – and won! We took the money!

The programme, hosted by Grampian's first continuity announcer, Douglas Kynoch, quickly attracted the desired audience, good press coverage and convinced GTV management that quizzes with local contestants were a sure-fire way of winning high local viewer percentages.

So began a succession of locally-produced quiz programmes beginning with *A' the Airts* in 1962 and ending with *Snap!* in 2005. These quiz shows gave me, a Perthshire-based freelance journalist, a pathway into television work – initially providing questions for quiz shows and later devising and writing documentaries. Over the years I worked for no fewer than five programme directors - Alan Franchi, Jim Brown, Mike Lloyd, Gordon Thomson, and Graham Mcleish - and devised over 65,000 questions for the quiz programmes:

Win A Word was presented by Lesley Blair who was a good quizzer but occasionally had concentration lapses. I recall one occasion when two opposing contestants were each called

Lesley Blair

William. "Oh dear!" said Lesley, "this could be confusing." Short pause "Ah! I know what I'll do. I'll call you both Bill!"

The *Try For Ten* question master, Billy Raymond, was a cabaret singer and entertainer from Renfrewshire who was a great hit with the studio and viewing audiences. At the beginning of every programme there had to be sixty envelopes in a rack of pigeon holes with each envelope holding twenty questions. Three envelopes were selected by the contestant and handed over to Billy. Pronunciation wasn't Billy's strongest suit, so ideally before the recording I sat down with him writing phonetic spellings over words he found difficult.

Junior Try For Ten & Know Your Country were quizzes for teenagers, both programmes hosted by Jack McLaughlin, who was superb at getting the young folk to relax and enjoy the experience.

Top Team was a knockout quiz for teams representing schools and youth, sports, and hobby clubs in the Grampian area, with a cash award for their school or club. The question master was announcer/presenter Jimmy Spankie and *Top Team*'s success in attracting a high percentage of the local viewership confirmed the production team's hopes for quiz programming of this kind.

An adult version was devised as a general knowledge quiz series for teams representing clubs, sports teams, universities and colleges. Called *Top Club* it was launched in 1971. *Top Club* became an annual series of fifteen programmes featuring sixteen teams, the series finalists earning four figure sums for the charities of their choice. Selecting the teams for recording meant holding auditions throughout the North of Scotland and the Outer and Northern Isles which meant much travelling throughout the viewing area. I still recall finding myself in Lerwick one year on January 4th, Kirkwall the following morning, and Aberdeen that evening after enduring some of the scariest flights I have ever experienced.

Jimmy Spankie was question master from 1971 to 1983. He was succeeded briefly by radio broadcaster Jimmy Mack, and then finally by sports reporter and journalist, Frank Gilfeather who was *Top Club's* host until its last series in 1998.

The programme consistently earned very high ratings and on more than one occasion attracted almost 50% of the area's viewership, beating rival programmes such as the BBC's *This is Your*

Life. One series featured a team representing Aberdeen University Students. This was an outstanding team captained by a very bright local lad called Michael Gove. He went on to cut his journalistic teeth in the Grampian News Room. Who knows what happened to him after that!

In the late 1970s and early 80s radio broadcaster Bill Torrance had been presenting a quiz show on Radio Forth about Scots words and their meanings,

A young Michael Gove

entitled *Shammy Dab*. Grampian adapted it for television. The contestants were well-known Scottish personalities – actors, singers, writers and so on. The original series was presented by Bill Torrance and subsequently by comedian Johnnie Beattie and then by sports presenter Dougie Donnelly.

George Duffus, the well-known local comedian and after-dinner speaker, hosted a general knowledge quiz entitled *Random Choice* which ran for a thirteen-programme series just at the point when Grampian TV was in process of being taken over by the Scottish Media Group. The very last of the Grampian-based quizzes was devised by Carrie Watt, who had come through the ranks with the company, and was called *Snap!*

Snap! was just about the last programme series to be recorded in the old Grampian TV studios in Fountainhall Road, Aberdeen. I'd been in at the beginning with my quizzes and was still there four decades later – a kind of "I've started, so I'll finish" situation. I don't think I was the only one with a tear in my eye when our question-times finally came to an end.

The Art of Sutter
Art Sutter

The Art Sutter Show was conceived one evening while I was compering a North East talent show in His Majesty's Theatre in Aberdeen, unaware that in the audience were Grampian Director of Programmes George Mitchell and programme director Alan Franchi. Alan became a great personal friend over the years we worked together, and it was easy to see why everyone in the industry loved the man. So the *Art Sutter Show* was born after George and Alan saw  something in my act they could present to the Grampian TV public. We started with a pilot show which thankfully was successful, and I remember researcher and producer, Marian Hepworth saying that this was going to run and run.

I was used to interviewing high-profile celebs and politicians because of my Radio Scotland afternoon magazine programme, so I thought TV would be quite similar. But of course TV is totally different to radio which is really background entertainment, whereas television demands your total attention. Doing an hour-long live show on a Friday night was a bit scary, but I did have a great production team, including Alan Franchi, Hilary Ling, Marian Hepworth, plus young Carrie and Theresa.

The first show was a bit of a blur as it was my first experience of a one hour LIVE production. I just knew I loved every minute of it although I can't remember a single guest from that night. Alex Sutherland with the boys in the band provided great support. Alex's band on that first occasion included Peggy O'Keefe the piano-playing legend. Every TV host needs a friend as floor manager. Tim Spring was that man for me and he kept me right with all my timings to ad breaks and obviously when to end the show on time. I must also add Graham Mcleish to the mix as he took over from Alan as director and brought new ideas and direction to the show. When I look at the credits showing the number of people it takes to produce *The Graham Norton Show*, for example, what we achieved on a

Friday night LIVE show was incredible. The 'Norton' show, of course, is recorded for transmission the following evening. *The Art Sutter Show* regularly achieved over 50% of the total viewing audience, surpassed only by *Coronation Street*.

Art holding Liz McColgan's medals

We tried to keep the show 'clean' with as little risky material as possible. The guests were asked to abide by Grampian standards which seemed right for the time. But when you had guys like Bradley Walsh, Joe Pasquale and Alan Stewart being themselves it was sometimes impossible to put restrictions on them! Bradley was a kind of law unto himself and had I succeeded in 'restraining' him he wouldn't have been as entertaining as he was with his 'off the wall' sense of humour.

The first thing he did when I welcomed him onto the floor for the first time was to go round the back of the set and declare 'this is like a Chinese takeaway'. He then proceeded to place an order for Kungo po chicken, fried rice etc and asked me what I was having. An unusual start to an interview to say the least, but a serious chat with Bradley Walsh was never on the cards. Over the years he was a great guest.

Art with Bradley Walsh and Alvin Stardust

One gag came close to a Mary Whitehouse complaint, however, when I asked him about his professional football career. His mother had encouraged him by telling him he was good for 'Sweet FA'. FA, of course, stands for Football Association, but Brad knew that wasn't the interpretation the viewers would take. He also got me into trouble at the Caledonian Hotel in Union Terrace where we were staying overnight. There was a grand piano in the lounge and he insisted that I should play while he and fellow guest, Jenny Powell, had a dance. Nothing wrong with that you may say, but it was 2am and the other hotel guests curled up in bed understandably didn't see the funny side.

Alan Stewart was an old friend and also great fun. Alan was a well-known eligible bachelor at the time and the interview got round to girlfriends. I asked about his 'chat up lines' to girls he had just met. He said he took them to his flat or home for a coffee. He recalled saying to one lass who seemed settled down for the evening. 'How do you like your eggs in the morning?' To which she replied:

'Unfertilised'. By today's standards fairly mild perhaps, but in the mid-eighties on 'the Grumpian' it was as close to the line as we got. But I have to say the live audience loved it!

Joe Pasquale was just Joe as he is today, brilliantly original and extremely funny. Sir David Frost was also terrific fun and so professional in every way. Not once did he make me feel uncomfortable with his erudition and experience.

Then there were people like Sir John Junor the eminent newspaper editor and the politician David Steel, who gave the impression he really didn't want to be there, but his publisher wanted to promote his book.

Alan Stewart

Art with Joe Pasquale

Hannah Gordon was as lovely a person as she was to look at and so easy to talk to. Apart from our distinguished guests it would be wrong not to mention some of the more local lads who added to the variety of the show and were every bit as entertaining – people like Grampian's Frank Gilfeather, footballer, Brian Irvine, and of course Denis Law who, although speaking with a more English than Scottish accent, had many happy memories of his home town.

Art with Hannah Gordon

Edwina Currie was the only guest who nearly walked off the show. Programme boss George Mitchell suggested I should mention in my introduction a passage which she'd included in her book claiming she hadn't had sex for three years. Her words NOT ours. When I mentioned this in rehearsal she blew a gasket. Actually, I don't blame her, as even although she had written it, I felt she was really invading her own privacy. She was going to walk off the show if the line wasn't removed, but after my fulsome apology she agreed to continue. Authors really should be more careful about what they write!

Other famous guests included Russell Hunter and Una Mclean who announced their engagement on air which was great and they were hilarious. This led to what was a longer chat than it should have been which had consequences on our next guest, Rikki Fulton. It meant Rikki's time on the show was reduced, and being live there was nothing we could do. Understandably, Rikki was very unhappy and I don't think he ever spoke to me again.

Finally, and I hear readers say thank God for that, I have one regret where I let myself down as well as the entire team and crew. Our guest was the actress, cake-maker, and one time girl friend of Paul McCartney, Jane Asher. Let me explain. It was I think the tenth anniversary of the *Art Sutter Show* and Jane was the main guest. To my surprise she brought with her a celebration cake in the shape of a grand piano. Director Alan Franchi had included a white grand piano as an essential prop from the very first show. Jane's 'piano cake' was absolutely stunning and I was so delighted that I fell over my own ego and took the cake home with me to let family and friends see it.

Art with Scotland the What ?

But of course Jane didn't really make the cake for me but for the whole team. Every show was a team effort and, in truth, I was just the front man. I was mortified and brought the cake back the following week, but to this day I still regret my action and would like to say SORRY to the entire team. Incidentally on the subject of the lovely Jane Asher we did raise a few eyebrows and had tongues wagging when we both appeared together for breakfast in the hotel dining room the following morning. She signed her book to me as 'my breakfast date', but I can assure readers, including my lovely Wife Janette, that it was all completely innocent.

I loved every minute of my time with Grampian - from the production meetings in Dizzy's restaurant on Thursday nights, to the close of play at the end of every Friday night programme. It was a pleasure to work with all of the team and a privilege to have been part of the Grampian Family.

Views from the fireside
Romper Room
Gillian Brand (nee Brown)

In 1964 I took part in the children's TV programme called *Romper Room*. I have some vivid memories of that time even though I was only four years old. I remember my mother driving us from Kemnay to Aberdeen to the studios on numerous days and I can clearly recollect the outside of the Grampian Studios with the logo on the wall.

Lesley Blair presenting Romper Room

I remember the presenter Lesley Blair and being led through the doors into the studio where filming took place. Two incidents from that time have stayed with me throughout the last 56 years. The first being asked by Lesley about a dog we used to look after at the family home. It was a very small dog and I do remember telling her that we took it for a walk and "it got awfy dubby feet! "

The other incident was a frightening one for me. I'm guessing the programme was teaching road safety that particular day. I can see the zebra crossing marked out on the studio floor with two black and white stripey poles either side, each with some sort of sack over the top. The sack was pulled off revealing an orange ball with a frightening face and a moving mouth. That was too much for me and I remember bolting for the doors to find my mother!

I feel privileged, looking back, at being part of the programme. Indeed when I talk to friends my age, they often ask how did I get to be on the show? I can also confirm that many still remember the scary Belisha beacons too!

And who can forget Lesley's Magic Mirror!

For Pete's sake!
Pete Moran
Film Cameraman, 1977-1989

I started with Grampian Television in
August 1977. As a former free-lance assistant
cameraman, I had initial reservations about
being a staff member, but soon embraced the
job and enjoyed working with a very talented
and friendly group of people at Grampian's
Queen's Cross studios in Aberdeen.

My first few days were spent sleeping in
my mini-van parked outside the studios. I
spent the evenings in Grampian's social club
before retiring to my spartan accommodation.
(Fortunately, I am of limited stature, so fitted in the van reasonably
well.) Breakfast was supplied by the wonderful staff in the canteen
(Doreen Gerrie and Liz). Brian Young, a film editor, took pity on me
and offered me the use of his flat as he was going on holiday for a
few days. This gave me the breathing space to look for a better living
space than the back of a van.

I was kept very busy at GTV and spent a lot of time travelling
the region as a 'mute' cameraman or as an assistant on the film
production unit. As an assistant my job was to keep the film
magazines for the camera loaded, operate the clapper board and
constantly check the camera for 'hairs in the gate' which involved
removing the lens and checking for any debris left on the film plane
which could ruin the shot for the cameraman and director. The
clapper board was to allow the film editor to synchronise the separate
sound and the pictures together using audible and visual means. Each
four hundred feet roll of (expensive) film would last for ten minutes,
so an interview could use up several rolls which kept the assistant
busy. As a 'mute' cameraman, I would be sent out to record news
events like floods, accidents, fires, boats running aground, etc and
the sound effects or music would be added latterly, back at base.

The oil boom was already well under way, and my first trip
offshore was to take some footage of Jim Callaghan (Labour PM
1976-79) visiting BP's Forties Field. Time was tight and I had to get

back to Aberdeen in time to get the film processed and transmitted 'down the line' to ITN and shown on *North Tonight*. The delicate film was whizzed through the processing machinery in record times. Talented film processors Sandy Knox and Alex Crombie got cameramen and the newsroom out of a hole on many occasions! Also housed in the processing unit was Johnny Thompson, a talented stills photographer and a lovely, gentle man.

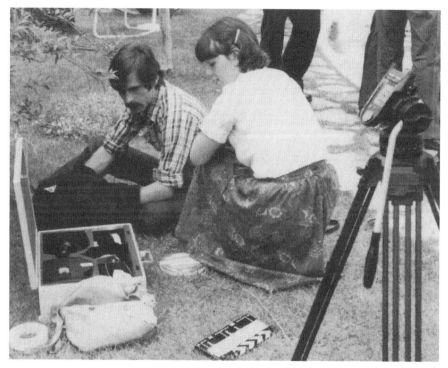

Reloading a film magazine in the 'black bag' so as not to expose the film to light.

The Electric Theatre Show was a long-running series on Grampian. It featured stars of the small and big screen being interviewed about their lives along with film of them on set locations. My first *ETS* was on the Greek island of Rhodes where the feature crew were filming *Escape to Athena*. We managed to get exclusive interviews with Telly Savalas, David Niven, Jenny Agutter, Roger Moore and Elliot Gould who proved to be difficult during his interview, as he turned on a loud 'ghetto blaster' every time he answered a question. Don't know why, but I think he was a bit miffed with his own PR department about something or other.

Another *ETS* I was involved with was on the set of *Local Hero*. A lot of the scenes were filmed over by Fort William, with the pub and telephone box scenes shot in the fishing village of Pennan on the Moray Coast. Our director was Graham Mcleish and the Production Assistant was the trusty Helen Straine, with John Doran as producer. We had a day off in the middle of the shoot as

Pete Moran filming Burt Lancaster

there was a 'closed set' to allow Burt Lancaster to film some of his scenes on set in a converted whisky distillery. The previous evening, we had a few drinks with actors, Peter Capaldi and John Gordon-Sinclair (as you do) and we all decided to hire a couple of boats the next day to float about on a loch. Armed with a load of beer, off we went. A great day out, with lots of jolly banter!

Filming of the filming of Local Hero on Camusdarach beach

I was very fortunate to be chosen as film cameraman on two of Grampian's most prestigious series. One was *OIL* directed by Mick

Csaky with Ted Brocklebank and Bjorn Nilssen as writer/producers and *The Blood Is Strong,* directed by Bernd Schulz, produced by Ted Brocklebank, with Ted and Angus Peter-Campbell as writers. Music was provided by the Gaelic group, *Capercaillie. OIL* was an eight-part series for C4 and *The Blood Is Strong* a three-part series for C4. *OIL* was a co-production with NRK of Norway. The GTV crew were to film in the USA, Europe the Middle East and China. The NRK crew filmed in Russia Europe, Mexico and Africa.

On these shoots, apart from the buzz of visiting far-flung parts of the world, I was very proud and still am, to have worked alongside such professional crew-members as Hilary Ling, Alex Duthie, George Leslie, Terry Wolsey, Steve Horrocks, Bruce Moroney, Pete Wolsey, Sheila Gordon, Barbara Dickie, Sandy Knox, as well as producers and directors, Ted, Bernd Schultz and Mick Csaky.

We worked long hours and were sometimes away from home for several weeks at a time. Each day after the shoot, back at our hotel, the production assistant had to produce a 'call sheet' (schedule) for the following day, the camera crew had to pack all the 'rushes' (exposed film ready for despatch to the London labs) and the sound recordist had to log his tapes. There was a very positive approach, by every member of the crew to achieve the best possible outcome to each day's filming, with everybody 'mucking in' to get the best results.

On some of these shoots, aerial footage was required. This involved me being strapped into the back of a helicopter with the door removed behind a 'helevision' camera mount. In Dallas I recall we hired a company called Pumpkin Airways to try to re-create the original *Dallas* TV series title sequence. As it turned out we were lucky enough to have the helicopter pilot who filmed that original sequence. It was a tremendous buzz to be able capture footage nearly identical to the original.

On another helicopter shoot, the pilot was descending into Los Angeles airport, and unbeknown to him, another helicopter was ascending into his flight path. The first thing I knew was our chopper rapidly rolling to avoid collision. I saw the other aircraft almost corkscrewing through the air at high speed. I was flung against the 'helevision' mount and got a couple of bruised ribs. On landing, both pilots were summoned to Air Traffic Control to file a 'near miss' incident. Now, that was a bit scary.

The Grampian Social Club

Grampian's Social club was run by members of staff, for members of staff. Two of the mainstays of the club were John McAdam and Bob Reid, who were founder members. The club offered facilities such as snooker, table tennis, darts, etc and also organised various events through the year including golf and skiing. A Christmas party for the children of staff was held with a guest Santa. A summer party for the children was also arranged with Jim Craib driving a bus full of children to Haddo House and or other locations. The club also did a great PR job for the company, as guests from various shows like *Bothy Nichts, Andy's Party, The Entertainers and Calum's Ceilidh* were invited up to the club after the shows before heading home.

Just after Aberdeen FC had beaten Real Madrid for the European Cup Winners Cup in Gothenburg, Leslie Taylor from the Education Dept. was returning from Sweden on the 'St. Clair'. The ship had been commissioned to take Aberdeen supporters on the return trip to see the game. I recall Leslie, standing on a table, giving an impromptu rendition of a medley of Connie Francis songs including Lipstick on my Collar to entertain the boisterous Aberdeen fans on their successful return. Leslie was also hosting a party that evening at her flat, to which we were all invited.

Meanwhile back at the Social Club, Jack Bruce the former bass player and vocalist of 'Cream' arrived in the club after appearing on *North Tonight*. Jack, resplendent in an Afghan coat, got steadily drunker as the evening wore on. Eventually, Ron Whichelow from Security arrived in the club and noticed the inebriated stranger sitting on a barstool. "Excuse me sir, are you a member of this club?" he enquired. "What club?" slurred Jack. I quickly explained to Ron who Jack was. Ron sheepishly turned back to the Rock legend and said,

"Mr. Bruce, I've always been a great fan of your music". "Where's the party?" responded Jack. Later that evening, we assisted one of the world's greatest rock musicians down the stairs and on to Leslie's homecoming party. That was a big, big night.

I left Grampian TV in 1989 to further my career in the up and coming 'Independent' sector. Over the years I've been fortunate to work on various network documentaries which, of course, are no  part of the Grampian story. But I'll always remember the tribute *North Tonight* programme editor, Alan Cowie paid me shortly before I moved on. "Pete" he told me, "You're the best film cameraman in Scotland... under five foot six inches." That's what I liked about Aberdonians – their directness!

But it was this directness and the privilege of working with a great community of dedicated and talented people who were also my friends that made the Grampian years some of the best of my life.

Always expect the unexpected

Craig Millar
Dundee/Aberdeen Reporter, 1986-2018

If there is one adage which should epitomise the thought processes of a news journalist it is 'always expect the unexpected'. For the occupants of the Grampian Television newsroom of the mid to late 1980s it could hardly have been more appropriate.

Within a 20-month period, two of the world's most devastating oil disasters shook the industry to the core. The shockingly abrupt downing of what was then the world's biggest civilian helicopter and the cataclysmic destruction of one of the North Sea's most productive oil platforms both happened on Grampian's news 'patch'.

The Chinook helicopter and Piper Alpha disasters took the lives of 212 men and will be forever remembered by the journalists and camera crews who covered them. I am proud to say I was one of a team which met the considerable challenges of covering both calamities. The memories are still vivid.

It must have been around 11.30 on the morning of November 6, 1986. The news agenda had a distinctly routine air to it. With cameraman Terry Farquharson and sound man Sandy Knox, I was dispatched to the gates of a primary school in the Aberdeen suburb of Bridge of Don.

Our task was to 'vox pop' parents who were turning up to collect their children.

We were trying to gauge their opinions about industrial action being carried out by Scotland's largest teaching union, the EIS. We had hardly started when we were suddenly interrupted. The phone rang in our Volvo crew car and the voice at the other end was that of *North Tonight* producer, Alan Cowie.

"A helicopter has gone down off the coast of Shetland," he said. "Get to the airport now. We've chartered a plane to get you up there."

Armed only with that sparse piece of information, we sped off to Dyce. Our plane was waiting and the normal airport formalities were dispensed with. With the camera gear on board, the captain emerged from the cockpit to ask, "Right, I understand it's Shetland we're heading to. Is it Unst or Sumburgh where we're landing?"

Bear in mind, this was very much pre-internet days. We had little more guidance than had been given on the car phone. And that was where our only phone was - in the car! Worse still, having just joined Grampian a few months before, my geographical knowledge of the Shetland Islands was limited to say the least, I gave it my best guess.

"I think it's Unst." Wrong answer. Unst is at the northern end of the Shetland islands. Unbeknown to us at that point, the helicopter had crashed into the sea near Sumburgh Airport at the southern tip of Shetland's Mainland, about 80 miles away.

Then an unlikely ally came to our rescue. The pilot told us our take off was being delayed as we had to wait for a BBC crew to arrive. Damn, I thought. I had hoped we would depart ahead of our local rivals. But when reporter Jane Franchi appeared she saved me from major embarrassment. Armed with a bit more information than us she said, "It's not Unst we're going to, it's Sumburgh!"

The doomed helicopter was a giant Boeing Vertol Chinook which had been carrying oil workers back from Shell's Brent Field. It had suddenly plunged backwards into the sea at 11.32am after a catastrophic gear box failure which led to its twin rotors colliding with each other. Remarkably, we were in the air well before 1pm. Bad news travels fast. On arrival at Sumburgh at around 2pm, Jane and I were rapidly briefed by local journalist Jonathan Wills. Neither of us had much time to complete our reports because the charter flight was returning to Aberdeen at 4pm in time for the evening news bulletins.

While I was doing a piece to camera near the end of the runway, a speeding car stopped beside us. Inside was Andrew Anderson, then working for BBC Shetland, but soon to join Grampian TV. He tipped us off that the coastguard helicopter pilot, Captain Gordon Mitchell, had a story to tell.

In the nearby Bristow's hangar, Captain Mitchell spoke of how he and his crew had been on a training exercise when they spotted an oil slick and wreckage from the Chinook. They then rescued two survivors from the sea, the pilot Captain Pushp Vaid and young oil worker Eric Morrans. Tragically, the 45 other men on the Chinook perished in what was the world's worst civilian helicopter disaster.

Captain Mitchell's account was detailed - and gripping. Jane Franchi then announced she was heading back to Aberdeen on the plane. I asked if she would take back the Grampian TV tape containing all our footage as it had been decided we would stay on in Shetland. To her credit, Jane did so and handed it over when she arrived in Aberdeen at around 5pm.

A Boeing Vertol Chinook Helicopter

Once edited, it meant my report was the lead item on *North Tonight* at six oclock.

It was broadcast not just across Scotland but on ITV stations in the north of England as well. It had been a mammoth effort by all concerned at Grampian - those on the scene and the production staff back at base. But despite the exhilaration of a job well done, there was the sobering reminder that 45 men had died.

The next day, we were joined in Lerwick by producer Bob Kenyon who had flown up to assist. The two survivors were relatively unscathed - miraculously. Outside the Gilbert Bain

Hospital we interviewed the Shell Chief Executive, Sir Bob Reid, who reminded viewers just how hazardous the exploitation of oil in the North Sea could be. Behind him, off camera, I could see Shell's communications chief from Aberdeen with tears running down his face.

By this time an ITN crew, with reporter Simon Cole, had arrived on the island from London equipped with very new and state of the art mobile satellite equipment.

We were able to feed our material directly back to Aberdeen - a big advantage over the opposition!

A few weeks later, we conducted an exclusive interview with Eric Morrans. Fortuitously, his sister, Irene, worked at Grampian and helped to arrange it. Eric's story was both electrifying and horrific.

When he boarded the Chinook offshore, his allocated seat had been taken so he sat at the top end of the cabin looking back towards the rest of the passengers. It was their stunned faces that would be forever printed on his memory when, within two minutes of landing, there was a huge bang, like an explosion, and the helicopter hurtled towards the sea as glass and bits of metal flew around the cabin.

The Chinook tragedy happened on the sixth of the month. Who would have thought that on July 6, 1988 something even worse was to occur?

It was a Wednesday night when the phone rang in my house at around 10.45. On the phone was Grampian news editor Steve Mylles. The news was chilling - there had been an explosion on a platform called Piper Alpha. Steve's tone was ominous.
"It sounds like a really bad one," he said.

Incredibly, the first blast on Piper had only happened about 45 minutes before his call. We were still in the days of no internet and mobile phones and the problem for our newsroom, and others, was that we were unable to visually convey anything of the dreadful events occurring 120 miles north east of Aberdeen.

As casualties would be ferried back to Aberdeen Royal Infirmary's helipad, it was to there that I was dispatched to meet up with camera crew George Leslie and Pete Wolsey.

Also gathering at the hospital were anguished relatives hoping beyond hope that their loved ones would survive. As we waited, it became increasingly apparent that the scale of the disaster was massive. When the first helicopter arrived, we saw the initial signs of the human cost of Piper Alpha.

Some of the casualties were walking wounded, some had obvious burns injuries and others looked shell shocked. The more seriously injured were stretchered into the hospital. However, there would not be an ongoing procession of helicopters returning to shore - too many men had either died or were missing as Piper disintegrated.

Piper Alpha

In 1988 there were no rolling news channels so TV schedules were being adjusted as the disaster unfolded. I returned to edit a report at Grampian for a 9am news bulletin. At about 8.15am, during the editing process, senior producer Bill Mackie popped his head round the door.

"The Time The Place is coming from Aberdeen this morning," was his news.

"Sorry Bill, I've got to get this piece edited," was my somewhat brusque reply.

The Time The Place was a studio-based current affairs programme produced by Granada TV in Manchester for the ITV network. It was hosted by the energetic and highly-experienced Mike

Scott who bounded about amongst the studio audience.

Bill Mackie returned to the editing suite at about 8:45, "Craig, like I said *The Time The Place* is coming live from Aberdeen this morning... and you're presenting it."

Well, that *was* unexpected! We had little more than an hour to prepare for 60 minutes of live television being broadcast across the UK. Grampian staff arriving at Fountainhall Road that morning were commandeered into the studio to make up an audience. Bill Mackie had rapidly assembled a smattering of experts, trade unionists and politicians - including Margaret Thatcher's Energy Secretary Peter Morrison - to offer their initial understanding of what had happened on Piper Alpha.

It was to some extent 'seat of the pants' television - but it worked.

The sense of tragedy was conveyed to the nation. Not known for being emotionally demonstrative, Bill Mackie, or 'the major', as he was known at Grampian, gave me a hug on meeting me at the studio doors as I emerged! 'Herograms' were later faxed from ITV in London.

My colleagues in the newsroom could not have cared less. They were working furiously to cope with a whirlwind of breaking news as survivors emerged to tell their stories about how they escaped the world's worst oil disaster.

On the night of July 7, Grampian, STV and ITV were able to broadcast dramatic and graphic pictures of the blazing Piper Alpha platform through the complete coincidence of having cameraman Paul Berriff on board an RAF helicopter from Lossiemouth as part of a previously-commissioned documentary series called *Rescue*.

Over the next few weeks the likes of Bill Mackie, Alan Cowie, Steve Mylles, Alan Fisher, Frank Gilfeather, Ross McWilliam, Andrew Anderson and Donald John McDonald all served the newsroom with distinction and the department received plaudits from ITN in London. It was a sombre time in Aberdeen. A feeling of numbness was widespread as people tried to come to terms with the magnitude of the terrible loss of life. Looking back, I think the newsroom achieved the difficult balance of reporting the reality of what had happened in a way that totally respected the sensitivities of the viewing public. After these two dreadful events, there was a rather more cheering postscript for me some three decades later.

In 2016, I was preparing a news report to mark the 30th anniversary of the Chinook disaster. I knocked on the door of Captain Pushp Vaid's home at Westhill outside Aberdeen. He agreed to do an interview with us and as the camera was being set up we discussed our mutual love of golf.

A few months later we played golf together - over 30 years after I reported on the world's worst civilian helicopter crash - one which he survived against all the odds.

Spankie Doodles 4
Jimmy Spankie

Pittodrie blues

Sometime during the 60s Aberdeen Football Club raised its turnstile prices for a league game from, I seem to remember, 5/- to 5/6d (25p to 27.5p). This prompted Alastair Beaton, our sports programme producer at that time, to suggest I take the camera down a busy Aberdeen street to ask people what they thought about the increase and whether it would stop some fans from attending home games at Pittodrie.

These quick interviews are called 'vox pops' derived from the Latin 'Vox Populi' (who said Dundonians are thick?) meaning the voice of the people. In my view they could be fun and occasionally funny but not usually of any great value to the issue being discussed. The interviewer can help to make the item more interesting to watch by trying to ensure: All interviewees do NOT look in the same direction. There is a range of ages. A balance of the sexes (although I discovered quickly there are only two in Aberdeen). Before the cameraman had to stop for lunch I decided we could stop one more person.

'Hello, you may have heard Aberdeen F.C. have raised the price of admission to 5/6d. Would you be willing to pay the extra money to go to Pittodrie on a Saturday afternoon?'

Pause –'Yes I think I would'

'Why?'

Longer pause – 'Because I'm their centre forward'.

Collapse of Spankie, Sports programme host who had not recognised Ernie Winchester who led the Dons' frontline.

Yes - we did transmit the item! Nobody 'phoned to complain. Not even Ernie.

This sporting life – GTV style

The Sportscope team

Following Innes Wright's successful *Grampian Golf* our first sports programme was a Friday evening look ahead to the weekend's activities in our area, *Sportscope*.

Al Beaton produced it while I assisted and presented each Friday evening at 6.45 for 15 minutes with a budget of £15. Alastair quickly assembled a small team. Archie Glen was happy to be our football expert. He was the Dons left half and skipper for many years and had been capped for Scotland. On the programme he either analysed two or three of the following day's games or interviewed an appropriate player or official.

Between Perth and Aberdeen there were several first and second division teams and, of course, we also covered the Highland League. It was a little more difficult to find a rugby correspondent. The Scottish Rugby Union were not at all keen to allow players or officials to speak to the media. Alastair found a gem in A.J.M. Edwards - Freddy to all. Although he had been a football trialist many years previously rugby and cricket were two of his passions. Locally he was a rugby referee. How clever was that? One person two sports. Freddy was a delight to work with and being a retired headmaster was readily available. He didn't appear every Friday but when he did he came to the studio in the morning with a typed sheet of paper. My questions were in red, his answers in black. What a gentleman. Questions and answers provided before we even went on air!

On the programme we also tried to introduce variety by highlighting minority sports. One such was basketball. Yes, the Harlem Globetrotters were in town. A world famous group skippered by their genial giant Meadowlark Lemon. I reckon he could have picked me up with one hand. Whether I would then have made it through the basket is doubtful.

To plan each Friday's programme a pattern quickly emerged. Alastair and I went on a Tuesday evening to Archie's home. This had two obvious advantages. Archie's attractive wife was able to offer a female slant for the programme, but more importantly she produced supper! This was a wonderful bonus for two bachelors, although Aileen unsportingly usually included Archie!

One Tuesday evening we were faced with a Rangers v Celtic Scottish Cup Final. Nothing to do with the North East, but how to recognise the fact that the two weegie giants were in the final again? I had an idea. "What about asking the referee to appear?" I was immediately rewarded with another can of beer. So it was that the match referee 'Tiny' Wharton flew at his own expense from Glasgow to be interviewed by Archie . The interview was filmed for inclusion that night. The programme budget paid for his lunch. And ours. No doubt you will have guessed that his nickname was 'Tiny' because he stood over six feet tall. Reminded me of Meadowlark Lemon!

One of the world's greatest golfers of the time agreed to appear on the show. Australian Peter Thomson. Here's how I began the item: "Now, golf and we're delighted to welcome to the studio one of the world's greatest. From Australia Peter Thomson. Thank you for joining us Peter. You won our Open Championship in 1954, 1955, 1956 and 1958. What happened in 1957?"

"Someone else won it" replied Peter.

Stupid question. Perfect answer. Collapse of Spankie.

Our first sports Outside Broadcast was in Perth. It was one leg of the Dewar Cup Tennis Tournament. I co-commentated with Gerald Williams a sports journalist who married Joyce Barclay, one of Scotland's best players. There were a few venues for the preliminary rounds in various British locations culminating in the   final at the Royal Albert Hall. Players such as Virginia Wade, Roger Taylor, Jimmy Connors and Julie Heldman were regular competitors in the Tournament which began in 1968 and ran for nine years. It was a tradition that the finalists were piped on to the court. One year Dewars

Jimmy with Julie Heldman and Virginia Wade

own piper was unavailable. The Hon. John Dewar (now Lord Forteviot) was the sponsor and organiser and I'd like you to guess who was asked to play the finalists on to the court! Be honest - how many people do you know who have played solo bagpipes in The Royal Albert Hall?

'Home at last'
Ted Brocklebank
Head of Documentaries and Features 1986-1995

The news desk had received a tip-off that an Ulster policeman planned to do what had proved impossible for more than a century – to lift the famous Dinnie Stones across the bridge at Potarch on Deeside. Legendary local strongman, Donald Dinnie, had allegedly carried the granite blocks, inset with metal rings for lifting-purposes, across the Potarch bridge around 1860. But no one had done it since. We piled into the crew car and set off at high speed.

The legendary Dinnie Stones

But as we passed through Banchory, some 20 miles into the journey, our senior cameraman, the local shop steward of the powerful ACTT (Association of Cinematograph, Television and Allied Technicians) union, drew the car to a halt. 'Time for practicables' he announced. I'd already been shown the clause in the union agreement with ITV that ACTT members should be allowed a morning break 'where practicable'. New to the job I pleaded with the crew to film the lift-attempt first and then have a coffee break later. It was to no avail. Half an hour later, 'practicables' duly observed, we screeched to a halt outside the Potarch Inn, only to hear a burst of applause and ragged cheering. We had missed the big event. The Dinnie stones had been carried across the bridge for the first time in a century. Worse, the BBC TV crew from Aberdeen who had arrived on time had filmed the whole story. It was a salutary lesson at the beginning of my career as a TV reporter that in the early 70s news coverage came a distant second to abiding by the ACTT rule book. Indeed, so powerful was the TV technicians' union that in September 1974 Grampian members went on strike for two weeks when a programme director was fired after screening a copy of the banned pornographic film, *Deep Throat*, on the internal ring mains system. It didn't help that on the day of the screening the new Chief Constable of Grampian Region, Alex Morrison, a 'Wee Free' from Lewis was visiting the studios.

The early days of the new documentary department were fraught with union problems over crewing. Bernd Schulze who'd directed our successful early films was an ACTT member, but after he left to set up his own production company the union decreed that future documentaries for the network would be directed by Grampian staff. Since network commissioning editors held the purse strings and preferred directors with network experience, an uneasy compromise was reached whereby a Grampian programme director would come along on shoots as 'assistant director'. The logic was understandable. How else would Grampian directors get experience of network productions unless they worked on them? But ultimately this was financially untenable. For regional news coverage four of a crew, including reporter and electrician, was the norm. But for network documentaries it wasn't uncommon for 'doubled-up' crews of eight or even nine, all of whom apart from the producer and electrician, were members of the ACTT union. Bob Christie, Grampian's labour relations chief, and Graham Good, the financial controller, were supportive during this period as we sought a solution which would include an element of Grampian crewing but still allow us to work to network budgets and standards. Equally supportive was Channel Four's Commissioning Editor, Caroline Thomson. Caroline was the daughter of Labour peer, Lord Thomson of Monifeith, a former editor of The Dandy in his days with magazine publishers, DC Thomson. With her father fiercely pro-union after his baptism in journalism with Dundee's non-union Thomson group, Caroline, better than most, understood the union delicacies we were struggling with.

Thanks to Caroline we won our first locally produced and directed film for Channel Four. *Last of the Hunters* was researched by Terry Wolsey, directed by Mike Steele, shot by Grampian crews, edited by the talented Grampian film editor, Charlie Main, and written and produced by myself. It told the story of the families of three prominent North East fishing skippers, Terry Taylor of Aberdeen, Andrew Bremner of Wick and the brothers, Andrew and

Willie Tait from Fraserburgh. With songs from Archie Fisher, Maureen Jelks and Zetta Sinclair, it remains one of my personal favourites. Continuing the fishing theme, and again with Grampian's Mike Steele directing and Charlie Main editing, Channel Four next commissioned a documentary about the burgeoning fish farming industry in Scotland and Norway, entitled appropriately *Sea Farmers*. The department was now well into its stride. Terry Wolsey became our full-time researcher and Hazel Deans who'd been my PA and secretary in the news-room now handled our administration, including travel and hotel booking, visas etc. She became the department's anchor, the calm, efficient and tireless Broch lass she's always been, and still is as STV North's last remaining production assistant. They're lucky to have her.

From the days we launched our first Gaelic news programmes I'd been fascinated with the language and culture of the Gaidhealtachd. We'd filmed extensively in Skye and Wester Ross for the Oil series and witnessed at first hand the difficulties the area was facing. I'd also long recognised the talents of Angus Peter Campbell, fast becoming one of Gaeldom's foremost men of letters, and Maggie Cunningham who at this stage was free-lancing from her home at Plockton. What if we could interest Channel Four in a documentary series charting the history and culture of the Gaelic Scots? We'd shoot it against a backdrop of the most breathtaking scenery in the Gaidhealtachd as well as in the American and Canadian outposts where the diaspora still thrived, with Angus and Maggie, native Gaelic speakers, as key members of the production team. Grampian's Charlie Main would edit and Terry Wolsey would be our researcher. I even had a title for the series, borrowed shamelessly from 'The Song of the Canadian Fishermen':

From the lone shieling of the misty island
Mountains divide us and a waste of seas
Yet still the blood is strong, the heart is Highland
And we in dreams behold the Hebrides.

All we needed to make *The Blood Is Strong* a reality were musicians capable of producing a fresh Gaelic soundtrack and a director with the talent to bring the story, the pictures and the music together. Oh, and then the small matter of convincing Channel Four to pay for the three hour-long programmes I felt would be necessary to tell the story. It was Bob Kenyon who suggested that I listen to a new group on the Gaelic scene. They were called Capercaillie. Two youngsters from Taynuilt had founded the band, Donald Shaw on keys and accordion, and his vocalist girlfriend, now wife, Karen Matheson. Later they'd be joined by Charlie McKerron on fiddle, Marc Duff on whistle, and Manus Lunny on guitar.

I went to hear Capercallie performing in Edinburgh's Usher Hall and was blown away, especially by the purity of Karen's voice. Later, in a film I made with Sean Connery, I had the great man describe her in commentary as having 'a throat touched by God'. And so it seemed that night. All we needed now was the right director. The only choice for me was Bernd Schulze, with whom I'd cut my network teeth more than a decade previously. With Bernd on board, Capercaillie producing the music, Professor Jim Hunter joining Maggie Cunningham as programme consultants, and Angus Peter Campbell speaking as well as co-writing the commentary, *The Blood Is Strong* would become one of the most successful documentary series Grampian ever produced. After premiering in 1988 it sold throughout the world, and Capercaillie's soundtrack album quickly went 'gold'. The lovely Karen Matheson singing 'Sri Machair Aignis' (Aignis on the Machair) brings tears to my eyes to this day.

While making *The Blood Is Strong* I had learned about the sinking of the troopship Iolaire on New Year's Day, 1919. It was Britain's biggest-ever peacetime loss of life at sea. More than 200 returning WW1 veterans from Lewis and Harris drowned within sight of Stornoway harbour. Yet the story was virtually unknown outside the western isles. Graham Mcleish made a fine job directing *Home at Last*, Grampian's 70th anniversary commemoration of the loss of the Iolaire. Having found my creative home the title seems particularly apposite for this chapter! *Home at Last* was screened again by BBC Alba on the centenary of the disaster in 2019 to considerable acclaim, including the Mail's John McLeod who deemed it 'the best film to emerge from the Iolaire disaster'.

The sunken Iolaire's mast - the only thing visible the following day

The Thatcher years of 1979-90 saw the breakthrough that the UK television industry, and ITV in particular, so desperately needed. The advent of the satellite broadcasters, Sky and BSB, brought much-needed competition. Tory legislation to end the closed shop meant breaking the union stranglehold of restrictive practices. Added to this, legislation enforcing both BBC and ITV to acquire 25% of non-news programming from independent producers brought an end to the chronic over-manning that had long dogged TV documentary-making. Finally, new technology, including more compact VT and then digital cameras, was to transform the whole sector including, vitally, the morale of all who worked in it.

This brave new dawn allowed our department not only to pursue joint ventures with independent producers but also to commission documentaries from 'indies' based in the Grampian transmission area. Memorable 'indy' productions around this time included Tim Neat's *Journey to a Kingdom* about folk legend and poet, Hamish Henderson, Frieda Morrison's lyrical *Troubled Fields* about the crisis in North East farming, Mike Marshall's popular food series with Derek Cooper, *Scotland's Larder* and Al Beaton's film about nutritionist, John Boyd Orr, and his founding of Aberdeen's

Rowett Research Institute, *A Candle Burning Brightly*. While they were independently produced, most used Grampian crews and editing facilities, and as executive producer I had responsibility for budgets and final editorial approval. Simultaneously we continued to produce our own network documentaries, including *The Energy Alternative*, a three-part co-production with William Woolard's Inca Productions for Channel Four. This saw Grampian crews working in San Francisco, Colorado and New Jersey in the States, as well as in Scandinavia and Japan. I recall the company financial controller, Graham Good, commenting that our documentary locations all seemed to involve 'exotic and expensive places that Brocklebank hadn't yet visited'. He was not altogether mistaken! *Scotland the Grave*, for Channel Four, brought us back home to Dundee, which had one of the worst records for coronary heart disease in the country. It also allowed me to renew acquaintances with director Bernd Schulze. It won a BMA award and ended my decade-long association with Channel Four on a high.

A phone call from Selina Scott allowed us to target the wider viewership of the ITV network for our next series of documentaries. Selina had become hugely popular first as an anchor for ITN then as the first co-presenter of BBC's *Breakfast Time*. Stints in America presenting CBS' *West 57th* followed and she had now set up her own production company, Bellendaine. Along the way she had become acquainted with Prince Andrew, Princess Diana and indeed to the heir to the throne, Prince Charles. Selina confided that Charles might be interested in filming a return visit to the Hebridean island of Berneray where on a fact-finding visit he'd once B&B'd with crofter Donald 'Splash' MacKillop and his wife, Gloria.

ITV jumped at the chance of a TV exclusive. In total secrecy, again with Bernd as director and a Berneray-born chum of mine, John Archie Morrison, as programme consultant, we filmed Charles gathering potatoes and dipping sheep as well as ceilidhing into the night in the MacKillop living room. Charles chatted movingly with Selina about his love for the western isles and the crofting lifestyle. We called the show *A Prince Among Islands*, and with Charlie Main editing, added music by Capercaillie. It was a huge success and launched Grampian on a series of documentaries featuring Selina.

The second in the series, *A Year In Spain*, featured the Spanish

Prince Charles planting potatoes

royal family filmed during the year which culminated in the Barcelona Olympics in 1992.

The film was a co-production with Spain's Canal Plus and contained unique footage shot by Grampian cameramen on the Spanish royal yacht and at the holiday palace in Mallorca where, famously, Selina upstaged King Juan Carlos, whose motor bike was refusing to kick-start, by simply pulling out the choke. Honour was restored when the king pushed her off his yacht deck into the Mediterranean.

Such intimate scenes of their royals at play had never before been seen by the Spanish people. Not surprisingly our documentary was the most widely-viewed ever in Spain, a record I believe it still holds.

While filming *A Tale of Two Cities* in Texas back in the 70s I had befriended an articulate young journalist who worked for Texas Monthly. His name was Harry Hurt III, and he it was who provided the subject for our next special with Selina. At the time few on this side of the Atlantic had heard of a New York property magnate called Donald Trump. Harry sent me a copy of a biography he'd written about Trump called The Lost Tycoon. It was fascinating stuff detailing how the billionaire Trump had lost his fortune by overextending himself buying gaming clubs in Atlantic City, the closest gambling mecca to the Big Apple. But the most fascinating fact for me was that Trump's mother, Mary Anne, hailed from the village of Tong in Lewis. She had emigrated to the States in the wake of the Iolaire disaster. What's more she was still alive, and as I discovered on a recce trip to meet her in Manhattan's Trump Tower, she had absolutely no doubts that her favourite son would come back bigger than ever. How big even she could not have imagined!

Selina with King Juan Carlos

Using a Grampian crew we filmed Trump in New York, Atlantic City, and with his financial comeback on track, at a giant party at his holiday palace, Mar-a-Lago, in Florida. All smiles and bonhomie, Trump had flown us down from NY in his enormous private jet, showing off his movie theatre and bedroom to Selina en route! But the atmosphere changed when at the end of our keynote interview Selina quizzed him about how much New York real estate he actually owned. The interview over, I suspected we were on the verge of being thrown out of Mar-a-Lago when Steve Horrocks, our cameraman, came to me ashen-faced. In her contribution Selina describes in detail the near-disaster of our camera apparently losing colour which actually turned out to be the making of the film. Cannily, Selina, through her production company Bellendaine, retained sales rights. Years later when Trump was launching his bid for the presidency she sold it, allegedly for megabucks, to an American network who were prepared to risk being sued by the future president.

I first met Sean Connery back in the 60s when he was making a documentary about Fairfield's shipyard for STV. Our paths crossed again when I tried to interest him in a film about the St Andrews golf legends, Old and Young Tom Morris. Understandably, the ever-young James Bond star, didn't want to appear in a film where the real hero was Young Tom. But we kept in touch. Sir Fitzroy Maclean upon whom Ian Fleming allegedly based the Bond character, had also become a mutual friend of 007 and myself. Through Sir Fitzroy I met Michael Gill, the director of the seminal BBC

Ted Brocklebank with Sean Connery

documentary series, *Civilization*, and we came up with the idea of a truncated *Blood Is Strong* with Sir Fitzroy consulting and Connery providing the commentary. ITV jumped at the idea. Again, Grampian crews shot most of the sequences, including a dramatised landing of Bonnie Prince Charlie on Eriskay. My abiding memory of *Highlanders* was recording the commentary track at a studio near Connery's home on New Providence Island in the Bahamas. It was there reading from my script that he described the throat of Karen Matheson as being "touched by God". His own throat was bothering him at the time and he had a bit of a head cold, but when he heard Karen's voice on playback he croaked, "God, you were right about that girl. What a voice!"

Other network documentaries followed, mostly shot by Grampian's tireless Alistair Watt, including *A Talent To Abuse* about Gaeldom's answer to Billy Connolly, the hugely gifted but alcoholic

Norman Maclean.

The Year of the Braer in 1993 saw a return to my oil roots when a tanker grounded, spilling thousands of tonnes of oil into the sea off Sumburgh Head in Shetland. The star of that show was Rhoda Bulter, a wonderful Shetland poet, we had discovered and recorded for *Black Water-Bright Hope* all these years before. Now she recorded and spoke her diary entries for the year following the Braer disaster as we marked the impact on Shetland of the biggest oil spill since the Exxon Valdez. *Braer* marked my debut as producer/ director/writer. It was the role I was to assume, guided by experienced cameramen like Al Watt, for the rest of my TV career.

The Braer, grounded off Sumburgh Head

Elsewhere, Alistair Gracie, my successor as Head of News & Current Affairs had turned *North Tonight* into the most watched nightly news show in Scotland. Grampian gained huge network praise for its coverage of the Piper Alpha oil disaster in 1988 when 167 men died in a conflagration on Occidental's production platform in the North Sea. It was the world's biggest offshore oil disaster. Tragically, in 1998, aged only 50, Al Gracie, like our mentor, Charlie

Smith, died of a massive heart attack.

By 1995, and recognising that SMG were hovering with takeover plans, I formed my own TV production company. Over the next five years I went on to produce and direct Scottish and network documentaries under the Greyfriars Productions label. They of course are no part of the Grampian story, but many featured the western isles which had become a kind of spiritual home. Future challenges would lie ahead as a Member of the Scottish Parliament and in free-lance journalism. A quarter of a century has passed since I walked out of the Queen's Cross studios for the last time. Yet, semi-retired and living in my native St Andrews, I still look back on the quarter century I worked for Grampian as the time of my life.

Catering for every taste
Doreen Gerrie
Restaurant Manager

The canteen, or restaurant as it became in 1988, was the place where the staff came to eat, sleep, laugh, moan (a lot) and to rest their eyes from the 'bright lights'. Hence the pink décor of the dining room, pink being considered restful on the eyes. We even had a pink Christmas tree one year which had people craning their necks in disbelief. It was fondly known as 'the lavvie brush'!

The canteen area was really split into 3 - the dining area, the front which was used for entertaining, and the separate and famous Green Room which has its own stories. Many of the studio guests, especially in the early years were glad to visit for a coffee. Kenneth More, the actor, who was also famous for the Birds Instant Coffee advert took a good laugh when Liz told him we only served Nescafe. Joan Collins in her pre-*Dynasty* days arrived in her hair rollers, hidden under a huge fur hat. Vidal Sassoon, the famous hairdresser, provided my first 'starstruck moment'. He joined us on our coffee break. What a gentleman... no free haircuts though!

Great excitement on the day Princess Alexandra and husband Angus Ogilvy opened the new frontage in 1987, with Angus desperate for a bag of chips. Did he get one? No... Well it was 2.30pm and the fryers were off. He gallantly declined the offer for us to put them back on again.

Princess Anne also came along as part of the BAFTA Shell Film Rally in 1990 when she enjoyed afternoon tea in the restaurant. All went smoothly on the day but the lead up to it was quite frantic. A huge police presence checked every nook and cranny, even the bars in the Green and Board rooms, smelling all open bottles. No one was allowed to use the front ladies' toilet in case Princess Anne wanted to powder her nose

Speaking of noses, on the first ever Comic Relief 'Red Nose Day' a 'Throw Custard Pies at Management' was held in the front of the restaurant. Bob Christie bravely smiled while Ann Cairns took great delight in throwing the first plate. Graham Good and Eric Johnstone were also willing targets. A huge sum of money was raised on the day.

Princess Alexandria, Alex Mair and Doreen Gerrie

On numerous occasions we had to go beyond our job descriptions - like the time we had to run along to the chemist to buy a hot water bottle for Lady Margaret Tennant, the wife of the chairman. She was on her way to stay with the Queen at Balmoral. "Its always freezing out there" she explained.

At the Scottish BAFTA Awards at the Beach Ballroom 'Mrs Mac' from *Take the High Road* forgot some of her underwear and Liz dutifully went into town to purchase same. Result? One very happy 'Mrs Mac'! We also had the pleasure of amusing Elaine C. Smith's months-old baby while she had lunch. The feeding was fine, but the nappy-changing cleared the canteen !

Special Theme days were always popular - Indian, French, Italian, Mexican to mention a few, but with Indian always the favourite. The Indian recipes, music and décor were all borrowed from the Light of Bengal restaurant and the Italian from Little Italy The first ever Indian day we had 100 people queuing for lunch when Chef George, while chopping chillis, inadvertently rubbed his eye. Taxi for George to Aberdeen Royal Infirmary. Let's say George never made that mistake again!

Soup was very popular, especially as a hangover cure for certain members of the newsroom. So was my magic cure for sore throats, which the announcers and newsreaders would drink before going on air. What was it? My secret, but it certainly worked .

Some programmes we dreaded. *Pick a Number* was the worst as gallons of custard and jelly had to be made for props, and also up to 240 packed lunches for the kids. *Stovies* was another nightmare, as huge pots of stovies had to be cooked. Poor Karen spent all day peeling onions and potatoes.

Telethon was also a very busy show with us hosting lots of events, including a fashion show which Diana Speed compered while a bevy of Grampian lovelies modelled.

Staff enjoyed the free frothy coffee we served, but modernisation meant a new coffee machine was installed and a token cost of 10p imposed. Needless to say WW3 nearly erupted at the outrageous new charges!

Catering was also required at special events hosted at Drum Castle, Castle Fraser and Fyvie Castle where Daniel O'Donnell made his television début. It was the start of the Irish superstar's fame and Liz's life-long infatuation. She became the envy of my mum's friends because he apparently touched her knee! Catering was hard work but great fun and brought a host of lovely memories, too many of which are unprintable!

Welcome to the Tom and Jerry show

Eileen Doris Bremner
Production Assistant/Programme Director, 1963-1993

The first two staff members I met in Grampian TV Reception that August morning in 1963 were called Tom and Jerry. 'This bodes well' I thought 'for a fun-filled future.' It was indeed the start of 30 years of – yes, a lot of fun – but also a lot of hard work, nerve-wracking situations, sometimes very long hours and the making of lifelong friendships.

Half of my job as a trainee production assistant was secretarial, the other half, among a multitude of technical chores, was timing each programme to the second. Making sure the programmes did not impinge on the all-important commercial breaks. After all Heinz beans, Oxo cubes and Esso Petrol were our bread and butter.

I worked for fifteen years as PA to ten different programme directors, each with a different personality and way of working. Some are more memorable than others. More than half are sadly no longer with us.

Adrian Malone, a Londoner, was a baptism of fire for me as a trainee. A self-styled perfectionist he reckoned that people worked harder and quicker for a raging bull. "When I am in the control room I am God" he would declare. I later found a wonderful response to this in a newspaper referring to somebody else's misgivings about their personal deity, "Sometimes I have doubts, I think that after all I may not be God". I cut it out and pinned it on our office wall with Adrian's picture. He was awful but I liked him.

Mike Bevan was a young cockney whizz-kid who grappled admirably with the local Doric dialect. He directed mostly light entertainment. We even had a *Strictly* then. *Strictly Scottish* was a long-running music show, very popular with the viewers. *Aye Yours* was another of his successes as was *Cairngorm Ski Night*, an aprés-ski evening of variety. And of course many a live *Hogmanay Show* with all the attendant pressures that brought on artists and production staff.

I worked for two Alans. Number one, Alan Wallis, fired my ambition to become a programme director one day. He drew me into his domain, showing me the designer's sketches for the studio sets he required. He discussed where to place the cameras and move them around and how he prepared his camera scripts. He had a wonderful sense of humour and spoke with an Oxbridge accent, but he too quickly familiarised himself with the Doric. He produced shows like the *Pop Scotch* series which featured artists like Deep Purple, Cat Stevens and Marmalade early in their careers.

Of course all directors had to work on the mainstay programmes too – news, sport, political discussions, documentaries, religion, quizzes, childrens. It was a hugely enjoyable learning curve, helping to put these different formats together, especially as only the director and PA worked with the programmes from conception to transmission.

Alan, number two, was a scion of the Dundee-Italian Franchi family. He was my last 'boss' before I became Grampian's first female programme director. During the ten highly enjoyable years I worked with him he was the company's senior programme director. However, he frequently drove me and other production staff to distraction because he liked to work right up to the wire. Everything was left to the last minute, so I would regularly be in the office until late at night typing up his camera script for a show the next day. On one occasion he left the office to go home and automatically switched off the light and closed the door, completely forgetting that I was still there typing away. His Italian heritage made him temperamental, argumentative and thrawn, but his charisma always saw us through whatever bickering we'd shared on all types of programmes.

Our trip to Russia to film a Burns Supper was classic Alan Franchi. Alan had discovered that a tour operator organised trips for Scots to go to Moscow to enjoy a Russian Burns Supper. Why didn't a Grampian film crew go along too? Alan was a great ideas guy!

In mid-January our crew flew by Aeroflot from Glasgow to Moscow where the temperature was -35 degrees. Grampian had rigged us all out with padded, high-viz, mountaineering gear. I had scarlet salopettes, a vivid royal blue jacket and moon boots. With all the crew dressed similarly we looked like psychedelic Michelin men, a vast contrast to the sombre grey and black-clad citizens and military men posted every here and there on the streets of Moscow. It was cold, but I have to say I've felt colder filming on many a summer's day in Aberdeenshire! Having said that the moustaches of two of the crew froze solid - more frustratingly so did the film camera motor which had to be constantly heated back to life.

We filmed Lenin's tomb in Red square where the guards changed duty every hour and at a school where Russian kids sang and recited Burns works. There was a troika-ride through snow-covered woods. Very Dr Zhivago. And then of course the highlight – the Burns Supper in Moscow.

But our classic Franchi episode had nothing to do with these. It happened after we'd been to visit the Moscow State Circus. The circus was held some way out of town and after an excellent show we went to reclaim our Michelin men outfits, glowing bizarrely among the dark Russian outer garments. But guess who had lost his ticket? The attendant refused to hand over Alan's jacket without one. When the vast cloakroom area eventually emptied, there in glorious isolation was Alan's bright blue jacket. But 'Niet' was the response when Alan identified it. Heated words followed. Louder and louder, in Russian and Scots, including words I didn't think Alan even knew. Eventually our researcher, Marian Hepworth, smoothed things over and Alan was reunited with his jacket.

But our troubles were far from over. Our coach had long gone and a bus we eventually boarded turned out to be going in the opposite direction from the town centre All around were tall, grim flats. It was 10.30pm, pitch dark, and there was that eerie hush deep snow exudes. Suddenly we were alerted by the glow of a match which illuminated the face and outline of a figure in uniform. As he lit his cigarette he enquired in broken English, "What is it that you want?" It seems he'd been following us for some time.

Sergei (at least that's who he said he was) saw us back to our hotel and agreed to join us for a drink. Whisky and vodka were then consumed in industrial quantities judging by the headaches next morning. At breakfast our Courier told us Sergei was with the KGB. We were probably lucky not to have ended up in the lubyanka!

After fifteen years supporting male directors 'them upstairs' finally relented after regularly turning me down when I'd applied for director posts. It was nerve-wracking at the beginning but I got a lot of support from the studio production staff and I soon got into the swing of the new job.

As a director location filming was much more interesting than studio production. Film (or nowadays electronic) cameras are very different from their studio counterparts. Likewise, I found studio crew amenable, polite and co-operative whereas film crews tended to be taciturn, glum and complaining. I could never understand why they were so unhappy doing one of the best jobs in television. But I recall there was one particular exemplar of the breed who occasionally showed his lighter side. On a particular shoot I needed about 30 seconds of seagulls flying about. "Are you sure it's just seagulls you want?" asked the cameraman. I was going over notes with my PA in the car at the time. "Only seagulls", I assured him, wondering at the sudden burst of enthusiasm. Ten minutes later he was back. "Got the seagulls OK. We saw a mermaid sitting on a rock, but since it was just the seagulls you wanted ..."

On another occasion I recall a rather startled reverend gentleman who was about to be interviewed in his church when the cameraman shouted out to the electrician, "Bring me two blondes and a redhead". This was normal film speak for differently powered lamps, I should explain, not the cameraman suddenly showing an interest in the female sex.

But there was one very important happening in my early days at Grampian. As with most new companies we were regularly auditioning for staff as well as artists. An early job was attending to people as they arrived, putting them at ease and seeing them out again. One of them was a tall, dark, dishy guy. He failed the audition, but won me instead. Yes, dear reader, I ended up marrying him. So it's fair to say that my time with Grampian introduced me to a lifetime of happiness.

Salmond owes it all to me!

Frank Gilfeather

Sports Correspondent, 1980-1988

As a 21-year-old, I had dallied with the idea of presenting on Grampian TV. It was a couple of years after Jimmy Spankie and a camera crew filmed me at the Camperdown boxing club in the Lochee area of Dundee for his Friday evening Sportscope programme. That three minutes-long report in 1965 when I was a Scottish champion and internationalist, excited me and later, when I fired-off a 'let me do a weekly spot on the boxing scene in the north and north-east' to managing director  Alex Mair, I received a call from Charlie Smith, Head of News and Current Affairs. "Come to Aberdeen and discuss it".

Weeks later, I was on screen, oozing the opposite of confidence and wondering, every time I sat in the studio and stared down the lens of the camera, what made me believe I could do this. I did a round-up of the boxing scene every fortnight and received my five guinea fee (£5.25p) – worth around £95 in today's money – in vouchers for my chosen department store, Cairds, in Dundee's Reform Street.

The Scottish Amateur Boxing Association would not allow me to receive a straight financial payment on the grounds that it would deem me a 'professional' sportsman and impact on my career. I recall exchanging six of the vouchers on a navy leather reefer jacket, the cost of which were it today, would equate to around £600, a sum I wouldn't dream of spending on a new coat. Still, being on the telly gave me a certain cachet with many of my fellow Dundonians making up their own narrative along the lines of, "See that Frank Gilfeather, he's earning a fortune."

I was a trainee reporter on the weekly title, the Arbroath Guide, but my little taste of TV ended when I joined Aberdeen Journals, publishers of The Press & Journal and the Evening Express as a news reporter and later as a sportswriter.

In 1980, having worked secretly writing the *Sportscope* script as well as those for the children's show, *Wings and Things*, I joined the Grampian staff as its first specialist sports correspondent for the *North Tonight* programme. I also put together a half-hour show at 6.30pm on Fridays.

It was then that Aberdeen FC and Dundee United, the two main teams in our transmission area, started to make their presence felt in Scottish football with their respective managers, Sir Alex Ferguson and Jim McLean, guiding their clubs to remarkable success at home and abroad and loosening the Celtic and Rangers grip on the game north of the border.

But while a successful football team like the Dons offered me travel throughout the UK and Europe, from Ipswich to Iceland, from Merseyside to Munich, the Fergie-Frank dynamic wasn't exactly sweetness and light. While it was thrilling on the pitch, off it the Ferguson regime ensured that the media's relationship with the players was broken. Fergie had to sanction or block requests to talk to a player thereby controlling the agenda.

This presented me with an unpredictability that often made work unnecessarily unpleasant; arguments over fees for interviews, tetchiness about unwelcome questions, and irritation surrounding opinions on performances that were not in line with those of the manager. Happy days!

A memorable clash came following a 3-1 Aberdeen defeat at Dundee United where Jim Leighton, the Reds' international goalkeeper, had an off day. Six days later, on the eve of a home game against Hibernian, Ferguson joined me live in the studio to preview the fixture during which he revealed Leighton was injured and unavailable for selection.

Around 1.45pm the following day, I bumped into an Aberdeen FC director in the Pittodrie car park where he mentioned that Leighton was dropped and not injured as the manager had told print and broadcast journalists. I had a Saturday job reporting for Radio Clyde and, without revealing my source, transmitted the story that what he had told us about Leighton was not exactly accurate. Injury? What injury?

The fallout on Monday morning was explosive. The noise levels on the line from the boss's bunker at Pittodrie were red hot with expletives raining down like confetti at a wedding. Fergie had heard from somebody in Glasgow, where Radio Clyde ruled the wireless airwaves at the time, about my Leighton exclusive and he didn't like it.

"You're banned," he screamed. "You will not be allowed back at Pittodrie. The doormen will be instructed to prevent you coming in." I tend to leave histrionics to others. I asked for clarification. Would I be stopped from reporting games, which I did for Clyde and a couple of Sunday newspapers? The silence on the other end of the line told me of a potential reticence to impose a total prohibition.

"You will be banned from attending the post-match press conferences. You will not have access to me."

"Ah, is that all," I replied. "I thought it was something serious."

It was just one of numerous Fergie flashpoints that punctuated our working relationship.

Alistair Yates and Frank Gilfeather live from Gothenburg

Sir Alex Ferguson's Pittodrie legacy, however, cannot be overstated. The mere mention of the word Gothenburg to a Dons fan, for example, evokes memories of their astonishing 2-1 win over Real Madrid in the final of the European Cup-Winners' Cup final in the

Swedish city in May, 1983. It presented Grampian with the monumental task of producing its flagship news programme live from the Ullevi Stadium. Just as we went on air for North Tonight the heavens opened and gifted a downpour of monsoon proportions.

Alan Saunders at Real Madrid's Santiago Bernabéu Stadium

My opening introduction from outside the stadium meant that I returned to the specially-built studio inside the ground like a drookit rat. Still, we rattled through all the preview stories, one or two filmed in advance with the Real Madrid team and presented by Alan Saunders, one of two Dundee-based reporters. There was a pre-match chat with Ferguson, vox pops with the Aberdeen fans and two or three one-to-ones with people like Alex Collie, the Lord Provost of Aberdeen, and Jock Stein, the legendary Celtic manager.

Not only did the Dons' victory offer us tales of heroism and triumph on the field, there were numerous stories of the supporters who'd travelled from the north-east to witness the club's greatest-ever achievement. Five hundred of the 10,000 wearing red and white favours had managed to drink the bar dry on the P&O ferry, the St

Clair, on the journey over the North Sea. The famous victory made sure that achievement would be repeated on the return trip. And, of course, Grampian was there to interview those sea dogs staggering off the ship at Aberdeen harbour. The entire occasion over a few days, however, didn't end when Fergie and his (extremely) merry men touched down at Aberdeen airport.

"Don't take your coat off," head of news, Al Gracie, told me as I entered the newsroom. "Get down to Pittodrie. You're presenting a live outside broadcast on the return of the team and we have crews out covering their open-top bus journey from the airport to the ground."

Stimulating times indeed. But I was grateful that, despite my years as a sports journalist, I never lost my news sense, built through years as a reporter covering everything from golden wedding anniversaries and council meetings for the 'Arbroath Guide' to being at the heart of the Fraserburgh Lifeboat Disaster of January 1970 for the P&J.

This ability to adapt was called upon in 1983 when, along with arts correspondent Alan Cowie, who'd also taken the news route earlier in his career at the BBC, I headed for the Cults area of the city where six people had died in an explosion at the Royal Darroch Hotel.

Alan and I just happened to be first into the office that morning. When we arrived in Cults it was to a scene of carnage. One neighbour I spoke to, whose property backed on to the hotel, showed me various pieces of heavy duty, industrial cooking equipment scattered around his garden. It was a shocking tale, but nothing compared to the Piper Alpha Disaster of July 6, 1988, when because of the demands of the story, it was all hands on deck in the Queen's Cross newsroom.

I was given the task of finding survivors who would tell us what went on out there as Occidental's oil platform exploded killing 167 men. In the immediate aftermath of the disaster, without the presence of PR and media advisers, reporters could use their wit and guile to extract information. When I asked a friendly nurse at Aberdeen Royal Infirmary's A&E department if she knew the names of any survivors, she mentioned one – Derek Ellington – who, she said, was the first man off the rig.

These were pre-mobile phone days. The internet and broadband were words not yet part of our language. There were three Ellingtons listed in the phone book. We visited two addresses - no luck. The third one turned out to be the home of the mother of the man I sought. This, remember, was the morning after an unimaginable tragedy, and as we – George Leslie (cameraman) and Ian Murray (sound recordist) – approached the house in Garthdee, Aberdeen, I suggested we started the camera rolling before the door was opened.

Piper Alpha

Derek (for indeed it was our man), looked as if all life had been drained from his face. His eyes stared straight ahead as if the horror of what had happened the previous night 120 miles into the darkness of the North Sea, would never leave him. Thankfully he recognised me and invited us into his cosy home. I joined him on the living room sofa. Then with cameraman George, on one knee, focussing on the face of this man, still traumatised by his experience, we spoke for 20 minutes as he described in graphic detail the sheer hell he had undergone. The interview led the ITN News at Ten that night.

But there were lighter, equally memorable TV moments, away from sports journalism. In 1987, I spent an enjoyable time shooting profiles of parliamentary candidates for the Banff and Buchan Westminster seat. They included profiling the sitting MP, Albert McQuarrie, nicknamed the Buchan Bulldog because of his pugnacious approach to politics, as well as his young opponent representing the Scottish National Party, Alex Salmond.

On one occasion we were filming Salmond at Fraserburgh Harbour where he was explaining his party's policies to local fisherman. As cameraman Gordon Watson gathered his shots, a woman accompanied by her Newfoundland dog, a breed I'd never seen before and the size of a small bear, approached. She'd come along to tell the man who would in time become Scotland's First Minister that she supported him.

Alex Salmond

Captivated by her dog, I had an idea. What if we could velcro an SNP rosette onto this enormous animal and persuade it to stand on its hind legs and place its front paws on each of Salmond's shoulders. The voice-over was already in my head, "Could this young pup (Salmond) upset the odds in this, his first stab at Westminster, and unseat the Buchan Bulldog?"

Years later the young pup told me, "That piece you did with the dog won me the election. I'd never experienced so much feedback." There was a price to be paid, however. He revealed that the dog's excessive licking of his face gave him a rash that took a week to clear.

Although I left my Grampian staff role at the end of 1988 Alistair Gracie had me back for many years to present the *Summer at*

Six programme while *North Tonight* was off the air. Various producer/directors continued to use me for documentaries and outside broadcasts. I was also invited to take the chair for a programme that had been hugely popular with audiences stretching back to 1971 when my original mentor, Jimmy Spankie, was at the helm. Programme director, Alan Franchi, a fellow Dundonian with a warm personality and impeccable manners, thought I'd be the right quizmaster to breathe new life into the format. I went on to enjoy a nine year stint at the helm before SMG took over Grampian and ditched the programme, which was of course *Top Club*.

Frank with Jim Munro, his ex-boxing coach

Without Grampian TV how else could this working-class lad from Dundee's Lochee have met and interviewed household names from the worlds of sport, politics, literature and the arts? How else could I have chatted with Hollywood icons like Charlton Heston, top political figures like Sir Roy Jenkins, comedians like Dave Allen, Des O'Connor and the incomparable Dame Edna Everage? Or jousted with Fergie and Jim McLean, two of the greatest football managers Scotland has ever produced?

For these and other memories I'll always be grateful to Grampian, the little TV station with the big reputation.

Frank with Dame Edna Everage

Welcome to Icarus Airlines!
Graham Mcleish
Producer/Director, 1973-2000

Friday 10th November 1978 is a date I won't forget in a hurry. I was on the Isle of Skye for the first transmission of colour television in the area. Grampian had a big public relations event organised in a hotel in Portree with members of management present, and we were there to film the mid-day switch on. We spent the morning filming an item for that night's news programme, interviewing local worthies with on-screen stars Kennedy Thomson and Lesley Macleod in attendance. Bob from our sales team was canvassing local businesses seeking future advertisers.

The previous day, accompanied by my loyal voice of reason, Production Assistant Helen Straine, and our film crew, we had driven over in benign weather from Aberdeen to a beautiful winter sunlit Skye. But today a November Atlantic storm was brewing with menacing weather warnings all over Scotland. Grampian had hired a small aircraft to get the film back to Aberdeen in time for that night's news. For reasons lost in antiquity (and possible incompetence) Helen and I had also been ordered back to base to direct that evening's programme. It was with a tinge of excitement but growing apprehension that we set off from a now distinctly breezy Portree along with Kennedy, Lesley and Bob for Broadford airport.

I recall our vehicle rounding a corner to a scene from a horror movie. We were about to drive from rainy, breezy, grey into the blackest darkness and howling wind of the predicted Atlantic storm. The mood in the car went suddenly quiet. Helen and I glanced at each other for reassurance. Bob lit a cigarette. Kennedy and Lesley stared silently ahead.

Broadford 'airport' back in the seventies did have a short tarmac runway but that was about it. The 'terminal building' was a glorified portacabin. We fought our way from the car with our luggage and precious film. By the time we had splashed through the puddles to get inside the rain was lashing horizontally from a cloud base that looked no higher than a hundred feet. Once inside the violently-buffeted building Lesley and Kennedy headed ashen-faced for the toilet. There was only one so I don't know what happened there! Bob lit another cigarette.

Helen and I went up to the man at the table. Before I could speak he said, "I didn't expect to see you lot in this weather". I opened my mouth to say something but he barked, "On the scales". I turned to get my luggage. "Not the luggage, you get on the scales. I have to weigh you for where you sit on the plane". Helen and I glanced again at each other for reassurance.

The aeroplane was a Piper six seater where each of us, by weight, had to sit in specific seats in order to keep the plane balanced in flight. At the sight of me standing on the weighing machine, the normally amiable Bob, now with a lit cigarette in each hand, nervously asked what the bloody hell was going on. I tried to calm him by saying, "It's just for weight," avoiding adding that it was for balance as well. Lesley and Kennedy were obediently weighed without a word.

I looked out through a rain-battered window hoping to see a break in the low cloud, but there was none. The man at the desk suddenly announced, "Here he comes" and a roar of revving engines could be heard approaching. I looked up and saw this tiny aircraft cavorting down through the gusts and cloud towards us. It went shooting past at about a metre off the ground and then climbed back up and disappeared into the clouds again. Bob's reaction was a heavily expletive-peppered question, "What the hell happened there?" The man at the desk said it was ok, the pilot was just scaring the sheep away!

When the plane finally did touch down the runway was covered in water and there was a spectacular splash and spray everywhere with beautiful spirals of water from the twin propellers. I remember feeling relieved that the plane at least had two engines. But my relief was short-lived. "I'm not going on that bloody thing!" yelled Bob who by now must have had four lit cigarettes in each hand.

While Helen tried to reassure Bob we waited for the pilot to appear to get permission to approach the aircraft. The door opened and out stepped what appeared to be a young boy passenger. My heart sank when the desk man said, "Hmm, he's a young pilot today". Having successfully negotiated my three score years and ten anyone below the age of sixty-five is young to me nowadays. But I was only 27 at the time and this guy looked about 12!

Beckoning us over into the monsoon deluge the youngster asked me to give him a hand removing two massive kerbing blocks from the nose of the aircraft which we dumped on the grass. "For keeping the nose down when there's no luggage," the youth explained. I was so glad Bob didn't hear that. All luggage loaded we went back to get our passengers. Lesley and Helen were the lightest so they went to the back where the plane was quite narrow. Kennedy and I were in the middle row and Bob, being the heaviest, was in front of me in the seat beside the boy pilot. I didn't know what magic Helen had worked with Bob but he'd entered the co-operative, suspended-animation mode and boarded the plane without incident.

We splashed our way to the end of the runway for take-off and with a roar of the engines we started moving. Usually at take off you are pushed into your seat with the acceleration. This time there was none. With engines screaming we didn't seem to be going fast enough for take off. The water-logged runway was restricting our acceleration. I had the nightmare vision of being Charles Lindberg on his first transatlantic flight in 'The Spirit of St Louis' splashing down the runway and barely clearing the power lines. We eventually lumbered our way off the ground, but I'm sure we left tyre marks in the moss, scraping the top of the dry stane dyke at the end of our runway. Once up above the storm clouds the flight was relatively uneventful - apart from our boy pilot handing me a paper map, and pointing down through a break in the clouds to ask where I thought the place below was!

As we approached Aberdeen the weather brightened and the rain clouds dissipated, but the wind had actually got worse. It was now gusting at up to 80mph. Severe turbulence in a large plane is unpleasant and can be dangerous. Severe turbulence in a small six seater is terrifying and extremely dangerous if the passengers start panicking!

At about a mile away from the Aberdeen runway there was a particularly violent bump followed by a freefall drop which stirred Bob in front of me from his slumbers. I later discovered that Helen had cracked open a bottle of Grampian whisky, which we always carried as 'thank you' gifts, and given Bob a stiff dram to calm him down back at Broadford. But the effects were now wearing off. At the same time Lesley at the back wakened from her previous zombie state into full-on screaming terror. Bob, in loud expletive mode again, grabbed the pilot's arm which sent us violently sideways. We were then hit by another gust which sent Bob's head forward into the dashboard, setting off some sort of squawking alarm. It felt like we were in a flying tumble drier a thousand feet above the ground. I grabbed Bob and pulled him back while trying to prise his grip from our now very alarmed boy pilot.

With more screaming and jolts and drops Bob now grabbed at the door with the clear intention of getting out of the plane. I don't think you can open a door wide enough to get out during flight as the wind pressure is too high, but I wasn't going to let Bob succeed. I do however remember during the struggle looking through a fresh air open gap down onto the Overton car dismantlers yard!

Our visibly-terrified pilot shouted, "The turbulence will stop soon, there's a cushioning effect at around fifty feet." To which Bob, frantically gesticulating towards the fast-approaching runway, yelled "That's not a cushion! That's bloody concrete!"

With Bob still fighting to get out and lots of screaming and shouting the plane bounced at least three times, sliding sideways with screeching tyres and roaring engines onto the runway. I was still holding on to Bob as we stopped at our parking area. With much lower wind pressure he could now get out of the door, but after all we'd gone through I didn't want him walking into the propellers. When the engines finally stopped and the dashboard's electronic beeps and buzzers ceased, a wonderful silence reigned. It was at that point, realising that he wouldn't have to radio his mum for help after all, that our boy pilot's sense of humour surfaced. He turned and said, "Ladies and gentlemen, thank you for flying Icarus Airlines".

Lesley, Kennedy and Bob set off for home in a taxi. Helen linked into my arm and with a lovely smile said, "You done good, pet". I answered in my best Dundonian attempt at a Weegie accent, "You did no bad yersel, hen" and we both laughed. We then went off in our taxi to do something much more mundane, like directing that night's live news programme.

Views from the fireside

Colin Lawson
Aberdeen Businessman

How can a TV station hold an entire community together, especially one as diverse as that formerly covered by Grampian TV? Throughout the North East and across Scotland to the Western Isles we had been brought up listening to our own local dialects through the medium of television. We knew how folk in Inverness and Orkney talked because we heard them on Grampian. Although hundreds of miles away, thanks to GTV, they were our neighbours.

Many of the Grampian presenters and broadcasters became household names in the poorer part of Aberdeen where I grew up, as familiar as 'the tick mannie' and 'the provie cheque wifie'. Kennedy Thomson frae Aiberdeen, Frankie Gilfeather frae Dundee and Norman MacLeod frae the Hebrides. 'The Grampian' was part of our local family community. My boyhood memories during the early seventies were of black and white TV with a 50p meter on the side which sometimes became the weekly 'bankie'.

We grew up to the songs and banter of Andy Stewart and Calum Kennedy. Andy was from Arbroath and Calum from Lewis, but they were our TV stars, their music was our music. When the Rediffusion mannie came to empty the TV money box, my mother pretended to be out the house as the meter collector counted out the pennies. But he treated us all the same. TV was our only escape. They were hard times and he knew the score. Eventually, he knew he would get his money.

Our local TV presenters seemed far more natural than their network counterparts. I wonder if they realised what their tongue and twang meant to the surrounding areas and how important 'local' was to us. In these days we were totally unaware of what lay ahead, with today's fast-moving media circus, multi-channels, streaming and the like. We have far more choice, but are we really any better served by our TV?

I can well remember when SMG took over Grampian TV. Now our broadcasters spoke with strong Glasgow accents. People like Jimmy Boyle and Billy Connolly came to mind. Overnight it seemed we had been transferred from Garthdee to the Gorbals, and my friends from Bieldside felt they had been re-located to Bearsden. Suddenly our local TV station had been taken over by a complete new wave of broadcasters with strong west coast accents, all very good broadcasters no doubt, but for my ears they didn't have the magic that Grampian had to hold the community together.

Television has lost its identity. Twenty four hours of anything and nothing, hundreds of channels and technology allowing us to watch programmes from any country and in any language. But it is programming without heart. We Aberdonians who thought we struggled with the Dundonian pronunciation of Jimmy Spankie when he was at his prime, now long to hear TV accents from anywhere north of the Tay.

Now I find myself tuning into BBC Alba for genuine local TV coverage. Okay, the people speak a different language from the Doric I grew up with and I have to be content with sub-titles. But the issues covered are the issues that interest me, local topics featuring the views of ordinary people. The music is the kind I used to tune in to Grampian to hear – fiddle and accordion music and ceilidh bands.

Where are they in the schedules of STV North? Nowhere it seems. How I wish there was still a local TV channel that showed real people going about their day to day business. That was something Grampian had in spades, or 'barry loads' as we would say, and made it the envy of the country. Dear auld Grampian, fit wye did ye hae to ging awa'?

'The old order changeth'
Rachel Innes
Reporter, 1985-Present

Grampian Television went on air in late September 1961 - beating my own arrival into the world by just a few weeks. Although it was to be another 24 years until I finally became a member of staff at Queens Cross, 'the Grampian' featured prominently throughout my early life.

My father was a professional musician who regularly performed with Musical Director Alex Sutherland on various shows, and my mother worked on the *Miss Grampian* beauty contests. She was a model who ran her own agency, even drafting me in as a model for an item filmed at Aberdeen Art Gallery for an afternoon show called *Flair*. I must surely have been a last-minute stand in!

As a student I worked across the road from Grampian in Dizzy's and the Albyn – the station's unofficial social club. And so I was delighted and privileged to start work as a reporter on *North Tonight* in December 1985, and not only because I could then enjoy the benefits of the still very much-missed official social club!

Professionally, I really felt that I'd arrived – Grampian was everything I'd hoped it would be – dynamic, exciting with an incredible range of departments producing an impressive range of programmes. News and current affairs, numerous Gaelic language offerings, entertainment shows and educational programmes for schools. The opportunities seemed endless. Though there were hundreds of employees it was a very friendly and welcoming place, very much like an extended family with a joint pride in our endeavours and plenty of opportunities to celebrate them!

Our then Head of News, Alistair Gracie, gave me my big chance, as he did for so many young journalists. Alistair presided over a period of major news events in the North, such as the Piper Alpha disaster, and guided us into winning the BAFTA Scotland Award for Best News Programme for *North Tonight* in both 1995 and 1997. A year later, not long after being appointed Controller of Grampian by the new owners, Alistair tragically collapsed and died while on one of his regular lunchtime runs. He was only 50 years old.

Donald John Macdonald was another young reporter who had much to thank Alistair for. DJ, as he was usually known, hailed from South Uist and was initially recruited to beef up the Gaelic news team. But his news-gathering skills meant he was soon broadening his horizons into general reporting. I came to admire his passion and enthusiasm for a story, his tenacity in pursuing every possible interview and angle and his determination to seek out and expose any injustice.

DJ found it easy to talk to people and put them at ease. To me he just seemed to be a genuinely decent, kind and compassionate human being. In case that makes him appear too good to be true I should add that he was also great fun, with a mischievous sense of humour and a love of a party, and in particular a sing-song. No news-room gathering was complete without his rendition of 'Mary Ann MacRae'.

His very human qualities were in no way diminished as he progressed over the years to

Donald John Macdonald

become a producer and ultimately editor of *STV North*, as Grampian Television became known in 2006 – along the way helping and encouraging many young people to launch and progress their own careers.

In the years since the Grampian name disappeared from our screens there have been many changes and challenges in the industry. Now we are mainly a news-only operation based at Tullos in Aberdeen, with staff numbers counted in tens rather than hundreds.

DJ at Kisimul Castle, Barra

But throughout the changes DJ, and indeed all the Grampian veterans who were part of the new team, were determined to ensure that the stories and issues that mattered to the audience across Grampian's vast and diverse transmission area continued to be represented on screen. That determination was rewarded when STV North's *News at Six* programme – still referred to as *North Tonight* by many - was named best news programme at the RTS awards in 2018 and 2020. DJ was so ecstatic after our first win that the morning after the night before he posted a photograph of himself on social media still lying in bed – the RTS trophy cradled in his arms.

He was right to be proud though. His work earned him respect throughout the Scottish media industry and I know that it literally changed lives for the better. He produced a documentary in 2016 called *Who Cares?* which directly led to the Scottish government launching a root and branch review of the entire care system.

DJ seemed to know everyone, and everyone seemed to know

him - even a doctor performing a minor procedure on me last year asked, upon hearing where I worked, if I knew 'that Donald John Macdonald?' In fact anyone you met anywhere would ask the same thing, often saying his name in their attempt at his Hebridean lilt. And this continued long after he ceased to be a regular on screen.

Ian Simpson, Michael Armstrong, Carol Frost and Rachel Innes in the gallery of STV North

While his career trajectory was never in doubt, DJ's South Uist sense of direction was legendary. Just four days before Christmas 2020 he set off to drive to the Dundee office. Nearly two hours later he called me from his car.

"Gosh you've not been gone long" I said, "are you heading back up the road already?" "You'll never guess what I've done" he said. It transpired that, not for the first time, a roundabout had got the better of DJ. He'd headed north rather than south on the bypass, wondering why he was passing an airport en route to Dundee. Secretly, he seemed quite tickled that here was another elaborate tale to add to his repertoire. DJ loved to tell a story, the more dramatic the better. Sadly, there was little time left for story-telling.

Just two days later, on Christmas Eve, he passed away, so suddenly, so tragically at the age of only 60.

STV North's loss is as nothing compared to the Macdonald

family's. Above all Donald was a devoted family man, with such love for his relatives and especially his son Ben, of whom he was so proud. It was a terrible end to a year like no other, during which DJ had continued to lead our news operation as Covid 19 changed the world forever.

I feel honoured to have shared my career alongside DJ Macdonald. Neither of us probably expected when we started out on our Grampian journey that we'd spend the best part of 40 years happily working together. But family life apart, it has been exactly that – the best part. And I'm certain that like me DJ just couldn't imagine wanting to work anywhere else.

With the passing of DJ Macdonald *STV North* is sadly that little bit less Grampian. But hopefully there is still enough of the old guard left to ensure that the values he held so dear will continue to be honoured, and that his legacy will live on.

The way it was and might have been
Ted Brocklebank in Conversation with former Grampian Chief Executive, Alex Mair

Alex Mair joined Grampian nine months before the company went on air in 1961, initially as company secretary. He later became Chief Executive and oversaw many of the 'firsts' which won Grampian the accolade of 'the little TV station with the big reputation'. Alex retired after 27 years at the helm in 1988. In this interview recorded shortly after his 98th birthday he tells Ted Brocklebank about some of his career highlights.

Alex Mair

TB: Just how important a role did Grampian play in your life?

AM: Well, for nearly thirty years Grampian WAS my life. I loved every minute of it and feel very privileged to have seen it all from day one. The greatest year of my life was undoubtedly 1961, the year we opened the station.

TB: Many of our contributors have described Grampian as uniquely friendly among TV stations. Was this something you worked at?

AM: Well, I'm not sure we really worked at it. We were very small and from the beginning felt that our job was to reflect the region we covered to the outside world and to bring the outside world to viewers in our region in a way they would understand. This meant I was on first name terms with all MPs in our area and understood the issues we debated in programmes like *Points North*. But coming from Aberdeenshire I could relate to local productions like *Bothy Nichts* and *Aye Yours* and make sure they had a place in our schedules. So, we were seen as local but not parochial. It's a fact that Aberdonians are also very hospitable and generous people and we always made visitors to the studios very welcome.

TB: What did you see as your greatest strengths in building the company Grampian became?

AM: Well, first and foremost I was very lucky in having Sir Iain Tennant as my chairman for most of the time I was in charge. I respected his judgement and he seemed to respect mine. Neither of us knew very much about television at the start. We made our mistakes but we learned on the job. Our first managing director only lasted four weeks and there were other poor managerial appointments. But Iain and I had a shared confidence and trust in our ability to get things right. I think my greatest strength was as a judge of character. Pick the right people, put your trust in them and then let them get on with the job. Iain felt the same way. It's a fact that when I became managing director no fewer than four of the fifteen ITV CEOs had started their careers with Grampian: Ward Thomas of Yorkshire, David McCall of Anglia, Lord Windlesham of ATV and myself. Grampian may not have been a finishing school but we were a great starting one. The same was true of the calibre of in-vision people we recruited: Donny B Macleod, Renton Laidlaw, Isla St Clair and Selina Scott all went on to become network stars after beginning their careers at Grampian.

TB: Which of the key early appointees stand out in your memory?

AM: Well, although I was an accountant I realised that as well as safeguarding the pennies we had to have strong creative heads. Jim Buchan and Charles Smith were ideal choices. Jim's people hailed from the North East. Like me he had served in tanks during the war and he was a highly-experienced BBC producer. And although Charles had limited television experience he was an outstanding and highly-respected newspaper journalist. There was a bit of creative tension between them but they rapidly built the company's reputation for excellent regional programmes. It was my job to see they had the money to pay for them, and as an accountant I can say with some pride that after year one Grampian was always in profit, and our programme ratings continued to grow apace.

TB: What are your outstanding memories of your time at the helm?

AM: Well, I suppose they break down into two – the technical 'firsts' and the programming 'firsts' if you like. On the technical side we were the first company in British broadcasting to introduce ENG (electronic newsgathering) – much to the envy of BBC Scotland in particular. We were the first ITV company to introduce computer graphics, the only small regional company with its own Outside Broadcast Unit and the first regional company to link subsidiary studios – in Dundee, Inverness and Stornoway - into our headquarters, thus giving immediacy of news coverage to the biggest transmission area in the ITV network. Much of the credit here should go to Alex Ramsay, our brilliant chief engineer and to Bob Christie, who had the difficult job of negotiating these 'firsts' through the technicians' unions. Again, what I could provide was total support and the necessary funding.

On the production side we were the first ITV station to broadcast live from a North Sea Oil rig, the first region to schedule locally-produced musical entertainment in 'peak', the first small region to set up a dedicated documentary department aimed at network production, and the first UK TV company to tackle the difficult subject of sex education in a series for youngsters.

TB: One of our contributors, an English engineer now based in New Zealand, claimed that Grampian had very high professional standards because it only hired the best and paid over the odds to get them?

AM: I'm not sure about that. As Aberdonians we liked to get value for money. But I think it comes back to picking the right people, putting your trust in them and if they show potential promoting them through the ranks. Alex Ramsay and Bob Christie were good examples of that. Bob started as a studio cameraman but became our labour relations chief and eventually our production controller. On the news side, with respect, you're another example yourself. You had gone elsewhere, but when Charles Smith passed away I remember calling you and asking if you wanted to come back home to Grampian as his successor. I remember when we announced the *OIL* documentary co-production for Channel Four I was asked along to Shell headquarters for lunch. One of their senior people questioned our choice of director for the series. I explained that as major financial contributors Channel Four had recommended a number of directors with network credentials, but we as producers had the final say. Whichever director we decided to appoint Grampian and NRK producers would retain joint editorial control for the series. Again, it was a case of backing our judgement. In the event we stuck with our director of choice and the series was screened to great praise, including from the oil industry, in some fifty countries worldwide.

TB: Many in the industry felt that Grampian punched above its weight at network level. Apart from educational series such as *Living* *and Growing* Grampian documentaries like *Two of a Kind, Last of the Hunters, A Tale of Two Cities* and the *Oil* series won regular network slots on ITV and Channel 4. What part did you play in this?

AM: Well, it may have helped that I was chair of the network finance committee and my fellow CEOs, people like Lew Grade, the Bernsteins and John Freeman, preferred to keep me on-side. But I think there was an acceptance that Grampian produced quality programmes, and especially with the arrival of North Sea Oil, we were the right company in the right place at the right time to tell what was a huge on-going story.

TB: You retired as chief executive in 1987 but were invited to stay on as a board member. Why did you refuse?

AM: I felt it would be unfair to my successor for me to remain a member of the board. A bit like back-seat driving. I wouldn't have enjoyed it had that been myself with my predecessor still on the board.

TB: So how did you feel less than a decade later when Grampian announced it was to 'merge' with SMG?

AM: I thought it was the wrong decision. Some years later as the industry continued to contract it might have been necessary to merge, but it wasn't necessary at the time and I didn't see SMG as a good fit.

TB: Some argued that the company had to act in the best interests of its shareholders.

AM: Grampian's shares were at an all-time high. I don't think the purchase price of £105m – although 700 times the £150,000 which was Grampian's net original share capital – reflected the real value of the company. I don't believe the shareholders were best served by the merger and in my view SMG weren't the right company to merge with

TB: So are you saying it was more a takeover than a merger?

AM: A merger is when two partners have a fifty-fifty deal. When one partner can outvote the other that is no longer a merger.

TB: You say that some years later Grampian might have had to merge. If not SMG, who might have been suitable partners?

AM: I always fancied an east-west split in Scotland. That's why we set up studios in Edinburgh. As you know the ITA put paid to that. But when major amalgamations started to happen who's to say whether a partnership of the UK's eastern regional companies might not have worked – Anglia, Yorkshire, Tyne Tees and Grampian might have been worth exploring.

TB: We've discussed whether the merger was in the best interests of shareholders. But how about the viewers? Do you think it has been in their best interests?

AM: Well, obviously STV North is a totally different animal than Grampian. It's simply a northern news outlet for STV. I think that under Alistair Gracie and DJ Macdonald a lot of the high standards Grampian set in news-gathering have been retained. But of course Grampian was far more than just a TV news station.

TB: So let's be clear. Had you still been in charge in 1997 would the merger have taken place?

AM: Had Iain Tennant and I been there it would not have happened.

TB: Alex, many thanks.

Footnote
Jimmy Spankie

At the start of our anthology of memories I paid tribute to YOU, the viewers, interviewees, advertisers and all who helped make Grampian TV such a success. As we near the end of our trip down memory lane it is a privilege to do so again. YOUR loyalty and support were vital in making Grampian the little TV station with the BIG reputation.

As well as having that big reputation for quality TV, Grampian also had a big, big heart, and contributed generously to local charities. In that spirit I'm delighted to say that all proceeds from the sale of *The Way It Was* will go to Alzheimer Scotland – Action on Dementia*. Can I add that we are eternally grateful to those who had confidence in our book from the start and particularly those who matched that confidence with financial support! They know who they are and I hope *The Way It Was* lives up to their expectations.

Sadly, since the publication of our first edition, my friend Renton Laidlaw has passed away. We send our sincere condolences to his sister Jennifer and family.

When we drew up our list of potential contributors we naturally approached all surviving Grampian board directors involved in the decision to 'merge' the company with the Scottish Media Group in 1997. Only Director of Programmes, George Mitchell, accepted our invitation. We draw absolutely no conclusions from this and thank George warmly for his valuable reminiscences in 'When Grampian Was Champion'. We applaud *STV North* for maintaining Grampian's reputation for news coverage over such a large transmission area and pay tribute to those, including former GTV staff, who have played a crucial role in maintaining these standards. However, as the company's long-time CEO, Alex Mair, reminds us in his interview Grampian was more than just a northern news outlet for ITV. The following Appendix demonstrates the rich diversity of Grampian's programme mix over the years. We can only apologise for any programmes we may have missed!

Donations to Action on Dementia can be made via www.alzscot.org

Some of the programmes produced by Grampian Television from 1961

Entertainment programmes
Andy's Party (1977–81)
The Art Sutter Show (1989–96)
Aye Yours
At Home with Kenneth McKellar
The Big Break (1989)
Bothy Nichts
Breakers (1990s)
The McCalmans (1986)
Cairngorm Cabaret
Cairngorm Ski Night
Strictly Scottish (1970s)
Ceilidh on the Caledonian Canal (1986)
Chartburn (1990–2000)
Hogmanay at the Palace
A Highland Hogmanay
Come Aboard
Country and Irish
The Entertainers (1977–81) :-
> Acker Bilk, Georgie Fame, Julie Felix, Patsy Gallant, Annie Ross, Judie Tzuke, Lindisfarne, Lisa Stansfield, Gilbert O'Sullivan, Stéphane Grapelli, Barbara Dickson, Mike Harding, Juniper Green, Dana, Tony Christie, Catherine Howe, Alistair Macdonald, Rokotto, Alan Price, The Pasadena Roof Orchestra, Grace Kennedy, Tom Paxton, Elkie Brooks, Spookey, Richard Digance, Iris Williams, The Nolans, Joe Sun, Suzi Quatro
First Light
Grampian Disco Dancing Championship
Guess Who's Coming To Dinner (1984–86)
The Highland Road (1984)
Ingle Neuk
It's George (1970s-1980s)
ITV Telethon (1988, 1990, 1992)
The Jim Macleod Show (1970s)

McCue's Music
Magic of the Musicals (1984)
Maggie! (1983)
Melody Inn (part networked)
The National Television Awards (ITV network, 1995–97)
Northern Nights
The Paul Coia Show (1986)
Pick of the North
Pop Scotch (1969-70):-

Deep Purple, Chicken Shack, John Mayall, Duster Bennett. Trader Horne, Matthews Southern Comfort, Johnny Nash, Taste, Blue Mink, Renaissance, Toe Fat, The Move, Manfred Mann Chapter III), Pentangle, Bridget St. John, Alan Price and Friends, Writing on the Wall, The Tremeloes, Marmalade, Desmond Dekker, Cat Stevens.

(Judy Dyble of Trader Horne said when appearing on Pop Scotch with Cat Stevens, "The flight back from Aberdeen was delayed by fog during which she listened to 'Tea for the Tillerman' being virtually written in front of her and singing along with it. That was magical.")

The Royal Clansmen
Runrig on the Rock (Edinburgh Castle)
Random Choice (1986),
Richard Clayderman (1985)
Scotch and Irish (1993–96)
Scotland the What?
Shammy Dab (1980-89)
Silver City Folk
Sounds 73
On Camera (1974)
A Touch of Music
Talking Loud
Thomson at Teatime (early 1970s)
Top Club (1971–98)
Try For Ten (1965–67)
The Video Show (1985)
Video Jukebox (1987)
Welcome to the Ceilidh (1976–82)

Win a Word
You'd Better Believe It! (1990)
Let the Music Take You
Musical Journey
One over the Eight: Nine varied Music and Arts programmes, two
of which were with *Demis Roussos* 1974

Documentary programmes
Black Water – Bright Hope (TRICS Award) (1975 – ITV Network)
A Tale of Two Cities (1977 – ITV Network)
OIL (AMANDA Award) 8x60 - Channel Four Network
Last of the Hunters (1987 – Channel Four Network*)*
Sea Farmers 2x60 (1988 – Channel Four Network)
The Blood is Strong (1988 3x60 - Channel Four Network)
The Energy Alternative (1990 3x60 – Channel Four Network)
Scotland the Grave (BMA Award) (1991- Channel Four Network)
The Year of Spain (1992 – ITV Network)
A Prince Among Islands (1993 – ITV Network)
A Talent to Abuse (1993 – Channel Four Network)
Highlanders (1995 – ITV Network)
Selina Scott Meets Donald Trump (1995 – ITV Network)
Eagle (1984)
The A9 Mystery (1978)
Commando (1983)
Till a' the Seas Gang Dry(1996 4x30)
The Berryfields o' Blair (1996)
The Tartan Tallies (1996)
A Glen For All Seasons (1997 6x30)
Fisherfolk (1998 3x30)
Around the World in 80 Hours (1993)
Beyond Explanation
Blowout at Bravo (1977)
Carnoustie: A Town of Golf,
Columba's Way (1972)
*Elizabeth of Glamis (*1985)
Cop College,
A Day in the Life (2003)
Fife: Andrew's Kingdom

The Glovers of Nagasaki co-produced with Fuji TV, (1995)
The Highland Heartlands (1986)
Home at Last (1989)
Hot Property - ITV Network
The Man Who Changed the World (1986)
The Masterbuilders,
Medics of the Glen - ITV network
Northern Eye
Picnic at Whitehill (1986)
A Place in the Sun (1981)
The River
Storm on the Mountain (1988 - Channel Four Network)
Please Keep Your Feet Off the Stage (1983)
City Out of Time (1983)
To Russia with Burns (1978)
Two of a Kind (1971 – ITV Network)
Unsolved (2003)
Valhalla
The Woman Who Ate Scotland (2006)
The Old Grey Ladies of Lossiemouth
Cinderella from the Sea
The Year of the Braer
Fall-out at Pentland
In The National Interest
Highland One
Flare-up at Shetland
Troubled Fields
A Candle Burning Brightly
Journey To A Kingdom
The Balmoral Connection

News Special programmes
What Price Oil? (BAFTA Award) (1974)

Feature programmes
The Way It Was (1980s–1996)
The Electric Theatre Show (1976–1984 - ITV network,)
Country Matters (1990s)

Naturally Scottish
The Scottish Tourism Supreme Awards
Fix It
Get Real
Walking Back to Happiness
The Grampian Garden (1963–1980),
Grampian Midweek
Grampian Weekend
We the Jury
Pennywise (for the ITV network, 1985–88)
The Scottish Soldier (1975)
Wednesday People
Put It in Writing
Summer at Six (1980s)
Under the Hammer (1997–99)
Out and About (late 1980s)
Pin Money (1987)
The Great Outdoors
Grow for It
Movie Date
Off the Wall (2004)
The People Show
Rude Health
Desert Island Chefs
Spend Spend Spend
Sign a Story
BAFTA Scotland Awards 1995 (Beach Ballroom, Aberdeen)
On The Road Again
Scotland's larder
Drawn From Wild Places
Portraits of the Wild

Drama programmes
Just Robert, Shanty Burns and Mr Fixit
 1974 Written by Watt Nicoll: produced and directed by John
 Sichel. (With actors Russell Hunter, Collette O'Neil, Molly
 Weir, Callum Mill and Derek Anders. All have a Scottish
 setting but *Shanty Burns* was aimed at the North-east in

particular dealing with the effects of oil on the people in the area.)

Childrens programmes
Get Fresh (ITV network, 1986–88), Presenters Charlotte Hindle and Gareth Jones(Gaz Top) with slime covered alien Gilbert. Aberdeen Beach, Scone Palace Perth, Aberdeen Exhibition Centre, The Waterfront Dundee, Eden Court Theatre Inverness with Kylie Minogue.
Ghost Train (contributions for the ITV network, 1989–92), Hayfield Riding Centre Aberdeen, St Andrews Sea Life Centre, Tolquhon Castle Aberdeenshire, Grampian Motor Museum Alford.
Isla's Island
Bill's Magic Box
The Birthday Spot
James the Cat (1984–86 - ITV network)
High Time
Pick a Number (1987–96)
Furry Tales
Rumblie Jumblie
Ron & Friends (1972–74)
Seamus
Scene on Saturday (1976 – early 1980s)
Superbox (early 1980s)
Top Team (1972-77)
Win a Word (1970)
Wize Up (1996–98)
Zoom! (early – mid-1970s)
Wings and Things

Sports programmes
1983 *North Tonight live outside broadcast by satellite from the Ullevi Stadium Gothenburg* for Aberdeen FC's 2 - 1 victory over Real Madrid to win the European Cup Winners Cup. Grampian was the first regional ITV company to transmit live by satellite.
Highland Cross : 50-mile duathlon from Kintail to Beauly.
The World Orienteering Championships,

Grampian Sheepdog Trials (ITV network and Channel 4)
Pure Strength
Sportscall
Sportscope
The Western Isles Challenge (co-produced with S4C and *Trans World International)*
The Back Page
Outside broadcast coverage of *Scottish League football*
Scottish Cup football
European Cup football
Cross Country Championships
Lawn Bowls Championships
Scottish Shinty Championships
Professional Wrestling (also for ITV network's *World of Sport*)
Marathons
City Centre Cycling (Aberdeen and Dundee)
Exhibition Tennis
Squash
International Amateur Boxing
Curling
Triathlon
Mountain Bike racing

News programmes
North Tonight (1980–2009)
Grampian Headlines (1988–2003)
Grampian News (2002–06)
Grampian Today (mid-1970s – 1980)
News and Views (1961 – mid-1970s)
News Review (early 1990s – 2013)
North News (lunchtime bulletin, 1980–88)
North Headlines (late night bulletin, 1980–87)
Police News

Current affairs programmes
The Time the Place (Live ITV Network topical discussion)
The Buck Stops Here
Craig Millar Reports (latterly The Craig Millar Files, 2003–04),

Country Focus (1961–84)
Crossfire (1984–2004)
Grampian Week (1970s)
Inquisition,
One Life to Live
Personal View
North Tonight Specials
Points North (1961–84)
Scottish Questions

Scots Gaelic programmes

Cuir Car (Children's)
Ar Duthaich
Am Fasach, Blas (1994–98)
Beathainchean Neontach (Nature)
Beagan Gaidhlig (1971–74)
Bocsa's An Fidhle
Ceol na Fidhle (Traditional music)
Coille is Cuan (Nature, 1995–96)
Le Durach (Gaelic version of *The Birthday Spot*)
Crann Tara (Current affairs/features, 1982–1990s)
Comhla Rinn (Chat show)
Deanamaid Gairdeachar
Duirn Chelteach
Failte (Features)
Fionnan Feior (Documentaries)
Muir is Tir, Nochd Gun Chadal (Contemporary music)
Seall (Documentaries)
Seudan a chauain (1995–97)
Seachd Laithean (Current affairs)
Sgeulachdan Na Cagatcile
Spors (Sport)
Tacsil
Telefios (Regional news, 1993–2000)
Telefios na Seachduinn (News review, 1993–2000)
Aite Mo Ghaoil 6x30
Eilean Mo Chridhe 6x30 – MG Alba Network

Picture Gallery
From Tram Shed to Television Station

Ten months before opening

Removing the front roof

Cutting up the rails

Rear garage stays as scenery store

Six months before opening, front and rear of building take shape

Completed frontage of the building
(The central flowerbed was initially a pond with fish in it!)

Everything broadcast goes through Master Control

*Harry Carson operating Grampian's first video tape machine
(A mobile phone gives better pictures than this monster!)*

Jimmy's Adventures

Up a snowy mountain with Ted Heath

Grampian Personality of the Year 1966

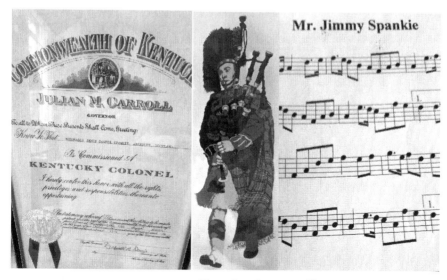

Kentucky Colonel
Jimmy Spankie

Piper Spankie
in full regalia

Very own pipe music

Bothy's Got Talent

Bothy Nichts was a hugely popular talent show set in the pre-war farming communities of the North East where appropriately dressed teams could actually lose points by being too professional.

Andy's Party

In addition to his popular songs Andy Stewart entertained with his humorous character sketches.

*Andy 'thrilling' the ladies in his more traditional style as a guest on
Calum's Ceilidh.*

*Multi-talented Gaelic entertainer Norman Maclean filming inserts for Ho
Ro Gheallaidh Thormoid (Norman's Musical Stramash).*

At Home with Kenneth McKellar

Ronnie Corbett on Kenneth McKellar's music and chat show

Welcome to the Ceilidh

Johnnie Beattie hosted this popular traditional music, dance and comedy series.

Behind the scenes

Romper Room with Lesley Blair (Cameraman Tom Leslie was Grampian's longest serving employee... at 6'4" tall he was great for the high shots!)

Electrician Ian Murray 'directing' Alistair Yates on Orkney

Tale of Two Cities

Houston Space Centre

*Eileen Doris Bremner and Marian
Hepworth on the crew's transport*

Oil

Exotic paddy field in China

The Esso tiger - choosing which one is lunch

The Great Munro Challenge at Devil's Point in Cairngorms

An era before drones - Leith Hall in 100ft tower

OB2 on its travels on the west coast

Film crew

Atop the spectacular cliffs at Eshaness on Shetland

THE ENTERTAINERS

ALAN PRICE

GRAMPIAN TELEVISION LIMITED

invites you to

the studio audience at

Queen's Cross, Aberdeen

on **TUESDAY 16th MAY 1978**

at 9.15 pm

DRESS CASUAL

The Entertainers rehearsals with Juniper Green

STV's current Managing Director Broadcast, Bobby Hain (left) in 1985 presenting computer programme Bits'n'Pieces

Only at 'The Grumpian'

Anne MacKenzie presenting a farming debate in a freezing cold cowshed complete wi' coos!

Riggers Mark Lynch and Ron Whichelow herding the audience.

Trucking shots around the world

Tianamen Square

Great wall of China

Lake Geneva and Riyadh Saudi Arabia

Grandfather Mountain, North Carolina

Highland games in North Carolina

BAFTA Scotland Awards 1995 from Beach Ballroom Aberdeen

The Electric Theatre Show

First Clapper Board

'Love from Gene Wilder' on the back of the clapper board

Autographs of people the back of the clapper board are a bit faded now but include:
Joan Collins, Liz Palmer, David Essex, Jenny Agutter,
Gene Wilder, Dyan Cannon, Suzanna York, Dennis Waterman,
John Thaw, Bonnie Langford, Sir John Mills, Robert Powell,
Karen Dotrice, David Niven, Sonny Bono, Richard Rowntree,
Roger Moore, Telly Savalas, O.J.Simpson, James Coburn,
Sophia Loren, Tony Franciosa, Zsa Zsa Gabor, Gerald Harper,
Iain Carmichael, Angela Lansbury, Arthur Lowe, Elliot Gould,
Anna Neagle, Michael York, Sir Richard Attenborough,
George Chakiris, Donald Pleasance, Jonathon Scott-Taylor.
Anthony Hopkins, Barbara Parkins, Neil Simon.
Only three wrote a comment - Jenny Agutter - 'Enjoyed being on your programme, many thanks', Bonnie Langford - 'With thanks' and Gene Wilder, 'Love from Gene Wilder'.

Technical areas
1971

Telecine film projectors

2" Videotape machine

Vision control

Transmission control

35mm film commercials

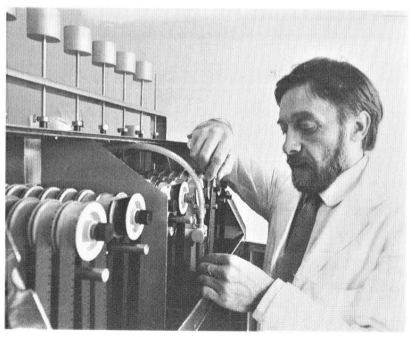

John Thomson developing 16mm film for Grampian Today

Graphics Department

Before computer graphics, name inlays and end roller credits were manually composed with Letraset lettering.
On screen captions were often hand painted with paint, pen and ink by the graphic artists.

This caption was about British Telecom disconnecting an old lady without warning

The Studio Gallery
(Where the programme director and team call the shots)

1979

1990s

Girl Power in the Gallery

1980s - £3.87m new facilities

Grampian's new frontage

Technical and transmission control

*35mm film commercials are now gone and are on 2"video cassettes - a
sort of commercials jukebox*

Broadcast quality computer graphics appears

1"video tape machine being installed which now give slow motion and still frames

Multi-format video editing

Staff bothy nichts

The only remaining video example of the ethos of Grampian's most famous local series 'Bothy Nichts' is an in-house, lighthearted presentation by members of staff recorded on 12th May 1979

OB1 in Bulgaria

Eight cameras in OB1(left) and sixteen cameras in the trailer

The Social Club

Social Club Bar 70s

Grampian's Set Designer, Eric Mollart, was the club's own Banksy or Matisse

The annual Social Club Christmas dance - 1973

The Adult Kiddies Christmas Party

Social club 1980s

1990s ... times changed - the club closed and became a much healthier staff gym !

Happy days

1960s Aberdeen

Edinburgh

Cairngorm Cabaret

1970s

Film Department 1970s

1980s - happy days and great memories

Printed in Great Britain
by Amazon

82037579R00172